P.D. OUSPENS

CW01626464

P.D. OUSPENSKY:
Pioneer of the Fourth Way

by

Bob Hunter

EUREKA EDITIONS 2021

© Eureka Editions 2021

ISBN-13: 978-94-92590-24-4

All rights reserved. No part of this publication may be reproduced, stored in a retrieval system, or transmitted in any form or by any means, electronic, mechanical, photo-copying, recording or otherwise, without the prior permission of Eureka Editions.

Contents

Chapter 1

LOOSENING HISTORY'S HOLD

THE FIRST WORLD WAR saved the Russian writer Piotr Demianovich Ouspensky from becoming famous in his lifetime. Circumstantially, that is, because it forced him to curtail a Far Eastern search for real knowledge and instead return to Russia – where he found the 'miraculous', as he termed it, on his doorstep. The direct cause of his subsequent wish to avoid fame was his contact with George Ivanovich Gurdjieff, whom he was neither the first nor the last to regard as a miracle worker in a psychological, even spiritual, sense. What Gurdjieff taught him evoked Ouspensky's determination to be more flexible in any future lives allotted to him than he conceived possible for a famous figure, and fixture, in history.

Before Gurdjieff arranged the first meeting between the two men, in Moscow in 1915, journalist Ouspensky had already made a name for himself in Russia through the depth of thought reflected in his books *The Fourth Dimension* and *Tertium Organum* and his lectures on occult themes. The latter book later made a stir in the West also. It is likely that had stable living conditions reigned in his motherland Ouspensky would have developed his views on man, life and the universe – at the risk of attracting wide acclaim.

Such a solo career is far from certain, however, for in the second decade of the twentieth century Gurdjieff worked in Russia and contact between the two rare minds would have been at least as likely in a calmer environment, if not so urgent.

As events happened, Ouspensky, benefiting from the knowledge that Gurdjieff passed to him, or rather, the understanding he acquired from it, took pains during the rest of his life to steer clear of popular recognition. Associates during his expatriate life in England reported that he prayed, 'Please, God, protect me from becoming famous during my lifetime.'

This prayer did not necessarily spring from any conventional theory of the hereafter. For one thing, Ouspensky nourished a suspicion, supported by experience, that any belief held confidently by the masses was bound to be mistaken. Thus anything applauded by the public was unlikely to be of merit, which made fame an unappealing goal. A deeper reason was based on what became regarded as his theory of eternal recurrence, although he was at pains to show that it was an ageless belief.

Despite the reasons, a self-perception that one is in danger of attracting widespread acclaim invites accusations of at least a degree of immodesty. Certainly, Ouspensky was not prone to false modesty. No shrinking violet would name his book *Tertium Organum* and subtitle it *The Third Canon of Thought, A Key to the Enigmas of the World*. Nor present it as the third instalment of percipient reasoning, following the efforts of Aristotle (*Organon*) and Francis Bacon (*Novum Organum*), while gently criticising both of his famous predecessors as dualists.

At the same time he did not pass off the system of 'superlogic' he had developed as being entirely original, claiming rather that in reality the third canon existed before the other two. On this reasoning, objective knowledge is always available; it simply requires a certain genius to recognise it. Still, Ouspensky's fear that fame was dangerously close, far from being a delusion of grandeur, was based on the reception of his ideas by, particularly, the intelligentsia and the growing number of people interested in the occult.

Apart from his antipathy to the herd mentality, Ouspensky's disinclination to be confined in the mould of a famous personality arose from a combination of his own belief in eternal recurrence and the psychological facts of life as taught by Gurdjieff. Ouspensky extended the idea of a psychological repetition of everyday events – in which, as can be easily observed, unconscious factors impel us to exhibit the same weaknesses, repeat the same mistakes throughout our lives – into a prospect of identical repetition of the whole life.

Largely as a result of his mathematical study of time, he saw life as a circle in which the points of death and birth coincided. It could be safely hazarded that such a tedious coincidence would not seem a sanguine expectation for many people. True, the occasional blessed person is heard to profess, 'If I had my life over, I wouldn't change a thing!' But one is tempted to suspect that in such cases the chief blessing involves a selective memory.

Fortunately for any who recognise the imperfections of their lives and are susceptible to Ouspensky's ideas, his recurrence theory contains an escape clause. We should expect he saw a way out of this vicious circle, otherwise he would have had to reject any prospect of human evolution, yet judging by most accounts he was at heart an optimist. Before meeting Gurdjieff, he had already thought deeply about time, space and higher dimensions and saw fallacies in conventional conceptions of temporal existence. His preoccupation with and writing and lecturing on these ponderings led colleagues and friends in Moscow and St Petersburg to nickname him 'Ouspensky Fourth Dimension'.

Under Gurdjieff's tutelage he further visualised, and experienced, ways in which heightened consciousness could open the way to a higher level of Being. If an individual could break free of conventional, mechanical ways of living he could inhabit different 'lines' of time. Worldly events would continue to recur in the familiar, mechanical manner but a conscious man would not be shackled to them. With unusual persistence, he could free himself from the rings of recurrence by realising their potential to become an upward spiral.

To Ouspensky, every moment contains different possibilities, and thus a potential choice. In eternal recurrence, opportunities not seized in one life become even more difficult to realise in the next. Mirroring individual lives, historic events recur relentlessly at the same recorded instant in circular time. Thus, identities who have impressed their stamp on worldly affairs endlessly repeat their assumptions of power, their mighty deeds, their horrific crimes; famous writers pen their beguiling stories with exceedingly well practised hand; all in fact who have earned their 'reward' on earth are obliged to go on endlessly earning it. In this scheme an historic figure gradually becomes so rehearsed in his or her role that it is repeated with an increasing sense of inevitability in recurrence. It becomes easier and easier for, say, the dictator to assume power, just as the ordinary man is inclined to do the easiest thing and so fall into the same errors in recurring lives. As a consequence, it becomes progressively more difficult to break free from this straitjacket, whether it be fastened by history or simply the mechanical action of 'doing the easiest thing' (an act in which the idiomatic 'doing' lacks any element of real will).

Ouspensky had no ambition to be such a puppet. If strings were to be attached to his life, he wished to have a say in choosing them. While he did not appear to follow the 'way of blame' practised by some Eastern mystics – and possibly to some extent by Gurdjieff – to avoid public adulation or even commendation, he certainly chose a life of anonymity. He continued to write but did not publish any new books after starting to teach Gurdjieff's ideas. When he led his own groups in England and the United States, Ouspensky of course became well known to, even deeply respected by, hundreds of followers, but they fell short of the number necessary to signify fame.

Even on this comparatively small scale of recognition, he applied strict rules that limited the number of his pupils: newcomers were admitted to his lectures only on recommendation or after having passed tests to determine whether they could grasp the ideas he presented, and they were forbidden to discuss these notions with anyone outside the group.

These precautions were not observed primarily so Ouspensky could avoid popular recognition. They were designed to protect the relative purity of the esoteric knowledge he was transmitting. Simply reducing it to verbal form drained some of its force, but exposing it to the general public, he and others feared, would have adulterated these ideas to the point of ineffectiveness.

Ouspensky evidently conveyed something of his theory of recurrence to his followers. It is recorded that at one lecture he was amused by a question whether his pupils might meet him sooner in the next round of life. 'It depends where I am,' he replied, with a smile. Even more, it would depend on where the pupils were in themselves, whether they had remembered anything from previous lives. For, as Ouspensky himself saw, measures like avoiding worldly renown were the simple part of the equation; Self-remembering was the difficult part and the key to increasing consciousness and actualising potentiality.

Ouspensky made it clear that, while recurrence did not violate any principles of Gurdjieff's system, it was not part of it. Gurdjieff's focus was on practical work in the present; people had more than enough to struggle against in their current life without expending energy on speculation about their fate afterwards. It seems unlikely, however, that he would have harboured any objections to Ouspensky's recurrence theory, considering it could stimulate people to raise their level of Being.

In view of Ouspensky's reluctance to become crystallised in one repeating circle of time, it is notable that already the figure he cut in a brief (sixty-nine year) span of history is being refashioned. Not many years ago, people interested in The Fourth Way, as Gurdjieff's system of psychological work is known, generally regarded Ouspensky as a fascinating lecturer, writer and teacher with a mind like a steel trap, a prodigious memory and an imperious bearing – but a severe, cold man with scant show of emotion.

It is now being pointed out more and more that he stressed that human evolution hinges on contact with higher emotions that are usually sealed from us, and that from the start his chief work was on transformation of negative emotions.

The few people who knew him well have attested that he was in fact an emotional man, even though he rarely let his feelings run away with his thoughts. His earliest writing shows that it was always in highly emotional states that he glimpsed significant insights into reality.

Those insights raise the point that we who visualise him only through his writing might not see why he would wish to change his life. The quality of thought expressed in *Tertium Organum* and *A New Model of the Universe* and the clarity of his exposition of Gurdjieff's teaching in the posthumously published *In Search of the Miraculous* might seem a greater contribution than any man could hope to pay for his existence.

If we look more closely at the record of his life, however, we may discern why Ouspensky aimed to become free of his life cycle, to live on a higher level and make even more effective use of his time on Earth. We may even pick up something of his own feeling that he had already lived many lives and his belief that opportunities for evolution are not endless, particularly when a person becomes aware of its possibility.

If we conclude that, spurred by this intimation of a cut-off point, he could well have fulfilled his aim, we might also entertain the possibility that he may be living now on a different level – a change that conceivably would be affecting the impressions he made, is making and will make on people linked to him through his teaching.

Chapter 2

LIFE IS MEANING

OUSPENSKY ONCE QUESTIONED a pupil and close friend, Dr Maurice Nicoll, about his aim in connection with recurrence. In other words, what would he wish to do had he the possibility of reliving his life? Nicoll replied he would like to have the power to feel meaning in all his experiences. He admitted that large parts of his life were like a dream and he had taken little in, with whole years blotted out of his mind.

'Yes, this is right,' said Ouspensky. 'As a rule we are not there. As Mr G. [Gurdjieff

said of someone: "He is never at home." '

Nicoll recorded in his diary that Ouspensky 'continued in something like the following words: "And this really applies to us all. We are never at home, or very rarely. We are nearly always out. So our experiences have little or no meaning for us." '

Nicoll remarked: 'But I am sure that you, for example, remember your life far better than I remember mine, and that your life has had more meaning.'

'Yes, but not quite in the way you mean,' said Ouspensky. 'I have noticed how much you have forgotten. In my case, as a child I did not play with toys. I was less under imagination. I saw what life was like at a very early stage.'

'Well, in my case I must confess that I never thought of life as a thing to think of,' Nicoll said. 'I took it all for granted.'

'Yes, that is why it had so little meaning for you,' his teacher replied. 'You were simply carried along by it, as by a torrent, thinking you were going somewhere – to some clear goal. It is only when you realise life is taking you nowhere that it begins to have meaning.'

Nicoll concluded: 'I carried away two clear impressions: one was that to formulate your aim in regard to the *possibility* of having to re-live your life at death, in terms of wishing to have more meaning, was right, and the second idea was that unless you saw the nature of life you could not get more meaning in living it.' (He may have italicised the word 'possibility' as a reminder that the theory of eternal recurrence was Ouspensky's idea, not necessarily backed by Gurdjieff's system. Or he may have been emphasising that another life was a real possibility that one should take into account. Again, it may even have been a warning that, if it were but a slim possibility, one was rapidly running out of chances to find meaning.)

'I realised that he had answered the question I had not asked – namely, "How can life have more meaning?" ' said Dr Nicoll. 'Although people do not realise it necessarily, they live by meaning, and when things become meaningless, they feel hopeless and useless.'

The foregoing exchange can be found in Nicoll's *Psychological Commentaries* (vol. 1, p. 63). He does not date the conversation but from his diaries, published in his secretary, Beryl Pogson's *Maurice Nicoll: A Portrait*, it could well have occurred at Alley Cottage at Sidlesham, West Sussex, which Nicoll and his wife, Catherine, rented from 1927 to 1933. Ouspensky regularly visited the cottage, on the sea marshes south of Chichester, for a weekend's relaxation.

In one diary extract, Nicoll recounts that, while talking about his childhood, Ouspensky told him that when he was a boy he realised many things which people do not realise until late in life, if ever. 'I saw many illusions,' he said, 'quite clearly and naturally.' (ibid, p. 102)

In an 'Autobiographical fragment' written in London in 1935 (*A Further Record*, pp. 299-303), Ouspensky talks of several mental pictures of events which happened before he was two. He could recall himself 'quite clearly' from the age of three. 'I remember the exhibition of 1882 in Moscow and the coronation of Alexander III in 1883, chiefly the illuminations,' he says.

His first memories were connected with his maternal grandmother's old-fashioned house in Pimenovskaia Street, Moscow. 'My grandmother was a very clever woman,' he says.

'I never forgot the wonderful stories of old Moscow life which she told me and my sister.'

On both the intellectual and emotional sides, Peter Damian had chosen his parents well. He was born in Moscow on 5 March 1878, the son of a woman who was a painter and had a taste for Russian and French literature and a man who was a survey officer, an amateur mathematician with an interest in the fourth dimension, and a talented artist. One of Peter's grandfathers, who died in 1882, had been an accomplished professional artist.

If, as is said, a male in the Russian society of that era was considered to be either a gentleman or a peasant, Ouspensky would seem to have been born every bit a gentleman. He himself said, however, that his family did not belong to any class but was in touch with all of them, a relationship he claimed (after an acquaintance with English and Indian social mores) was possible only in Russia.

Decades later he told his English pupils that he began to experience instances of *deja vu* early in life. At the age of six, while visiting a locality near Moscow, he was thinking that it was not quite as he remembered it from four years earlier, then realised he could not have been there before - not, at least, in his present life.

Again, when his mother became lost in the corridors while taking him to a new school, he 'recalled' the layout of the building accurately although he had not been in it previously.

Writing of these experiences later in life, Ouspensky says: 'With me these sensations (with a clear and distinct idea that this has happened before, that I have seen it before) began when I was about six years old. After eleven they became much rarer. One of them, extraordinary for its vividness and persistence, occurred when I was nineteen.' (*A New Model of the Universe*, pp. 296-7)

He then gives the usual psychological theories that attempt to explain such sensations. One is that 'they depend on breaks in consciousness, when consciousness suddenly disappears for one quite imperceptible moment and then flashes out again. . . .

The 'breaks' themselves are explained by the possibility of the same psychic function being carried out by different parts of the thinking apparatus . . . producing the impression that the same situation has occurred some time previously.'

Another theory is that 'the same sensation may be produced by an associative resemblance between two totally different experiences,' when any object may remind a person of someone, a place or an incident.

Ouspensky comments:

'Neither of these theories explains the reason why in most cases the sensation that this has happened before occurs chiefly in children and almost always disappears later. On the contrary, according to these theories, the sensations described should grow more frequent with age.'

As children, Peter Damian and his sister shared a faculty of foretelling the immediate future, which they tested – successfully, he reports – by predicting the turn of everyday happenings, although they kept this talent a secret, considering that their elders would not believe it. Later, Ouspensky would link 'this special kind of foreknowledge of people, things, places and events' with his theory of recurrence of lives.

When he was 'about six', Peter read romantic poet Mikhail Lermontoff's 1840 novel *Hero of Our Time* which, he recalls in *A New Model of the Universe*, produced in him a strong feeling of 'the repetition of events'.

Lermontoff's allusions to presentiments, expectations and 'remembering that which seems to have happened in some unknown past' may well be reflected in Ouspensky's own novel, *Strange Life of Ivan Osokin*.

Ouspensky's brief "Autobiographical Fragment" (1935) gives some faint clues as to why Lermontoff's work and another novel he reports having read at an early age, Ivan Turgenev's *A Sportsman's Sketches*, remained in his memory.

It is not remarkable that they should have come into the ken of the young bookworm as they were among the most popular Russian writers. Turgenev is credited with having penned the first Russian psychological novel and Lermontoff sprang into fame with his 1840 eulogy of the country's greatest poet, Alexander Pushkin, on his death after a duel.

Pushkin's superfluous man, Eugene Onegin, the hero of the poem of that name, is depicted as lacking inner integrity, moral discipline and a useful occupation or serious purpose in life, despite being outwardly smart, good-hearted and liberal in attitude. His weak character is contrasted with that of a sincere country girl with whom he has a relationship.

A similar distinction between the sexes is seen in Lermontoff's meditative *A Hero of Our Time*, which is taken to be frankly autobiographical but which the author described as 'indeed a portrait, but not of one man; it is a portrait built up of all our generation's vices . . .'

Peter Ouspensky may have perceived, appreciatively, that this imbalance between men and women had become a popular theme in Russian literature, combined with a condemnation of the wealthy ruling class and sympathy for the serfs and peasants.

Turgenev illustrates these disparities in his novels – and in a short story aptly titled *The Diary of a Superfluous Man* (1850) – in which noblemen with good intentions but an inability to direct their energies beneficially share the pages with practical and strong-willed female characters. His *A Sportsman's Sketches* is a collection of empathic portrayals of Russian peasants.

All this may have struck a chord in the young boy's feelings. As we have seen, he enjoyed the nurturing and protective presence of women, having been brought up by his mother and delighted by his grandmother's tales, while sharing secretly with his sister an ability to foretell everyday events. Later he would wed a strong-willed and perceptive woman who would complement his Work teaching – and as a final contribution permit posthumous publication of his magnum opus.

It is readily assumed from the adult Ouspensky's own words that what he signifies by remarking on Lermontoff is that author's intuition of eternal recurrence. For he writes: 'The feeling of the repetition of events was very strong in Lermontoff.

He is full of presentiments, expectations, "memories". . . ."The Fatalist" is practically written on the theme of repetition and of remembering that which seems to have happened in some unknown past" (*A New Model of the Universe*, p. 472).

However, in the following verse, which Ouspensky quotes to illustrate this form of remembrance, the notion of 'return' seems rather too well disguised to suggest the idea of recurrence to even an exceptionally advanced boy of six, even though 'awakening' may prompt an alternative to the conventional idea of an afterlife:

'Would it not be better to finish the path of life in self-forgetting
And to fall into an unending sleep
Looking for a new awakening.' (Valerik)

Although Ouspensky recounts that his father was interested in the fourth dimension, a subject that in the son's hands leads to Time, Eternity and the possibility of repeating lives, all his writing on this was lost. It was not until Peter was sixteen that he 'found Nietzche' who 'contributed a great deal to the popularisation of the idea of eternal recurrence' although 'Ouspensky Fourth Dimension' (as he was nicknamed) faulted his proposed proof of the theory (*A New Model of the Universe*, pp. 467-8).

So, even though, as already mentioned, he experienced feelings of deja vu from the age of six, it could well be that only later did he detect a similar sentiment in Lermontoff's writing pointing to eternal recurrence. (Ouspensky, after he received instruction from Gurdjieff, also attributed his deja vu intimations to moments of Self-remembering, which he recalled as having occurred at an even younger age than six years.)

Another thought that occupied Lermontoff was whether life was subject to fate or chance. The last of the five stories in *A Hero of Our Time*, 'The Fatalist', has one of the hero's friends survive a potentially deadly game of Russian roulette, only to be killed on the way home by a drunken Cossack's sabre.

Searching for an answer to the fatalism question may well have exercised Ouspensky's mind, too, and more so in later years when his sister died in jail while still young. Later still, he would be able to add to the equation Gurdjieff's 'Law of Accident', to escape from which requires a significant rise in consciousness.

Lermontoff felt an understandable loneliness as a lover of freedom confined in feudal Russia. He believed that only a 'storm' could purify the nation and free the common people, a possibility presented in meteorological metaphor by his poem about 'A lone white sail' that is neither fleeing happiness nor seeking joy . . .

> 'The blue waves dance, they dance and tremble,
> The sun's bright rays caress the seas.
> And yet for storm it begs, the rebel,
> As if in storm lurked calm and peace!'

(*Mikhail Lermontoff: Selected Works*, translated by Irina Zheleznova, 1976)

Again, though, it seems more likely that what impressed the young boy was simply the passionate concern of both Lermontoff and Turgenev for the oppressed in their country, and recognition of women's innate potential. The masters at his gymnasium apparently soon confirmed for him that the male of the species did not evidence much capacity of understanding; he was to extend that judgment to priests and professors too. At six, however, the dreams, visions and fantasies of romantic literature – romantic in the sense that its psychological and spiritual ideals are expressed symbolically – might appeal only generally as a justifiable reaction against the status quo.

Soon after that he became fond of reading poetry and looking at paintings, engravings and prints. 'Poetry and painting became the arts for me,' he says.

'I could also sketch at that time. About eight years, I began to dream of travels and of the sea. About twelve, I began to feel a great interest in natural science; everything about plants and animals had an enormous fascination for me.'

On the other hand, work at the Moscow Gymnasium 'was dull; I was lazy; I hated Greek and school routine in general.

Happily the boys at school were left very much to themselves and although I lived in school I managed to read a great deal'.

'About thirteen I became interested in dreams and consequently in psychology. At sixteen I first found Nietzsche [the 19th century German philosopher and superman advocate].

In 1896, when I was eighteen, I began my first independent travels, and the same time I began to write. I was very anarchistically inclined at that time. I particularly distrusted all forms of academic science and took a firm decision never to pass any examinations and never to take any degrees. At the same time I worked very intensely on biology, mathematics and psychology. I was enormously excited by the idea of the fourth dimension and, subsequently, terribly disappointed by the usual "scientific" treatment of it.

I mistrusted and disliked all kinds of socialism even more than industrialism or militarism and did not believe in any kind of secret revolutionary parties, with which all Russian 'intelligentsia' sympathised. But when I became interested in journalism I could work only on 'left' papers, because 'right' papers did not smell good. It was one of the complexities of Russian life.'

He felt there was a 'dead wall' everywhere in science. 'I used to say at that time that profesors were killing science in the same way as priests were killing religion.'

While working as a journalist Ouspensky travelled in Russia, in the East and in Europe. He wrote *Strange Life of Ivan Osokin* in 1905 during months of strikes and riots that culminated in armed insurrection in Moscow. The theme of the novel, not published until a decade later, shows that by the time he was 27 Ouspensky had a strong inkling of the psychological principles he was to learn more fully from Gurdjieff. To his associates later, he agreed the story is largely biographical, but professed he was never as foolish as Osokin, who can never act in his own best interest despite memories of past mistakes.

Who would feel clever or reckless enough to call Ouspensky foolish? Nevertheless, aspects of the 'fictional' hero's role bear a remarkably close resemblance to events in Ouspensky's life; likewise, certain characteristics are shared by the two.

The description of Ivan Osokin's 'boring' school days sounds very similar to what Ouspensky has described as his own experience – notably his expulsion at 16 for a prank, and his mother's death within a couple of years. Osokin, like Ouspensky, taught himself enough Italian to read Dante, and apparently spent his inheritance travelling to Paris and other places.

The book character dislikes the 'party public', as he calls the revolutionaries of the day, even more than the arrogant and selfish 'official Russia'. This sentiment was held also by his author, as Ouspensky's Autobiographical Note makes clear.

In what can be seen as a tragic prophecy, Osokin says that although the revolutionaries were prepared to die for their ideals, 'they will probably cause a great deal of harm, but they will never create anything. Some of them are very nice people, quite sincere and terribly unselfish. But those will perish. Only scoundrels will survive'.

Ouspensky's sister, to whom he was close in their younger years, was jailed in 1905 as a revolutionary and died in prison three years later, reportedly in Siberia. It seems to have been too painful an episode for her brother to write about. He possibly mentions the tragedy obliquely in *A New Model of the Universe* in the chapter 'On the Study of Dreams' where he says:

'A young girl, a political prisoner who spent a long time in the Boutirsky prison in Moscow (in 1906-8), told me during my visits, speaking through two gratings, that in her dreams the impressions of the prison were completely mixed up with the impressions of the 'Institute' (a Russian government girls' school with the character of French convents) which she had left only six years before. In her dreams the prison warders became confused with former 'class-ladies' and 'inspectresses"' (house-mistresses). Summonses before the prosecutor and cross-examination were lessons, the coming trial was the final exami-nation, and everything was similarly confused.' (ibid., p. 292)

His comment reflects his attitude to his own school life: 'In this case the connecting link was undoubtedly the similarity of emotional experiences, the boredom, the continual constraint and the general absurdity of the surroundings.'

The intriguing heroine of *Osokin*, Zinaida, apparently was based on a real woman, which naturally has led readers to speculate that romantic episodes in the book may have been modelled on the author's experiences as a young man. A respect akin to Osokin's belief that women belong to a higher 'caste' than men emerges elsewhere in Ouspensky's writings.

As the novel revolves on the reality of eternal recurrence, it naturally touches on man's psychological condition, and in this aspect Ouspensky seems to foreshadow the teaching he was to hear a decade later from Gurdjieff. The points of coincidence are so striking that some readers have suspected that Ouspensky revised the novel's ending to have the magician represent Gurdjieff.

'You must realise,' says the magician consulted by Osokin, 'that you yourself can change nothing and that you must seek help.' This approximates one of Gurdjieff's fundamental lessons: that man as he is cannot 'do'.

The magician also tells Osokin that 'in order to change anything you must first change yourself' (ibid., p. 194), advice that is basic to The Fourth Way teaching. He adds:

'And this is much more difficult than you think. It requires constant effort for a long time and much knowledge. . . . No one is capable of it by himself. People always repeat the same mistakes. At first they simply do not know that they move in a circle; and if they hear about this idea, they refuse to believe it. Later, if they begin to see the truth of it and accept it, they think that this is all that is necessary; they become fully convinced that now they know all they need to know and that they can change everything. And immediately they find charlatans who assure them that everything is very easy and simple.'

Changing requires 'different knowledge', says the magician. Above all, sacrifice is necessary. The sacrifice demanded of Osokin is that he give a period of his life to the magician.

He is told:

'For some very complicated reasons which are all in yourself, you happen to have guessed a very great secret which people generally do not know. By itself your guess is useless because you cannot apply it to anything. But the fact that you know this secret opens certain doors for you. You know everything repeats again and again. . . . If you could change something in yourself, you would be able to use this knowledge for your own advantage.' (ibid, p. 197)

This scenario conjures up the historic meeting of Gurdjieff and Ouspensky. The secrets that Ouspensky had already unearthed were not confined to his notion of eternal recurrence. But although at that stage he had accumulated and worked on an impressive amount of knowledge, he could not be said to have assimilated all of it into his understanding, a distinction that Gurdjieff would stress.

It needs to be said that there is less than universal agreement on this implication that Gurdjieff could put Ouspensky on the right track. Some admirers of Ouspensky's work contend that the quality of thought revealed in *Tertium Organum* and *A New Model of the Universe* show that in time he could have fully developed his mental powers without assistance. Indeed, it is sometimes claimed that contact with Gurdjieff slowed, and possibly misdirected, his progress.

Such views are usually advanced by those who fail to recognise Gurdjieff's teaching as a touchstone to genuine knowledge. This is something that Ouspensky himself never forgot; despite the differences that developed between him and his teacher, he always gave thanks for what he had gained from Gurdjieff. For, as the magician says of Osokin, Ouspensky had guessed a great secret but could not apply it without the practical knack that Gurdjieff, alone of any of the wise men he had met on his travels, could impart.

The magician reveals something else that is generally overlooked in considering Gurdjieff's work, although he himself made no secret of it. After warning that when a person has become aware of the 'great secret' he has only a few more lives and must make the most of them, the magician says: "You must understand that, for reasons of my own, I am interested in such people . . ." ' (ibid., p. 199).

Events were to suggest that Ouspensky did not realise exactly how these 'reasons of my own' applied to his dealings with his real-life 'magician'. Gurdjieff, too, had private reasons for taking an interest in all types of people, as may become clear as we trace Ouspensky's life. Gurdjieff had, as it is said nowadays, his own agenda. But if people helped him towards his big aim they could also help themselves.

It is also significant, in view of The Fourth Way teaching that Ouspensky would espouse a decade later, that his magician should stress: 'Nothing can be acquired without sacrifice.' He would discover through Gurdjieff that one of the hardest of sacrifices is, paradoxically, to give up one's needless suffering.

Ouspensky continues in his Autobiographical Note:

'In 1907 I found theosophical literature, which was prohibited in Russia: Blavatsky, Olcott, A. Besant, Sinnett, etc. It produced a very strong impression on me, although I at once saw its weak side. The weak side was that it had no continuation. But it opened doors for me into a new and bigger world. I discovered the idea of esotericism, found a possible angle for the study of religion and mysticism, and received a new impulse for the study of 'higher dimensions'.

In 1908 I was in Constantinople, Smyrna, Greece and Egypt. Early in 1909 I finally left Moscow and after that lived in St Petersburg. I studied occult literature; made all kinds of psychological experiments by the yogi and magical methods; published several books, *Tertium Organum* among them; and gave public lectures on the Tarot, on Superman, on Yogis, etc.'

As a journalist, Ouspensky met Count Leo Tolstoy not long before the great Russian writer's death in 1910. Tolstoy humoured Ouspensky by drawing a 'funny picture' of the fourth dimension on a tablecloth. Then he spoke about the way he had based some characters in *Anna Karenina* and *War and Peace* on his own family. He also said that the contact of

Pierre Bezuhov with Freemasons in *War and Peace* was autobiographical. Tolstoy said he had also tried to free himself from the domination of the Countess.

Ouspensky may well have been impressed by Tolstoy's attempt to found a religious and social system based on renunciation of violence and wealth and development of the inner self under a canopy of love for all living beings. Five years later he would discover why such fine schemes do not work as long as people remain as they are. Gurdjieff would demonstrate that the initial target for change must be oneself.

First, though, it should be interesting to see what glimpses of life's meaning Ouspensky was to gain by his own efforts. *Tertium Organum*, the book which made him known in the West as a thinker, can serve to make out a prima facie case as to the value of his ideas.

Chapter 3

THE WORLD AND CONSCIOUSNESS

THE REMARKABLE BOOK *Tertium Organum* created the public interest that made a way of life known as 'the Work' accessible to people in the Western world. Initially it seems surprising that, at a time when the author himself was engrossed in George Gurdjieff's profound teaching, it was Ouspensky's pre-Work philosophy that seized the attention of many Britons and Americans. It does not seem so puzzling when we realise how close Ouspensky came to Gurdjieff's System in his own thoughts and writing.

The possibilities revealed in the book aroused the interest of people seeking new meaning in their lives, warmed up and loosened their minds, as it were, and thus prepared them to tackle the demanding, practical tasks presented by Gurdjieff. In that second stage, it would have been difficult for anyone other than the authoritative Ouspensky to move up a notch on the scale of meaning and transmit Gurdjieff's message convincingly to a significant number of followers. Presented by a less sound thinker, a less precise lecturer, the 'System' may well have seemed to have emanated from just another Eastern cult.

Ouspensky's contribution to the Work did not end with his teaching mission; without the material support he attracted, the spread of Gurdjieff's ideas may have been severely limited. It was English money raised through Ouspensky's influence that financed the setting up of Gurdjieff's Institute for the Harmonious Development of Man in France. Later, Gurdjieff was able to 'shear', as he put it, rich Americans to maintain the outer form of his school. Of course, he possessed such skill in acquiring the wherewithal to extricate himself, his followers and dependants from desperate situations that if necessary he would have found another way of furthering his aim. The actuality, however, is that it was as a result of the large sales of *Tertium Organum* that the Work gained a foothold in Europe.

Just how an English translation of a copy of the book taken out of Russia after the 1917 revolution became instrumental in establishing Ouspensky in England and his teacher in France will be related in its chronological place. First, let us see what the book itself divulges – or rather, boldly pronounces – about its author's thought before it was influenced by knowledge claimed to have been bequeathed by a higher level of intelligence.

The manuscript was completed by 1911 and published in St Petersburg the next year, three years before the writer met Gurdjieff. In what amounts to the highest praise for its contents, and a backhanded compliment to its writer, Gurdjieff told Ouspensky that, had the author *understood* all he had written, 'I should come and bow down to you and beg you to teach me' (*In Search of the Miraculous*, p. 20).

The possession of knowledge alone did not impress Gurdjieff. Memorising and theorising with facts were mechanical acts, to his way of thinking. Being clever enough to weave those facts into an interesting form in a book was a smarter but still mechanical performance. In his estimation, all men, from dunces to geniuses, could be divided into machines and cleverer machines. Understanding was of a different order. It required a balance between knowledge and Being.

While Ouspensky might have lacked an esoteric key to the riddles of the earth and the cosmos, he was in advance of most of his fellows by evidently recognising they could not be solved by ordinary logic, or even by his special interest, mathematics.

He illustrates his dissatisfaction with ordinary life by means of an autobiographical episode reported in the Introduction to *A New Model of the Universe*. He identifies himself working on a Moscow daily paper *The Morning* on a day in 1906 or 1907 when he suddenly feels the futility and unreality of writing an editorial about a forthcoming meeting of the Hague Conference on an armaments convention and the customs of war. He pushes aside his papers and opens a drawer of his desk 'crammed with books with strange titles, *The Occult World*, *Life after Death*, *Atlantis and Lemuria*, *Dogme et Rituel de la Haute Magie*, *Le Temple de Satan*, *The Sincere Narrations of a Pilgrim*, and the like'.

He reports finding 'a strange flavour of truth' in these books, made all the stronger because he has been 'living in a desiccated and sterilised world'. By this he means that he has long held himself 'within artificial "positivist" bounds, have denied myself all dreams about things that could not be held within these bounds' (*A New Model of the Universe*, pp. 2-4). (Positivism was a late nineteenth-century scientific philosophy which stipulated that theories could deal only with observable, physico-mechanical phenomena. Ouspensky attacks it throughout *Tertium Organum* for affirming that the study of phenomena could show us reality, or that we could understand causes by trying to model noumena on phenomena.)

Through the occult books, he says, he suddenly 'began to find meaning in old fairytales and woods, rivers, mountains, became living beings'. Nothing was dead for him.

Contrary to the main criticism of Ouspensky, any imbalance would seem to lie in the emphasis on emotional qualities. That would be just as mistaken a view. However, Ouspensky realised he had become so accustomed to thinking 'scientifically' he was afraid even to imagine that there might be something else beyond the outer covering of life. He sees that much in the books that have attracted him is naive but when they touch the perceptive sides of his mind and emotions they open the door to 'the unbroken line of thought and knowledge which passes from century to century, from age to age, from country to country, from one race to another; a line deeply hidden beneath layers of religions and philosophies which are, in fact, only distortions and perversions of the ideas belonging to the line'.

Personal experiments aimed at discovering this hidden knowledge led him to judge, he says, that a 'constant or frequent sensation that the world is not all as it appears' is the first sign that a person may attain to a higher degree of consciousness. The implication here that a raised awareness is necessary to glimpse reality is one of many observations in the book that would signal to Gurdjieff that the writer might be ripe for Fourth Way recruitment.

His writing reveals the two sides of Peter Damian Ouspensky's character – the precise, cold-blooded scientist and the visionary who views the world with the perception of an artist or a lover. His professional life was divided also, into the hard-nosed world of journalism and the contrasting occupation of writing and lecturing on the fourth dimension and occult subjects, highlighted by poetic insights.

Ouspensky later told members of his London group that his given names, Peter Damian, had been passed down to the sons of his family tree for generations. The family had come to believe the 'Damians' were ascetic world-haters and the 'Peters' joyful lovers of life. He believed that both qualities had entered into him. As already noted, Peter Damian may have inherited his interest in mathematics from his father, while his mother bequeathed him an appreciation of painting and literature.

One of his English pupils, John G. Bennett, agreed that Ouspensky was a man of two opposing natures and commented that this dualism coloured his life and his writing. Bennett saw the ascetic, puritanical, Damian side in Ouspensky's attitude to Gurdjieff.

Both disciples and critics of Ouspensky the teacher tended to see only one side of his character, turning him into something of an enigma in that one person's impression that the lecturer was detached, strict and unemotional was contradicted by that of another who found him shy, warm-hearted, even romantic.

J.H. Reyner, a pupil of Maurice Nicoll, elaborates in his *Ouspensky: the Unsung Genius* on the idea that his Peter nature delighted in life's 'good' things, both physical and artistic, while that of Damian was world-rejecting and aesthetic. Ouspensky probably would not have objected to the tag of 'aesthetic', a quality he describes as 'the sense of beauty' and 'the *sensation* of the relation of parts to a whole, and the perception of the necessity for a certain harmonious relation'. Parts and wholes are key elements in his conception of higher dimensions.

'His artistic appreciation was enhanced by a visit to Paris with his mother in 1898,' Reyner says. When he returned to Russia and took up journalism, he 'enjoyed convivial company and good food and wine in the exercise of his "Peter" characteristics. He is described as being warm and generous, open-hearted and excellent company and it seems that it was not until he began to embark on his serious pursuits that he subordinated these aspects of his character to the more intellectual approach'.

Saddened by the death of his mother after their return from Paris, the young Ouspensky travelled to remote parts of Russia, experiencing different cultures.

Presuming that *Strange Life of Ivan Osokin* is largely biographical, Reyner deduces that 'the young Ouspensky was no paragon. He went through the usual adolescent experiences with the accompanying pleasures and pains, which helped him when he came to write on the subject of love in *Tertium Organum* a little later on'.

Whether or not he shared Osokin's susceptibility to women, it is not only the ordinary notion of love that he writes about in *Tertium Organum* but a 'cosmic phenomenon'. He reasons that if a negligible percentage of love's energy 'goes into the creation of the future by begetting, then the remainder must go into the creation of the future also, but in another way' (ibid., p. 169). The surplus, he says, is turned into other energy – demonstrably transformed into instincts, ideas, creative forces on different planes of life, symbols of art, song, music, poetry – and conceivably into a higher order of intuition and consciousness.

Possibly it was soon after an unhappy love affair, suggested by the Ivan-Zinaida relationship in *Osokin*, that Ouspensky was distressed by the death of his sister. He moved to the then Russian capital, St Petersburg, in 1909, working in journalism and attracting large audiences to his lectures.

It may well be, as Reyner considers, that the fresh ideas and experiences gained during his foreign travel, which included a study of theosophical literature banned in Russia, gave him the impetus to complete his 'philosophical treatise'. *Tertium Organum* is primarily a study of 'meta-psychology' and significantly has much in common with Ouspensky's major Work book, *In Search of the Miraculous*, in which he outlines the System taught by Gurdjieff. *Tertium Organum*, too, is the record of a 'quest of the wondrous' and proclaims that the meaning of life lies in 'eternal search'.

In large part, it springs from the author's experiments with a variety of techniques to raise consciousness, including altered breathing methods and probably the inhaling of narcotics. He was impelled on this course by his strong impression of the visible world's unreality and his deduction that, as answers to such questions as time, space, life, death and God still elude modern man's grasp, a method of thinking that transcends the logical process must be needed to understand them.

He does not report having used drugs to create ecstatic states; speculation that he did so is, however, strengthened by his defence of the practice with the claim that narcotics act only on what is already within the user. He also gives detailed descriptions in *A New Model of the Universe* of experimental results that could well have been produced with the aid of drugs.

He points out in *Tertium Organum*, however, that narcosis is not the only way to induce mystical states in ordinary men, enlarging on William James' advice in *The Varieties of Religious Experience* that 'certain aspects of nature' can awaken mystical moods with an assertion that 'in all conditions of encompassing nature this power lies concealed. . . . Sometimes these moods intensify and become the sensation of a complete oneness with nature' (*Tertium Organum*, pp. 302-3).

Ouspensky believes this common experience of mystics – a feeling of the unity of all – backs the findings of his study, and claims that they are theoretically correct according to what he calls the mathematics of the infinite and higher logic (ibid., p. 305).

The infinite, he says, is the greatest mystery. It looms large in his investigations into the dimensions of space, a particular dimension being the infinite repetition of the dimension immediately below it, as a line is an infinite repetition of a point, a plane of a line and a solid of a plane.

His determination to come to grips with this problem persuades him that man's chief goal should be to understand the world's genuine form instead of deluding himself that the sensations, perceptions and conceptions restricted to three-dimensional existence give a true picture.

Insights that he gained during higher states of consciousness convinced Ouspensky that there *is* a world, invisible to us, behind the image thrown up by our three-dimensional perceptions and conceptions. The notion of a projected image is ubiquitous in his study of man's thought processes; he frequently uses the analogy of a movie film in portraying the make-believe way we view our environment.

In *Strange Life of Ivan Osokin*, he uses the metaphor of a cinema to illustrate the 'infinite sphere' by which we represent the universe to ourselves. But it is not only in this novel, originally titled *Kinemadrama*, that he depicts a man's life as flicking through scene by scene like the frames on a strip of film joined in a continuous loop. The novel conveys the author's belief that a person's life – past, present and future – is already present and repeats endlessly, unless he remembers that he is imprisoned in this circle of fate. In the latter, rare event his life is transfigured into a real drama, for at that point he faces the ultimatum of either realising his potential or relinquishing to Ibsen's 'button-moulder' any aspects of himself that are worth recycling.

The cinema also features in his view of our three-dimensional outlook: we imagine the world as an infinite sphere, as on a screen, and through the focus of our receptivity runs a continuous film of feelings and impressions. Each impression, he says, defines the 'I' of a given moment.

This is remarkably close to the Work doctrine of perpetually shifting 'I's, which seize our attention and the next moment are themselves deposed by other 'I's.

Ouspensky urges us to study the cinematograph. 'Where are the pictures themselves? Where is the light throwing the image upon the screen? Whence do the pictures come, and whither do they go?'

He suggests that our consciousness is the light, penetrating the stores of impressions (pictures) in our psyche. We call the images on the screen life. What he regards as the most incomprehensible mystery of life as we see it is that the impressions come from the same screen.

A conclusion he draws from studies on our way of interpreting phenomena leads to the paradoxical assertion: 'I see it; therefore it does not exist.' By this he means that our sight is trapped, as are all our senses, in three-dimensionality and cannot see the complete picture. This holds true on a number of levels. On an elementary one, our eyes see the outside world in perspective, which is not its actual form. We realise, however, that perspective distorts and make allowances for this mentally and thus can conceive the actual three-dimensional form of the objects in view.

A more important shortcoming, and one we do not take into account, is that our eyes see only a *section* of a four-dimensional object or objects. In the terminology of the book, we see phenomena but not the noumena that contain it; we see effects but cannot even imagine their real causes.

Ouspensky indicates the extreme difficulty in comprehending the fourth dimension, in our usual states, by suggesting that to do so it is first necessary to be able to form an idea of the fifth dimension (*Tertium Organum*, p. 46). That is to say, 'it is impossible to understand the idea of time without conceiving in imagination the idea of eternity'. He says that eternity is not, as Immanuel Kant seemed to imagine, the infinite extension of time but the dimension perpendicular to it. (It is because 'extension in time is extension into unknown space' that time is the fourth dimension of space.)

In *Tertium Organum* Ouspensky arrives at 'facts' – psychological if not physical – largely by analogy with existence in the world of lower dimensions. His starting point is where Kant left off: that what we see as extension in space and comprehend as existence in time are not properties appertaining to things themselves but just the properties of our sensuous receptivity. That is to say, things exist independently of time and space. We see phenomena as sensory impressions by imposing our form of perception on them; this is the prism through which we view the world.

These ideas are still mind-bending today. Ouspensky, writing nearly a century ago, sets out his arguments clearly and patiently, at pains to demonstrate that he is presenting not a hypothesis but hard facts, even though they cannot be weighed, measured or examined under the strongest lens. Facts hard to grasp, for which reason, as one passage of text glides easily into the next, suddenly he resurrects a subject broached earlier, penetrates more deeply into the reasoning behind it, and the reader may feel himself to be a step closer to reality.

Detailed examples are essential because he is operating in fields largely untouched by science: the one-dimensional world outlook of a creature such as a snail, the two-dimensional perceptions of animals, the three-dimensional conceptions of man.

The extremely circumscribed comprehension (to us) of lower forms of life convincingly demonstrates the truth of the observation 'as above so below'. For example, the failure of two-dimensional beings to realise that the forms they apprehend on their plane world are but sections of solid objects is echoed in the inability of beings living on the next higher level to see the real causes of three-dimensional phenomena.

Ouspensky finds that animals 'must perceive the immobile angles and curves of the third dimension as motion, i.e., as temporal phenomena', and asks: 'Do not *we* perceive as motion, i.e., as temporal phenomena, the immobile angles and curves of the fourth dimension?' (ibid., pp. 114-5)

This is all very well, but as problems and possible solutions concerning noumena and phenomena are gradually unfolded, the reader may weary of the numerous analogies employed. Ouspensky, revealing a sympathetic side of his nature, agrees that 'the method of analogies is, generally speaking, a rather tormenting thing. With it, you walk in a vicious circle. It helps you to elucidate certain things, and the relations of certain things, but in substance it never gives a direct answer to anything' (ibid., p. 78).

The direct way to solve these questions is to find the conditions of the three-dimensionality of the world in our psyche. By this stage of the treatise, the two 'given' things on which he started his study of knowledge, *the world* and our *psychic life*, have become *the world* and *consciousness*. The 'direct' way, then, of seeking a solution to any of these problems, say space and time, is by studying our consciousness and its properties.

This aligns with the Work's injunction to receive and interpret life's impressions with increased consciousness. It is also one of the reasons that rather one-eyed supporters of Ouspensky believe he was capable, without anyone's help, of reaching the revelations presented by the Work. To claim this is to overlook the fact that that while Ouspensky knew in many cases what was needed, Gurdjieff understood how to achieve it.

The big unknowns investigated in the book are space; time; quantity, mass, substantiality; number, equality and inequality; identity and difference; cause and effect; the ether, atoms, electrons, energy, life, death – the very things that are ordinarily considered the foundations of our knowledge.

A reader may object that there is nothing mysterious about, for instance, identity and difference. However, Ouspensky suggests that objects we regard as separate in our three-dimensional experience can be seen to be connected in the fourth dimension – but only in the light of the fine energy of consciousness.

The direct path leads to a deeper examination of sensations, which leave traces in our memory, the character and timing of which remembrances lead to perceptions, which in turn lead to words and speech and concepts and ideas.

Ouspensky points out that the existence of visible and hidden sides of life was known to philosophy long ago. But on this he warns there is no greater error than the dualistic theory of a division between noumena and phenomena. Such division exists only in our minds, he says. 'The "phenomenal world" is simply our incorrect perception of the world.'

His opposition to a dualistic philosophy would be approved by Gurdjieff, for whom even spirit and matter were but finer and coarser degrees of the one substance, though he might have found Ouspensky dualistic himself in other respects.

In view of Ouspensky's later insights into the mysteries of time and space, it is appropriate that these subjects are introduced in *Tertium Organum*'s first chapter:

'Our relation to the objective world is most exactly defined by the fact that we perceive it as existing in *time* and *space* . . . In general, we say that the objective world consists of things and phenomena, i.e., things and changes in the state of things. The PHENOMENA exist for us in time; the THINGS in space. . . . In reality, we know only our own perceptions and conceptions, and we recognise the objective world by projecting outside of ourselves the causes of our sensations, presupposing them to contain these causes' (ibid., p.13).

It is a few chapters later that his abstract reasoning dictates that the fourth dimension of space – that is, the infinite repetition of the third dimension – must lie in time, that time is the fourth dimension. He says:

'We feel an infinite sphere as space; the rest of the world, that which was yesterday and that which will be tomorrow, we feel as time. In other words, every being feels as space that which is grasped by his space-sense: the rest he refers to time; i.e., the *imperfectly felt* is referred to time.'

He further explains that a four-dimensional body may be regarded as

'the tracing of the movement in space of a three-dimensional body in a direction not confined within that space – this is the direction of time. . . . The four-dimensional body is the infinite number of moments of existence of the three-dimensional one – its states and positions. . . . Four-dimensional space (time) is really the distance between the forms, states and positions of one and the same body. . . . The sensation of motion in time (and motion out of time does not exist) arises in us because we are looking at the world as if through a narrow slit, and are seeing the lines of intersection of the time plane with our three-dimensional space only.'

Along the way he throws up thought-provoking notions like:

'In the past, behind us, lies not only that which really happened, *but that which could have been*. In the same way, in the future lies not only that which will be, *but everything that may be*' (ibid., p. 45).

And, after lengthy expositions of the extension of dimensions, he asserts:

'It is impossible to understand the idea of time without conceiving in imagination the idea of eternity; it is likewise impossible to understand space if we have no idea of time' (ibid., p. 47).

Ouspensky accepts and builds upon the 'transcendental aesthetic' doctrine of Kant's *The Critique of Pure Reason*: 'The intuition (experience) of space and time are predicated upon forms particular to our sensibilities and not actual (objective) existents.'

Gurdjieff was to give Ouspensky a new starting point, specifically in an understanding of the various cosmoses, by pronouncing: 'If Kant had introduced the idea of scale into his arguments many things he wrote would be very valuable' (*In Search of the Miraculous*, pp. 304-5).

The abstract reasoning mentioned above requires a high degree of intuition, which further weakens the claim that Ouspensky was crippled emotionally, a self-mutilation by his Damian to devote all his energy to a theoretical analysis of Gurdjieff's ideas.

On the contrary, he remained attracted to the artistic side of life, especially poetry, throughout his life. The reason is apparent in a section of *Tertium Organum* where he is explaining why emotions cannot be expressed exactly in words: 'The interpretation of emotional feelings and emotional understanding is the problem of art.' He adds that life's emotional tones are best transmitted by music but it cannot express concepts. Poetry, however, tries to express music and thought.

Ouspensky patently had no misapprehension on the importance of feeling in attaining to 'cosmic consciousness', a term he borrowed from a writer on the occult, Edward Carpenter. 'High mental culture, high intellectual attainments, are not necessary conditions at all,' Ouspensky says in this connection. 'The example of many saints, who were not intellectual, but who undoubtedly attained cosmic consciousness, shows that cosmic consciousness may develop in purely emotional soil . . .' (ibid., p. 331).

So, before meeting the Work, he in no way confined the search for reality to a strictly cerebral exercise. The side of his nature interested in the arts is also evident when he says: 'Cosmic consciousness is also possible of attainment through the emotion attendant upon creation – in painters, musicians and poets. Art in its highest manifestations is a path to cosmic consciousness' (ibid.).

To Ouspensky, emotions are not merely 'organs of feeling for feeling's sake' but organs of knowledge; he says some things and relations can be known only emotionally and people fail to understand one another because different emotions rule their lives. He describes emotions as 'the stained-glass windows of the soul'. With this shade of bias, 'nothing gives one such a clear idea of things as the emotions, yet nothing deludes one so much'.

The following passage is so close to the Work teaching that it is hard to believe it was not added post-Gurdjieff:

'Emotions unite with the different I's of our psyche. Emotions apparently the same may be united with the very small I's and with the very great and lofty I's. . . . The continual shifting of emotions, each of which calls itself I and strives to establish power over man, is the chief obstacle to the establishment of a *constant* I. . . . The sign of the growth of emotions is the liberation of them from the *personal* element, and their sublimation on the higher planes. . . . the cognitive power of the emotions is greater in proportion as there is less of *self-elements* in a given emotion, i.e., more consciousness that this emotion is not the I' (ibid., p. 221).

On the manifestation of cosmic consciousness, he points to an important condition: 'it is necessary that the centre of gravity of *everything* shall lie for man in the inner world, in self-consciousness, and not in the outer world at all'. This reference to the positioning of one's centre of gravity again foreshadows a requirement of self-development in the Work.

(On correspondences between Ouspensky's early thought and the Work teaching, it should be borne in mind that in revised editions of *Tertium Organum* he probably substituted, for some terms, words taken from Gurdjieff's System. However, Ouspensky's integrity was such that it is unlikely any basic ideas were altered. He says in the preface to the second English edition that 'my chief concern has been to coordinate its terminology with the more developed terminology of those of my books written after the second Russian edition of *Tertium Organum*, from which the English translation was made'. He adds: 'The first word demanding a more careful use [of language] is "consciousness".')

It could be that his attraction for the occult produced in *Tertium Organum* an optimism that was not necessarily part of the System he was soon to adopt, nor with his own more sober view late in his life. This refers particularly to his confident claim: 'The future belongs not to *man, but to superman*, who is already born, and lives among us.' (ibid., p. 324)

He adds that 'a higher race is rapidly emerging among humanity' but stresses that a change for the better in the outer lives of the many will depend on inner changes in a few, and that 'conscious work is necessary'. He scoffs at reliance on 'natural growth' or the pictures of utopia promised by the fruits of science and technology.

These promises, incidentally, were not so different at the turn into the twentieth century to those of the twenty-first, judging by the catchcries he quotes:

' "Communication with the planet Mars", "The chemical

synthesis of protoplasm," "The utilisation of the rotation of the earth around the sun," "Energy imprisoned in an atom," "Vaccine for all disease," "Life to the length of a hundred years" – or even to one hundred and fifty! After that perhaps, "The artificial creation of men" – but beyond this imagination fails' (ibid., p. 307).

He counters these extravagant promises with the observation that at that time the number of unknown facts in every region of scientific knowledge was rapidly increasing; that the unknown threatened to swallow what was accepted as known. 'One might define the progress of science, especially lately, as a very rapid growth of the regions of nescience,' he comments, ignorance obviously being no more an acceptable excuse in our lives than in law.

When at the outset of his study Ouspensky presents 'the facts that can be proved' – that is, 'The existence of the world in which he (man) lives; and the existence of psychic life in himself' (ibid., p. 12) – he sees man as having three psychic lives. A list of these shows how close Ouspensky was to thinking along Fourth Way lines:

1. The psychic life of the body, which manifests itself in instincts and in the constant work of the body. (The physical body with its little understood mind.)

2. The psychic life of the personality, a complex and constantly changing 'I', which we know and in which we are conscious of ourselves.

3. The consciousness of all life, a greater and higher 'I'.

His idea of the soul as the reflected activity guided by impressions received from the external world and from the body, and consisting of sensations, perceptions, conceptions, thoughts, emotions and desires, may be too theoretical to match Work teaching. However, his definition of the spirit, comprising higher principles which may guide the soul-life, is closer to a Fourth Way understanding, particularly as he points out it is 'the region of the unknown – consciousness, will and the one "I"; i.e., those things that in ordinary man are in potentiality only' (ibid., pp. 203-4).

Gurdjieff would surely have agreed when Ouspensky says that our first fallacy when considering man's noumenon and psyche is that 'we are inclined to regard man as a certain unity, and to regard the different parts and functions of man as being bound together, and dependent on one another'.

The writer maintains that, as matter is merely the conditions of space and time in which we dwell, our consciousness can leave the conditions of materiality, when the moment would be expanded so that past, present and future would be seen at once.

He also anticipates Work teaching when giving a reason for the illusion of motion in space and time. It is, he says, because our 'I' is a complicated quantity within us that is in continuous motion, creating the illusion of motion around us.

Before he learns from Gurdjieff about the scale of intelligence throughout the universe, Ouspensky agrees with the following remark by one of his friends: 'Positivism assures itself that a stone is a stone and nothing more, but any . . . child knows perfectly that a stone from the wall of a church and one from a prison wall are different things' (ibid., pp.156-7).

Only the limitation of our minds prevents us from seeing life in all objects, Ouspensky believes. He reasons:

'If rationality exists in the world, then it must permeate everything . . . (ibid., p. 198).

Each stone, each grain of sand, each planet has its *noumenon*, consisting of life and of psyche, binding them into certain *wholes* incomprehensible to us (ibid., p. 200)

'Each combination of cells having a definite function is a living being also. Another higher combination – the organ – is a living being no less, and possesses a psychic life of its own. ... But even a complete organism is *merely a section* of a certain magnitude, of what we may call the life of this organism from birth to death' (ibid., p. 201).

The many instances where Ouspensky foreshadows Fourth Way teaching include his conviction that to develop man has not merely to improve but transform himself. It is a common mistake, he says, to think that we can remain as we are and simply add on what we would like to be. People 'do not want to recognise that man can and must become entirely different'. In saying this, he is already speaking the Work language – so much so that one might wonder whether some of his early writing could have given Gurdjieff ideas for the exposition of his System when he chose to present it in a form people could readily understand, which was by no means always his aim.

Ouspensky admits he does not have all the answers. Man has to turn in another direction, but the writer concedes that discovering what this is would be like finding 'the fourth perpendicular' that would open into the fourth dimension. Dismissing ordinary logic as a way to a solution, he says the psychological method 'gives a direct answer at least to the question of the immediate purpose of our existence'.

The meaning of life, as Ouspensky sees it before meeting Gurdjieff, consists in seeking knowledge. All life experience is knowledge. He writes that all the elements of a person's psyche – sensations, perceptions, conceptions, ideas, judgments, reasonings, feelings, emotions, even creation – are instruments of knowledge which the 'I' possesses.

'This process of acquiring knowledge, representing *our function in the world*, is performed not by the intellect only, but by our entire organism, by all the body, by all the life, and by all the life of human society, its organisations, its institutions, by all culture and all civilisation; by that which we know of humanity and, still more, by that which we do not know. And we acquire the knowledge of that which we deserve to know' (ibid., p. 216).

He comments that this will raise no doubts when it is taken to apply to man's intellectual side – but as for the emotions? He suggests that there is no sharp distinction between intellect and emotion and that in reality only emotions exist in man's soul. Spinoza saw this, he says, when he contended that emotion can be mastered only by another, more powerful emotion (ibid., p. 217) – an idea echoed with everyday importance, and application, in the Work.

The writing of Edward Carpenter and R.M. Bucke conceivably put Ouspensky onto the idea of higher degrees of consciousness, but at the same time he considered that they did not see the steps between the different levels of awareness. Carpenter regarded what he called man's existing 'self-consciousness' as a transitory form of 'cosmic consciousness'. But Ouspensky comments: 'Under the usual conditions of the average man the extremely misty focus of his consciousness is confined to the *psyche* perpetually going from one object to another.'

He adds that in saying 'I', a man does not mean his totality. 'I wish', words that he saw play the most important role in a man's life, usually refer not to every side of his Being simultaneously, 'but merely to some small and insignificant facet, which at a given moment holds the focus of consciousness and subjects to itself all the rest, until it is forced out by another equally insignificant facet'.

Ouspensky quotes eleven pages of extracts from Dr Bucke's *Cosmic Consciousness*, after which he criticises the expressed optimism that there will be advancement through social life, arguing instead that the only possible ground for favourable changes in the outer life can be changes in the inner life. Ouspensky asserts:

'All cultural conquests in the realm of the material are double-edged, may equally serve for good or for evil. A change in consciousness can alone be a guarantee of the surcease of wilful misuses of the powers given by culture, and only thus will culture cease to be a "growth of barbarity" '(ibid., p. 321).

This, though not unexpected, was prophetic in view of the Bolshevik Revolution that was to come.

In an example of the correspondence between Gurdjieff's and Ouspensky's ideas, Ouspensky notes that the psyche of man has often been compared to a dark, sleeping town in the midst of which night-guards with lanterns slowly move about, each illuminating a circle around himself.

'Each such little lighted circle represents an I, living its own life, sometimes very short. And there is continuous movement, either fast or slow, moving out into the light more of new and still new objects, or else old ones from the region of memory, or tormentingly revolving in a circle of the same fixed ideas. . . .

'The lighted circle runs quickly from one I to another – from one object, from one idea, from one perception or image to another: within the focus of consciousness rapidly changing I's succeed one another, a little of the light of consciousness going over from one to another. This is the true motion that alone exists in the world. Should this motion stop, should all I's simultaneously enter the focus of receptivity, should the light so expand as to illume all at once that which is usually lighted bit by bit and gradually, and could a man grasp simultaneously by his reason all that ever entered or will enter his receptivity and all that which is never clearly illumined by thought (producing its action on the psyche nevertheless) – then would a man behold himself in the midst of an *immobile universe*, in which there would exist simultaneously everything that lies usually in the remote depths of memory, in the past; all that lies at a remote distance from him; all that lies in the future' (*Tertium Organum*, pp. 204-6).

In noting 'this continual shifting of view from one subject to another', Ouspensky has hit upon what could be seen to be the basis of Gurdjieff's teaching on human psychology.

Studying Bucke's vision of a 'family' of men over the past forty centuries whose spiritual eyes have been opened may have helped prepare Ouspensky to combine with Gurdjieff's idea of Conscious Humanity.

He says that in moments of powerful emotion everything happening round about a man seems to be unreal, a dream. 'This is the beginning of the soul's awakening. When a man in a dream begins to be conscious of the fact that he is asleep and that what he sees is a dream, then he is waking up.'

Actually, 'the life of man goes on simultaneously on different planes, as it were, while the phenomena of one plane only at times and partially touch those of another'.

He recalls from his 1908 note book an experience of heightened consciousness of a type that arises when 'the sense of nature sometimes unfolds something infinitely new and profound in things which seemed to have been known a long time and in themselves contained nothing mystical. This event occurred while he stood at the rail of a steamer on the sea of Marmora on a rainy winter's day, looking at the waves as the ship heeled and shuddered.

'I watched this play of waves with the ship, and felt them draw me to themselves. . . . The waves were drawing my soul to themselves. And suddenly I felt that it went to them. It lasted an instant, perhaps less than an instant, but I entered into the waves and with them rushed with a howl at the ship. And in that instant *I became all.* The waves – they were myself: the far violet mountains, the wind, the clouds hurrying from the north, the great steamship heeling and rushing irresistibly forward – all were myself. . . . It was a moment of unusual freedom, joy and expansion. A second – and the spell of charm disappeared' (ibid., p. 304).

Tertium Organum contains many subjects treated in a refreshing and fascinating way, but the core subjects of space-time and consciousness are most closely connected with the Work ideas he was later to propagate. He sees that the latent energy contained in the phenomena of consciousness is boundless, that an idea can act for millenniums (ibid., p. 140). He notes that spirituality is not opposed to 'intellectuality' or 'emotionality'; it is their 'higher flight', a fusion of the intellect with the higher emotions.

He stresses that while the mind of man may assist in its own evolution it can also impede it, adding: 'And the individual who is not evolving does not remain in a static condition, but goes down, degenerates (i.e., some of his elements begin their own evolution inimical to the whole). And if we take into consideration what an infinitesimal percentage of men think and are capable of thinking of their evolution (or their striving toward higher things) then we shall see that to talk about the inevitability of this evolution is at least naive.'

Ouspensky also demonstrates an intuition of an impulse close to what Gurdjieff would explain as Third Force. Bucke maintains that the fundamental element of cosmic consciousness is a blending of thought and feeling. Ouspensky adds that it is not simply the blending but the result of this: 'thought and feeling plus something else, plus something else that is absent either in the intellect or in the emotional nature' (ibid., p. 323).

While arguing that reason and will can 'conquer' only by virtue of their emotional element – giving as an example the ascetic who kills all passion in himself by the desire for salvation – he states that 'will is the resultant of desires'. If this was entirely his own formulation before meeting Gurdjieff it shows a remarkable coincidence between the two men's ideas. He still had many miles to travel and many words to write before that meeting.

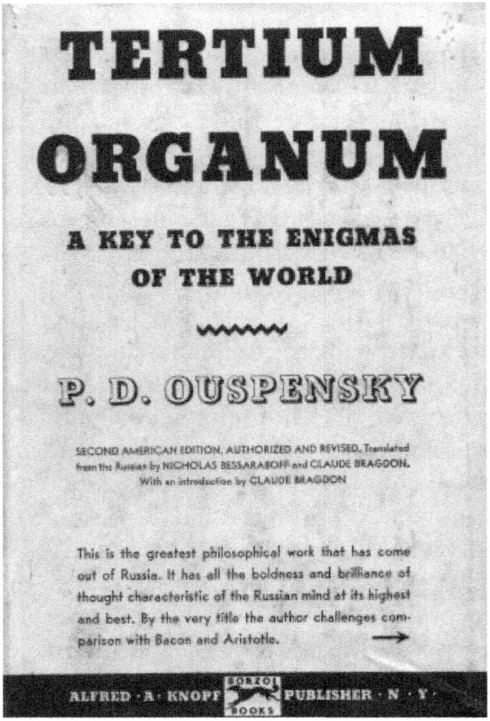

Chapter 4

CITIES WITH SOUL

IT was through contact with Theosophy that Ouspensky, who already had a constant interest in higher dimensions of space and time, became fully persuaded that it must be possible to experience a greater reality than our conventional perception of the world. Theosophy was banned in Russia, so he could not study it until he ventured to other countries.

He had left school in 1896 at the age of 18 and started work as a journalist and a translator. Exposure to the life of the community soon showed him contradictions that reminded him of the *Obvious Absurdities* he had read about in a children's book.

A year or two later, he and his mother visited Paris. Although he had vowed never to seek any academic honours, he attended university lectures in Russia and abroad. Perhaps he heard 'lectures by various professors' at the Sorbonne, as does the hero of *Strange Life of Ivan Osokin*.

In the absence of contemporary accounts of that visit, Ouspensky's sketch of his impressions of Notre Dame Cathedral in *A New Model of the Universe* may give an idea of its effect on him as a young man. He says that for him the view from the top of its towers always evoked strange thoughts. From that perspective he felt he saw two lines of life: the lives of the people in the city below and the lives of the cathedral builders. This led him to visualise history as being divided into two kinds, one of crime, the other of a real heritage as secret and invisible as the cathedral builders themselves. The need to keep unconventional ideas secret at the time of the cathedral building, he says, was a consequence of the Catholic Church's 'heretic-mania'.

His impression of the gargoyles was that they transmit the masons' psychological ideas, which stemmed from a school of esoteric knowledge, demonstrating in particular the complexity of the soul. Writing in 1922, he adds that these figures are the 'I's of Notre Dame, a description that appears to owe something to Gurdjieff's terminology.

However, it seems to have been Ouspensky's personal feeling that the gargoyles, along with the carvings of the twelve Apostles and the apocalyptic beasts, are aspects of the *soul* of Notre Dame, looking into a dimension invisible to ordinary people.

It will be seen that Ouspensky detected *soul* in other objective works of art in his world travels. On this, it is interesting to recall what he said when making an analogy with the cinema, in which pictures are thrown on the screen of our organs of perception. He regarded as a great mystery of life his deduction that both the images and our impressions of them come from our consciousness. This suggests that his insight into religious art works was based on his own psychological understanding, that he brought the 'film' of these ideas into the 'cinema' and projected them onto the 'screen', seeing the images more vividly because of that concentrated effort.

We will see later what different messages, and presentiments, he received from Notre Dame on visits in 1913 and 1921.

Presumably it was during his early Paris experiences that he contacted Theosophy. In his already mentioned 'Autobiographical fragment' he notes the then prohibited writings of its modern founder, Helena Petrovna Blavatsky, and others – adding that he immediately saw that system's weakness. Although it conveyed a mystical sentiment and spoke of higher dimensions and levels, it portrayed them as a continuation of the familiar third dimension and saw space and time as being separate from one another. Such a teaching could be of limited help in his struggle to grasp the complexities of higher dimensions.

When he returned to Moscow and journalism in 1898 the publication of his book *The Fourth Dimension* earned him wide recognition, including the respect of scientists, a regard that would be missing from the scientific response to the works that followed, even though he believed they showed the way to a clearer vision of reality.

Soon after their return home, Ouspensky's mother died. He then seems to have journeyed through remote parts of Russia, experiencing life close to nature. In the 1920s he told one of his English pupils, Maurice Nicoll, something of those days, disclosing that a mountain in the Caucasus was called Ouspensky after one of his ancestors, a general who had conquered a mountain tribe's stronghold by arming his men with extra guns so their rapid fire would give an exaggerated perception of their strength.

Peter Ouspensky, too, sometimes carried guns, but only as a means of showing courtesy to hosts. He spoke of gentle tribes people who sang a lot and were very welcoming to visitors but were easily offended if guests were careless in repaying them for their lavish hospitality. Ouspensky avoided offence by making use of a custom that obliged them to give a visitor anything of theirs he admired. He would praise a quite cheap object and when it was pressed on him would accept it only if they took something of his in return. He carried a number of cheap revolvers to offer as gifts.

Perhaps it was his Peter side that was impressed by Circassian tribesmen's ability to drink eleven bottles of a thick, red wine of which he – regarded by his city friends as being far from a novice in that capacity – could manage only two (*Maurice Nicoll: A Portrait*, p. 101).

By 1905, against the background of the Russian Insurrection, the suppressed start of the revolt that he predicted was inevitable, he had written the film scenario that he revised as a novel, published in St Petersburg a decade later as *Kinemadrama*. As we have seen, he saw in the new entertainment medium a reflection of the way he believed our lives are replayed again and again like a film, the light of our awareness projecting the recorded scenes on the screen of our senses.

The story was a way of popularising his theory of eternal recurrence, later set out clearly in his major books. The inner meaning of the story gives hints of Ouspensky's introduction to esoteric teaching. The underlying tone of most of the novel is pessimistic, with Osokin showing that even when he *remembers* mistakes of his past lives he still acts as though he had forgotten them and repeats them. The book's ending, however, gives cause for hope, with a new element entering the cycle of Osokin's lives. For the first time, the hero has genuinely asked for help. The magician agrees to show him the way, but warns that now Osokin has guessed a great secret his time is limited.

If Ouspensky did not visualise the magician as Gurdjieff himself – and quickly re-write the story's ending, before publication in 1915 – he certainly portrayed him as one who could live in higher dimensions; again, this is approximating Work teaching about Real I, the only one who can help a person become real.

One way of reading *Osokin* is to regard the other main characters as parts of the hero's nature, which is a method Ouspensky applied to his interpretations of meaningful literary works. He may not have planned the story from that perspective, but it still was likely to turn out that way, thanks to the new way of thinking he was developing. Thus Zinaida – as the heroine she would traditionally represent the man's emotional side – would view events of the day through the eyes of his quiet, passive side. Osokin's masculine, active side might entertain more inspired plans and hopes for the future, but the practical Zinaida would act to bring him down to earth in the present.

Evidently, even though he did not yet have precise Work knowledge or nomenclature, Ouspensky was approaching its precepts in his own terms, through his own inclinations. Zinaida's emphasis on acting now is close to the Work state of self-remembering, which necessitates being present in a real place in oneself in the moment. Perhaps the most significant aspect of this story is that, although Ouspensky had felt the reality of its theme of eternal recurrence before absorbing Gurdjieff's ideas, he found nothing in that teaching to contradict the theory that influenced him throughout his life.

Possibly financed by a small legacy, and certainly with an

arrangement to sell articles to newspapers and periodicals, in 1908-9 Ouspensky extended his travels to Constantinople, Smyrna, Greece, Egypt, and the east coast of the United States of America.

He had a brief preview of an aspect of Gurdjieff's teaching when he saw Mevlevi whirling dervishes in Turkey. They turned out to be the opposite of the frenzied dancers he had expected. Their whirling movements were part of a 'system' he could feel but not understand, although he believed that the turning dervishes represented the solar system, the planets revolving around the sun.

Using again the term that played an important part in his philosophy before meeting Gurdjieff, he felt that these dervishes were the *soul* of Constantinople. This word, which as employed by Ouspensky was more than a metaphor, also indicated his perception of cities, and of course other conglomerates and works of art, as living entities with parts corresponding to those of human beings though on a higher scale.

He realised that the dances demanded mental concentration, and it seemed as though that while turning the dervishes were solving difficult problems in their head. This was a challenge that pupils in Gurdjieff's Movements classes would face in coming years, so when Ouspensky saw the dervishes twelve years later he knew part of their secret: the principle of the mental work involved in their whirling, which made the 'miracle' even more significant for him. A deeper secret, he decided, was not how they did it but why, adding, disappointingly, that this could not be told.

Ouspensky was accompanied on at least the Egyptian leg of his trip by a friend, but has left scant record of this in his books. His main impression of the Pyramids and the Sphinx was that they, too, exerted a vital influence on those with eyes to see. However, as he came to grasp this fully only as the effects of his 1908 visit merged with those of another in 1913, it may once again be preferable to save his comments until we reach that stage of his journeying and understanding.

He made use of his knowledge of the United States at the

turn of the century in a short story, *The Inventor*, one of two tales in his book *Talks With a Devil*, which examines whether evil can be conscious. Although this story was not published in Russia until 1916, it was written before Ouspensky had heard Gurdjieff's ideas.

The invention in the story is a rapid-firing machine pistol and its inventor, who is shown to be unaware of his own nature, demonstrates the truth of the proverb about the road to hell being lined with good intentions. The tale is an allegory of the modern scientist – whose efforts focus on the material world – confronted by unanticipated consequences of new technology. In this respect, it is just as timely a warning now as it was eighty years ago.

In this story Ouspensky introduces his belief that it is the development of the emotions that are most necessary for man. His devil constantly opposes emotionally activated artists and mystics who can see a reality beyond the material world. The key point, as set out in the introduction, is that devils 'strictly speaking, do not even exist. It is you who create us'. Thus, when the inventor seeks an unselfish result from the material forces he has unleashed, and is no longer susceptible to suggestion, the devil vanishes beneath the earth.

The author makes his point but the 'happy' ending is only weakly substantiated by events. Perhaps the English edition's editor, John Bennett, culled some 'purely narrative' parts of the story that may have made it more plausible. As it is, the devil cuts off questioning by harking back to the condition set in the introduction, that no moral should be sought. It could be argued here that, rather than a weakness, this is a clever twist that emphasises the devil's weakness; that is, his impotence when confronted by lives that have found fufilment in other than the material world.

Ouspensky's central theme, that evil is mechanical, is also portrayed in the second of these short stories, *The Benevolent Devil.* In this 'fairytale', based on Ouspensky's impressions during his visit to India and Ceylon in 1913-14, the demonic force's aim is to prevent people realising that they could escape the prison of the material world by seeking a reality containing more potential than the realm of the senses.

The devil's role is remarkable in being a forerunner for that of Gurdjieff's hypothesis of the Kundabuffer 'implant'; both aim to keep mankind happy with his lot, for dissatisfaction might lead people to seek deeper meaning and purpose in life.

Incidentally, Ouspensky also makes an observation in *Tertium Organum* about instinctive actions that are interesting when compared with Gurdjieff's teaching about the Kundabuffer influence. He says that before the dawn of human intellect the actions of the animal kingdom were governed by a tendency to receive or retain pleasure or to escape pain (ibid., p. 88). He views instinct as a source of pleasant or painful sensations which repel or attract an animal in this or that direction, compelling it to perform whole series of complex actions, sometimes expedient to such a degree that they appear to be sensible, even founded upon foresight, like the migration of birds, the building of nests for the young which have not as yet appeared, the finding of the way south in the autumn, and north in the spring, etc.

He points out that this subservience to pleasure or pain was expedient; that is, it led to Nature's desired goal. By contrast, he says, our present slavery to the pleasure-pain principle is based on gratification of the senses and is not expedient to any goal useful to us.

Gurdjieff's view of mechanicalness would prove to be far more radical than that reached by Ouspensky through his own reasoning. In *Talks With a Devil*, Ouspensky draws a sharp distinction between the prosaic, flat, ordinary state of being 'immersed in matter' and the poetical, artistic feeling that responds to the 'voice of the miraculous'. Gurdjieff would assure him that both groups are equally mechanical.

This sweeping judgment is not one that many people can accept readily. Ouspensky could, so the fact that Ouspensky did not change the way he had already written *Talks With a Devil* would seem to be due to his honesty in what he presented as his own ideas.

The sometimes emotionally cloying passages in the book suggest that, for Ouspensky, it was an experiment in presenting a deep idea in a story that would appeal to a sentimental reading public. There is some subtlety in his approach but, despite the warning not to ask about morals, the author's message is occasionally stated plainly. The devil, for instance, hails a victory as 'the triumph of Great Matter, or the Great Deception, over the spirit, will and consciousness of man. . . . In order to come to it, the person must believe unconditionally in the reality of that which actually does not exist, in the reality of myself and my reign'.

Ouspensky also used some of the personal experiences he reveals in other writings. For instance, the hero becomes 'aware of the secret essences which lived and moved in all that surrounded him, embodied in the paintings of old masters, in ancient churches, walls and turrets, but always at one with the countryside from which they arose . . .'

Later, reviewing the overall effect in the light of Work teaching, Ouspensky was not keen on an English translation being published. Some of his followers have complained that *Talks With a Devil* does not reflect Ouspensky's mature understanding and criticised Bennett for releasing it in 1972. According to Bennett, Ouspensky had considered writing a third talk to relate the existing two to a Fourth Way scheme, showing that the Work could reconcile spirit and matter. He also suggests that one reason Ouspensky did not publish the book was that it 'does not adequately express the agony of indecision through which Ouspensky lived in the later years of his life' (ibid., p. 12).

That indecision was a result of his frustrating search for a source of the teaching he had received from Gurdjieff.

About 1907, after extensive reading on the occult, Ouspensky came to believe that an unbroken line of knowledge had passed down through the ages, and observed that few people realised this. Confident that it should be possible to correlate this hidden knowledge with ascertainable data by crossing the 'bridge' of the fourth dimension, he decided to write about all he had found. He plunged into unusual experiments in an effort to intensify his awareness of the world – but lost his enthusiasm for writing.

He felt a new method was necessary. His attempts to see noumena in place of phenomena gave him glimpses, he believed, of infinity, but he was not in control and could not remember these visions when he fell back into his usual state.

He did, however, retain a taste for reality. In fact, his experiments confirmed a sudden conviction he had had as a schoolboy – on reading about levers in a physics book – that many apparently different things were unified. Indeed, he records in *A New Model of the Universe*, perhaps with the benefit of a mature hindsight, that he had felt with awe 'the unity of all'.

These serious recollections may suggest that the severe, aesthetic, Damian side of Ouspensky's nature had become the driving force in his life. But during this period Peter, the pleasure loving aspect of his being, had plenty of opportunity to enjoy the company of his fellows. A rare glimpse of this part of his life was given in a feature article in *The New Age* by London journalist Carl Bechhofer in 1921. The English correspondent took the risk of seeking an interview with Ouspensky in the Caucasus during the Russian Revolution. He describes a drinking session with Ouspensky in a barn at beleagured Rostov-on-Don during the freezing winter of 1919.

Ouspensky recalled that in his social heyday in Moscow the police all knew him by his Christian name 'because, unlike most people, when I was drunk I always tried to resolve quarrels and not start them'. It also helped that he tipped the officers generously for their services. Apparently, restaurant porters, too, were well aware of Peter Ouspensky's calming ability, possibly also of his tips, and made a custom of phoning him to come round and settle rows, which were evidently a feature of Moscow cafe society. ("In Anti-Bolshevik Russia" article in *Gurdjieff International Review*, vol II, No. 2)

However, neither vodka nor the increasing inner knowledge of himself that he was gaining could counter a depressing feeling of the futility of everyday life. What was necessary, he decided, was a new technique to link the higher and the lower dimensions. He had read about the methods of yogis and Sufis, about schools that taught a special kind of knowledge, and was influenced by, among others, the author Edward Carpenter, who asserted that the path to 'cosmic consciousness' could be found only in the Orient.

In 1913 Ouspensky set out for the East with the aim of finding whether esoteric schools still existed. Before heading to Egypt, India and Ceylon, he called at London where he arranged with A.R. Orage, then editor of *The New Age* and destined to be, like him, one of Gurdjieff's chief instructors. 'They talked about their common interest in metaphysical teachings, and their belief that esoteric schools still existed. Before he left London, Ouspensky promised Orage he would send him accounts of his travels' (*Orage With Gurdjieff in America*, p. 19).

Ouspensky admitted later that at that stage he retained some 'fantastic dreams' about the likelihood of contacting not just physical groups of wisdom but mystic schools of Pythagoras, of ancient Egypt, of the men who built Notre Dame.

Chapter 5

GIVING TIME MORE SPACE

ONE OF OUSPENSKY'S main contributions to an understanding of the world is tucked away in *A New Model of the Universe* – his deduction that three dimensions are required to constitute time. That this theory was ahead of contemporary scientific thought indicates why the reasoning in many of the dozen long essays that form this book is difficult for the ordinary person. Still, while it was not a 'best-seller' like *Tertium Organum*, *New Model* has sold steadily since it was published in 1931 and today still strongly influences readers attracted by the thought-provoking ideas it introduces.

It also leaves little doubt that, before meeting Gurdjieff, Ouspensky had acquired a remarkable store of knowledge, and the emotive flavour of much of the writing suggests also a high level of understanding.

Ouspensky discusses time as the fourth dimension of space in his earlier book *Tertium Organum*. In *New Model* he says that this definition does not contradict ordinary views of life so long as time is imagined to be a straight line. 'But the idea of time as a *curve* of the fourth dimension entirely changes our conception of life. . . . when we begin to see how the curve of the fourth dimension is transformed into the curves of the fifth and the sixth dimensions, our views of things and of ourselves cannot remain any longer what they were,' he contends (ibid., p. 473).

Three coordinates are insufficient to describe the universe because it could then contain no motion, he explains. Four-dimensional space-time allows for motion, but motion has dimensions of duration, velocity and direction. 'Time is the measure of motion. If we represent time by a line, then the only line which will satisfy all the demands of time will be a spiral. A spiral is a "three-dimensional line" so to speak. . .'

In passing, Ouspensky suggests that the three-dimensionality of time 'makes unnecessary most of the elaborate hypotheses and suppositions which have been indispensable in the attempts to squeeze the universe into the boundaries of the three or four-dimensional continuum' (ibid., p. 425).

He points out that we cannot conceive the six-dimensional form of a body, which is *reality*, but see it as three dimensional, the sphere in which our senses function.

Interestingly, he sees that 'six dimensions constitute a "period", beyond which there can be nothing but the repetition of the same period on a different scale' (ibid., p. 426). Intriguingly, he adds:

'The period of dimensions is limited at one end by the point, and at the other end by infinity of space multiplied by infinity of time, which in ancient symbolism was represented by two intersecting triangles, or a six-pointed star.'

This symbol stands for the perfect union of the three space-dimensions and the three time-dimensions, 'where very point of space includes the whole of time and every moment of time includes the whole of space; when *everything* is *everywhere* and *always*' (ibid., p. 445).

Ouspensky also patiently lays out his reasons for stating that the number of dimensions cannot be more than six. It is worth taking a closer look at his reasoning as it gives an idea how his mathematical deductions and geometrical projections can be translated into important psychological and spiritual meanings.

Taking our usual conception of time as a line (rather vaguely representing the fourth dimension) divided into Before, Now and After periods, he proposes the addition of a number of Now lines perpendicular to the original line, each being 'the perpetual now' for a particular moment and in total representing the fifth dimension.

Despite the ordinary person's difficulty in conceiving of time in the plural, he also argues for the existence of other Before-Now-After lines of 'parallel times'.

Each moment of Now on one of the lines of parallel time contains a definite number of possibilities (and an infinite number of impossibilities). The actualisation of a possibility will determine what happens in the following moment, the next Now in one of the times. As this process is repeated, the line will trace a zigzag course in the fourth dimension and the perpetual existence of the actualisation will be in the fifth dimension, or line of eternity.

The actualisation of other possibilities in the time lines will take place in the sixth dimension, 'which is an aggregation of "all times" '. Ouspensky explains:

'The lines of the sixth dimension, which start from every point of 'time' in all possible directions, form the solid or three-dimensional continuum of time, of which we know only one dimension. We are one-dimensional beings in relation to time. Because of this we do not see parallel time or parallel times; for the same reason we do not see the angles and turns of time, but see time as a straight line' (ibid., pp. 429-30).

These straight lines are only imaginary coordinates used to measure spirals. This brings up the important point that a general line of 'great time' does not exist:

'each separately existing "system". . . has its own time', which is recognised but not explained by 'new physics'. Separate time is always a completed circle. . . . But a circle or any closed curve requires two coordinates for its definition. The circle (circumference) is a two-dimensional figure. If the second dimension of time is eternity, this means that eternity enters into every circle of time and into every moment of the circle of time. Eternity is the curvature of time. Eternity is also movement, an *eternal movement*. And if we imagine time as a circle or any other closed curve, *eternity* will signify eternal movement along this curve, eternal repetition, eternal recurrence.'

The next bold step in his theory is:

'The sixth dimension is the way out of the circle . . . one end of the curve rises from the surface . . . The line of time becomes a spiral. . . . The actual spiral of time is not analogous to any of the times we know, for it branches off at every point. And as there can be many possibilities in every moment, so there can be many branches at every point' (ibid,. pp. 430-1).

It is because our brains baulk at visualising such a figure that straight lines are substituted. A further caution, daunting if we wish to visualise true relations in space-time, is that 'direction, duration and velocity are not real dimensions but merely the reflections of the real dimensions in our consciousness'.

Ouspensky concludes that nothing can exist beyond the 'time solid'. Outside 'the space of the actualisations of all possibilities . . . we can think only of repetitions of the period of dimensions either on the scale of zero or . . . of infinity. But these are different spaces, which have nothing in common with the space of six dimensions and may or may not exist. . .' (Zero dimension refers to the point or the moment – 'a "figure" of the zero dimension, a point, is a solid of another scale'.)

Ouspensky says in a footnote (ibid., p. 442) that this essay, 'A New Model of the Universe', was essentially complete in 1912 and that none of the scientific theories that appeared up to 1929 had caused him to change his main conclusions.

He arrives at the idea of a space which expands and contracts in accordance with the size of the reference body. He says Einstein's 'mollusc' is the nearest approximation to this in 'new physics' but is too timid.

'In the old physics space is always space, and time is always time. In the new physics the two categories make one, space-time. In the new model of the universe the phenomena of one category can pass into the phenomena of the other category, and vice versa.

'When I write of space, space-concepts and space-dimensions, I mean space for us. For the electron, and most probably even for bodies much larger than the electron, our space is time' (ibid., p. 445). 'As three-dimensional bodies, electrons do not exist for us,' he says, adding that even their fourth dimension (their existence, the completed circle) is also too small for us to measure. 'Only the fifth and sixth dimensions of electrons have certain measurements in our time-space. The fifth dimension constitutes the thickness of the ray and the sixth its length' (ibid., p.461).

He argues that the basis for a theory as to the immeasurably short existence of very small units of matter will be found in the idea of 'different time in different cosmoses'.

The idea of time is inevitably linked for Ouspensky with eternal recurrence. Although it now appears to bear Ouspensky's trademark, he does not claim to have originated the idea of recurrence. He says European thought connects it with Pythagoras and with 'vague notions' of periodicity of the universe in Indian cosmogony. The idea disappeared after the first centuries of Christianity. He quotes Jesus Christ in the original Greek text speaking of *repeated existence*, translated as *regeneration*.

Nietzsche popularised the idea of eternal recurrence 'but added nothing new to it'. Ouspensky draws on his artistic side's interests to quote literary sources, from stories by R.L. Stevenson and C.H. Hinton to poetry by Alexis Tolstoy and D.G. Rossetti, for hints of eternal recurrence.

The difficulty for most of us in grasping the idea stems, as already stated, from the need to conceive of time as curves of five and six dimensions. To explain these curves, Ouspensky illustrates how life can be taken, not as a straight line, but as 'a series of undulatory vibrations'.

Studies in physical phenomena show that 'every wave comprises in itself a complete circle' and that every wave embodies smaller waves and is itself in a bigger wave. As an example, he proposes days as small waves inside waves of years, with the larger waves forming a greater wave of life. Using analogies between the wave of life rolling onwards in the fifth dimension and the quanta rotating in curved rays of light, he arrives at the notion of the point of death coinciding with the point of birth (ibid., pp. 473-5).

He even has answers for the tricky questions on recurrence, such as where those people go who have remembered their past lives (ibid., pp. 494-5). However the answers, including time adjustments when the soul touches eternity and different durations and speeds of time, may seem speculative. Such questions, however, may seem more amenable to being solved than the paradox of the fifth dimension being inside the fourth, by which Ouspensky gives a new meaning to the precept *As above so below.*

He says that 'a higher dimension is both above and below the lower dimension'. For example, 'the fourth dimension for us lies in the world of celestial bodies and in the world of molecules' and 'the fifth dimension lies in the moments of life eternally remaining where they are, and in the repetition of life itself, taken as a whole'.

This brings Ouspensky to one of his memorable formulations:

'*Life* in itself is *time* for man. For man there is not and cannot be any other time outside the time of his life. *Man is his life.* His life is his time. . . . Man dies because his time ends' (ibid., pp 476-7).

The clock is rewound and the same time begins for him again, and the tendencies of the preceding life are strengthened, good and bad.

Ouspensky concedes that everyone may not agree with all his deductions. His indifference to this is indicated by his next suggestion: that when the Angel of the Apocalypse says that 'there should be time no longer' (*Revelation* 10: 6), the death of humanity is implied. If this does little to ease a suspicion that the whole claim of repetition is ill-founded, he can reverse the familiar analogy of transformation to portray the situation of one who has seen the reality of time and eternity but cannot pass on the knowledge to others any more than a butterfly can tell the grub of anything it discovers.

This concession that the idea of eternal recurrence cannot be popular in its pure form is an acknowledgment that it seems absurd from a three-dimensional standpoint. Christianity, Ouspensky points out, talks of life after death but not before; Buddhism has adapted the idea so that 'their "wheel of lives" rolls along with the calendar', making it 'acceptable to the masses'.

The theory of eternal recurrence, it needs to be remembered, does not impose an absolute repetition of everything; a few people can make conscious changes in their lives without upsetting any universal scheme. This is no mere afterthought to make the idea more acceptable; Ouspensky has studied this aspect as thoroughly as he has the other implications. In suggesting where change is possible, he distinguishes five categories of people: those in whose lives everything is transmitted to the next; those whose lives vary slightly, upwards or downwards; those whose lives ascend definitely; those whose lives descend markedly and eventually vanish; and finally those with an inner ascending line which gradually leads them out of repetition to another level.

Despite the loophole, the proposed law of recurrence contains a condition designed to occasion pause for thought: 'the strengthening with every life of the tendencies of the preceding life, of those tendencies which grew and increased during life, both bad and good tendencies, those which were a manifestation of strength and those which were a manifestation of weakness' (ibid., p. 478).

Ouspensky's perception of the exact repetition of historical personages gives an idea why he prayed to be spared from fame in his lifetime. 'Every word they pronounce affects the destiny of nations. And they must know their parts perfectly. They can add nothing of their own, they can omit nothing . . .'

In explaining the categories in relation to recurrence, Ouspensky reveals his understanding of 'soul' before his views were influenced by Gurdjieff. He usually took the word 'simply in the sense of man's inner being, of his inner existence, of which his body is the temporary receptacle'. Few who believe in the existence of souls would find difficulty in accepting that, but some may hesitate to agree that 'souls are born and die just like bodies'. As he sees it: 'The soul may die on one plane of being and pass to a higher plane. And it may die altogether, become gradually reduced to nothing. . .' (ibid., p. 483).

Ouspensky claims the categories of dying souls were known of old. This is why, he says, that participation in the Eleusinian Mysteries was barred to people in whose lives great calamities occurred, because it was believed their continuous catastrophes showed they were going downhill, as in his fourth category of men.

What would seem to be the opposite category, comprising people who are exceedingly successful from the ordinary viewpoint, also becomes increasingly mechanical. As he sees it, nothing damns like easy success. In Ouspensky's view of life, men of real science, art, thought or action differ from these in seldom attaining success, being recognised only long after their death, a favourable factor towards escaping from the repetition of lives, for they start each life striving towards their unattainable aim, and sometimes 'remember' early.

This leads him to assert that evolution or inner growth cannot be accidental or mechanical.

'Evolution for all categories of people is connected with recollection. . . . as evolution means escaping from the wheel of the fifth dimension and passing into the spiral of the sixth dimension, recollection has importance only when it bears an active character in a certain definite direction, when it creates discontent with what exists and a longing for new ways' (ibid., p. 485).

A 'successful' type, he says, will attribute recollections to some personal flair; a 'descending' type see in them further cause of despair.

When he wrote this, presumably about 1912, he considered that the ways of evolution were typified by Raja-Yoga (development of consciousness), Jnana-Yoga (knowledge), Karma-Yoga (right actions), Hatha-Yoga (power over the body) and Bhakti-Yoga (right religious action). He notes ancient sages knew that man's powers could be greatly increased by right training and control of his body, mind, attention, will, emotions and desires. He sees that yoga increases the powers of man to struggle against not only nature but the delusions of his own consciousness.

It could well be that in revising this section (completed in 1929), he owed something to Gurdjieff, particularly what he divulges about esoteric schools. He adds that 'all five Yogas, that is each one separately, are an abbreviation and adaptation for different types of people of *one and the same general system*. This system is taught orally in particular schools, which differ from the Yogis' schools as much as the Yogis' schools differ from monasteries' (ibid., p. 270).

The Ouspensky of 1912 takes the Eternal Now as the state of Brahma, in which 'everything is everywhere and always' and every point of space touches every point of time, symbolised by the six-pointed star (ibid., pp. 327, 429, 445, 490).

On this scale man is a one-dimensional being, so that in leaving time at death he cannot enter the Eternal Now. Before this can be achieved, there are intermediate stages, which Ouspensky examines. Three ways lead to Brahma: movement into the future, movement into the past and movement on one spot in the present. The first is the process of life, or reproduction; movement on the spot is eternal recurrence; and backward movement is, according to Ouspensky, reincarnation. He obviously believed strongly in the notion of reincarnation into the past, an idea he was perhaps the first to promote in modern times – in a form, naturally, that bears no resemblance to science-fiction stories (see ibid., p. 486-7).

As an allusion to this backward movement, he quotes death-bed revelations in the *Old Testament* of King David and Joshua that they are going 'the way of all the earth', which he interprets as going into time, into the past. Similarly, Abraham and Isaac and Jacob were 'gathered to his/my people' and Joshua was gathered unto his fathers. As Judaism did not promise existence after death, Ouspensky decides that these phrases, never applied to ordinary men, portend more than burial in the family plot. He speculates they mean reincarnation into the past, as the only interpretation that explains evolution. His argument: any improvement must come from the past, as we cannot leave our sins behind, remembering that everything is eternal.

'We cannot go far forward with such a past as ours. The past still exists, and it gives and will give its results, creating new and ever new crimes. . . . There would be no possibility of thinking of the *evolution of humanity* if the possibility did not exist for individually evolving men to go into the past and struggle against the causes of the present evil which lie there (*A New Model of the Universe*, pp. 493-4).

It is not easy to comprehend fully the inner life of a man who develops such ideas as principles to live by, and who, furthermore, has arrived at them largely by his own reasoning.

As we have seen, 'Ouspensky Fourth Dimension' based much of his efforts to perceive reality on geometry (and meta-geometry) and mathematics. *A New Model of the Universe* affords glimpses of other methods he used. One of these was the examination of his dreams to discover whether any held messages from an inner part of his Being. A chapter on this also gives rare insights into his character.

Apparently he formed the idea in childhood that if he could *think* he should understand what dreams meant. By the age of twenty-two, having read all he could find about dreams in psychological books, he decided to observe his own systematically.

His detailed description of 'half-dream states' is informative on one hand because it presents logical reasons for ruling out any imagined significance from many dreams, particularly recurring ones. (One of his recurring dreams was of being sucked into a quagmire; he found it was caused simply by the entanglement of his legs in the blanket or sheets.) On the other hand, it gives the first inkling of the form of meditation that some of his later students came to believe his life's work was directed towards discovering.

He found that half-dream states – in which he had all his usual dreams but was conscious and could see how they were created – enabled him to see things in a new way.

A dream in which he saw himself scampering on all fours in times of danger gives possible clues to Ouspensky's make-up. He rationalises the crawling by comparing it with the action of a toddler who distrusts the new stance when faced by anything unexpected and drops to an on-all-fours posture (ibid., p. 278). Later we will see occasions in which Ouspensky, faced with a crisis engineered by his teacher, Gurdjieff, seems to drop back to his familiar position, afraid to trust his balance by venturing further in a new way.

His studies showed Ouspensky that it was incorrect to speak of the creation of *mental* pictures in sleep. Legs, arms, back, in fact, each part of the body also thinks, he says, and when 'the head-consciousness calms down and becomes clouded in the state of sleep . . . other consciousnesses begin to speak' (ibid, p. 281). Such an understanding may have prepared him to receive Gurdjieff's revelations about a person's different centres, each with their own thinking, feeling and moving functions.

In view of speculation that Ouspensky's nature was strongly divided into thinking and feeling parts, what he finds about dramatic or invented dreams is of particular interest. Observing that this type of dream contains subtle material of observation, memory and imagination that the dreamer does not possess when awake, he sees that it possesses artistic creation as well as memory.

One such dream 'showed me quite clearly that there was in me an artist, sometimes very naive, sometimes very subtle, who worked at these dreams and created them out of the material I possessed but could never use in full measure when awake. . . . this artist was . . . a playwright, a producer, a scene-painter, and a remarkable *actor-impersonator*. This last capacity in him was possibly the most astonishing of all . . . I had very little of this capacity when awake' (ibid., p. 285).

Some people who knew Ouspensky have protested that he did have some of these qualities, but usually suppressed them because he believed a detached, intellectual approach best suited his role as a psychology lecturer.

Ouspensky, however, denies that ordinary dreams reveal unknown depths of the dreamer's nature, claiming that 'dreams are always a caricature', contradicting nature as a means of compensation.

His studies convinced him that not only do we dream all the time in sleep, although remembering only those dreams that occur near awakening, but also in the 'waking' state. This, of course, connects his thought directly to the theme of the Work: that man needs to wake from sleep. His technique of observing his half-sleep states leads him to decide that what we call sleep and waking state is really '*sleep* and *sleep plus waking state*' (ibid., p. 296).

He remarks that it is easier to observe 'dreams' in the waking state than in dreams. It seems that this is meant only to emphasise the continuous nature of day-dreaming, for, as he is to find on meeting Gurdjieff, genuine Self-observation requires real effort.

His daydreams related to 'the sensation that this has happened before'. He recalls that these sensations began for him when he was about six but 'after eleven they became much rarer'. One reason for these dreams, he says, is the connection of an accompanying sensation of repetition with clear awareness and a heightened self-feeling. 'In some cases this special kind of foreknowledge of people, things, places and events can be verified.' Ouspensky saw in this further evidence in favour of eternal recurrence.

Superficially, it also seems a case of foreknowledge, in view of Gurdjieff's reputation in the field, that he associates the study of dreams with the practice of hypnotism. What is suggestive of Gurdjieff's System is that Ouspensky concludes that ordinary man's suggestibility is so great that his normal state could be called semi-hypnotic; in certain situations he can lose all independent decision or choice.

Further, his appreciation of the effect of suggestion in developing duality in a person takes him close to the Work teaching of Essence and Personality. 'From very early years [a child] learns to remember that he must show the feelings and thoughts demanded of him at the given moment and never show what he really thinks and feels. This habit becomes his second nature,' he says (ibid., p. 304), anticipating what he was to learn about the growth of Personality at the expense of Essence.

By 1911, Ouspensky, influenced by 'a fairly complete

acquaintance' with the literature on theosophy, occultism and magic, decided that new experimental methods were needed to explain the relationship between magic and mysticism (ibid., p. 311). He does not describe the methods he used, but it is widely assumed, judging by effects he reports, that it included inhaling nitrous oxide (laughing gas). He omits details of physiological phenomena that preceded changes in his psychic state except to say that his pulse rate sometimes reached a very high rate and sometimes slowed down, with an unusual direct connection between breathing and heart rate.

Upon a change in the state of consciousness, experiences flashed by so quickly that he could find neither words nor concepts by which to remember them. After about twenty minutes he would sense 'a strange duality' in himself, and found he was in a new world in which nothing was separate and all was visible at once at every point. The relation between the subjective and the objective was broken; they could change places. But, after his reading of Theosophy, he was astonished to find there was nothing resembling an 'astral' world (ibid., p. 313).

Describing the process of the experiments, he says that the pulsation of his body quickened until he felt a shock and he entered a transitional stage that was much like a 'half-dream' state except that he heard voices, which 'explained' everything but which he distrusted.

When he adopted a critical attitude, he passed a second threshold into an 'extraordinary lucidity of consciousnesses – and a world of mathematical relationships that were continuously transforming'. He became terrified of the abyss of infinity, but also laughed at himself for having been snared by 'beauty'. He saw that 'infinity was not infinite continuation in one direction, but infinite variation at one point' and that his terror arose from a wrong approach to it. Despite knowing this, he still felt a menace in it. He also heard constant warnings that he should stop his experiments because they were unlawful (ibid., pp. 320-1).

Words, he says, could not express the intense emotional

state, perhaps the most vivid characteristic of the experiments, for everything he understood came through it. He either loved or was horrified by the new knowledge.

The number three played an important part in this new world, with the entire universe sometimes appearing as a triad. When he tried walking in the streets during the experiments, again he perceived nothing was separate. Houses and other buildings were 'living beings full of thoughts, feelings, moods and memories', which were the people who lived in them. 'I mean that the people in relation to the "houses" played approximately the same role which the different "I"s of our personality play in relation to us' (ibid., p. 323).

This last comment suggests Ouspensky may have reworded his script in line with Work terminology, but there seems no doubt he is describing feelings he experienced in 1910-11.

When an experiment was successful, he felt he 'came into contact with myself, with the self that is always within me, which always saw me and always told me something that I could not understand and could not even hear in ordinary states of consciousness'.

In a result that evokes comparison with what Gurdjieff was to teach him about the lost art of sensing, Ouspensky found that in heightened states he was related differently to his body, being able to communicate with any part of it. The separate consciousnesses were completely immersed in themselves and continually spoke of what they needed, what they wished, what was pleasant for them, what unpleasant, and what dangers threatened them. Normally, Ouspensky comments, we feel only the general tone of these parts of the body as conveyed by our physical state or mood.

Another finding that connects with Work teaching was that the chief place in all that he had learned was occupied by his changed feeling of 'I'.

One experience of what he called 'experimental mysticism' is remarkably close to what he would later know as one of Gurdjieff's sayings: 'To know everything it is only necessary to know a little. But to know that little one must know a lot.'

Ouspensky, in trying to explain this new feeling of 'I', reports that when looking at a copper ash-tray during a heightened state of consciousness a 'whirlwind of thoughts and images' showed him all the connections between the ash-tray and 'an immense number of things'. He felt that 'to know an ash-tray meant to know all'. He wrote a few words to retain something of these thoughts and sensations. Next day he found he had written: '*A man can go mad from one ash-tray*' (ibid., p. 326).

A major discovery during his experiments into mysticism was the realisation that in ordinary life we think by a 'yes' or 'no' process, whereas in reality there are three elements. He saw in his questioning that the solution of a problem always came from a third, unknown side. He also realised that a rightly put question contains the answer, but it will always be unexpected, on another plane.

In a higher state of consciousness he thought not in words but by rapidly changing signs or hieroglyphs. If his ideas remained in words it meant they could not be expressed by hieroglyphs, and so had no place in reality. The many everyday questions that fell into the null category included the 'astral world' and 'evolution' as understood by orthodox science.

Some supporters of Ouspensky have argued that his 'mystical' experiences showed that he could have developed himself to an exceptional degree without the dubious aid of any other teaching. Gurdjieff, we can imagine, would simply ask what use it was to have these glimpses of reality if they could not be retained.

As for Ouspensky himself: 'I came to the conclusion that without the help of those who know another approach it is impossible to do anything' (ibid., p. 343).

He was not, however, without hope, because, as he says: 'Side by side with the idea of hidden knowledge there runs through the whole history of human thought the idea of superman.' He approved of the claim of Nietzsche's Zarathustra: 'Man is something that has to be surmounted' (ibid., p. 116).

Ouspensky's idea of superman is closely connected with time and eternity:

'There live in every man, as it were, two beings, one being comprising the mineral, vegetable, animal and human 'time and space' world, the other being belonging to some other world. One is the being of 'the past', the other the being of 'the future'. . . . It may be said without the slightest exaggeration that the soul of man is the battlefield of the past and the future' (ibid., pp. 118-9).

His superman does not belong to the historical future. 'If superman can exist on earth, he must exist both in the past and in the present. But he does not stay in life: he appears and goes away.' He maintains that an ordinary man cannot know of a superman's existence (ibid., p. 121).

Ouspensky's understanding that superman appears and disappears can be seen to have attuned him to the Work philosophy of messengers from a higher level emerging when needed to impart wisdom to a nucleus of human beings able to grasp their message and willing to accept the task of leading other humans in the way of increased consciousness. 'The idea of superman belongs to the "inner circle",' he says.

Ouspensky may be seen to have borrowed Work terminology in adding: 'Ancient religions and myths always pictured in the image of superman the higher "I" of man, man's consciousness . . . in a certain sense, living within man.' He says that the higher 'I' is superman in the past, present and future. Dismissing the 'tedious' notion of superman 'as a new zoological species', he insists that 'the idea of superman has never existed apart from the idea of higher consciousness' (ibid., p. 140). Superman is a possibility in man's soul – 'It rests with man himself to bring this idea nearer or to turn it aside' (ibid., p. 144).

Although he does not give a more precise specification of superman than man's higher 'I', Ouspensky seems convinced the main change in man must be the development of his emotional life. The Work similarly stresses the need for such a change, but the manner in which this belief is expressed in

A New Model of the Universe appears to be evidence that this was also Ouspensky's pre-Gurdjieffian view. He says that far from being a strictly rational being, superman enjoys ecstasy as his normal psychic state. This is so far beyond ordinary human emotionality that only art can convey what it is like, and then only feebly.

In other parts of the 'Superman' chapter, updated in the nineteen-twenties, the writer definitely appears to employ Gurdjieff's doctrine of 'I's. In contrasting ordinary man with superman, he says a person's 'I' continually changes as in a kaleidoscope, every suddenly aroused emotion becomes caliph for an hour, the 'will' being merely the 'resultant of desires'. (Ouspensky, as we shall see, had agreed not to publish Work ideas unless he understood them. Of course, were he making use of them in this chapter, he would have reason to believe he did understand what he wrote about.)

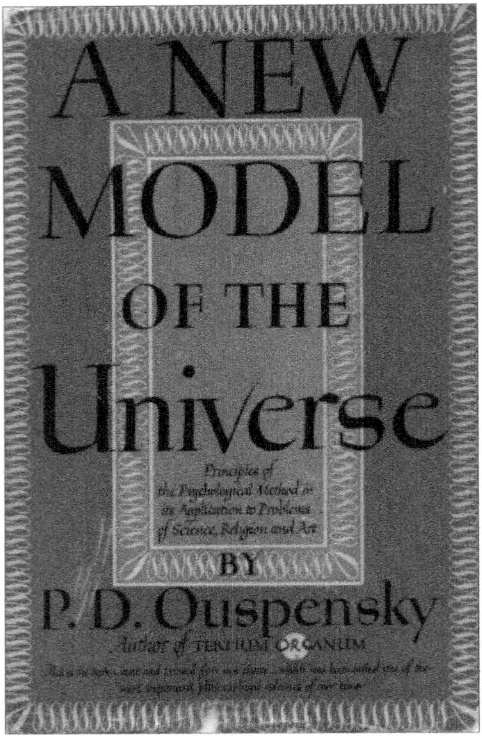
A NEW
MODEL
OF THE
Universe
Principles of
the Psychological Method in
its Application to Problems
of Science, Religion and Art
BY
P. D. Ouspensky
Author of TERTIUM ORGANUM

STRANGE
LIFE
OF
IVAN
OSOKIN
STRANGE
LIFE
OF
IVAN
OSOKIN
by
P. D. Ouspensky

Chapter 6

BECKONING TRACES OF CREATIVE THOUGHT

ON HIS 1913-14 JOURNEYS to Egypt and India, Ouspensky stopped briefly in Paris and before dawn walked around Notre Dame, thinking that he already knew the secret held by the cathedral's massive towers. The sight revived his confidence that a tradition existed apart from the history of crime. Nothing, he felt, could shake his conviction that the *thought* that created the cathedral still existed, and he was on his way to search for more traces of it, 'and I was sure that I should find them'.

Ouspensky believed the building of such cathedrals was 'part of a colossal and cleverly devised plan which permitted the existence of entirely free philosophical and psychological schools in the rude, absurd, cruel, superstitious, bigoted and scholastic Middle Ages' (*A New Model of the Universe*, p. 345). The 'schools of builders' have left us an immense heritage, 'almost all of which we have already wasted' as it concerned the invisible world. After noting the absence in Notre Dame's visible records of any word about the cathedral's construction work or architects, he remarks on the ironic circumstance that through the architectural schools 'for a time the Church was made an instrument for the preservation and propagation of the ideas of *true Christianity*, that is, of true religion or true knowledge, which were absolutely foreign to it'.

Schools of masons in the eleventh and twelfth centuries contained 'inner schools in which the true meaning of religious allegories and symbols was explained and in which was studied "esoteric philosophy", that is, the very "magic" for a mere thought of which people were put on the rack and burnt at the stake'.

Though much of the cathedral has been altered, Ouspensky was entranced by the view from the towers over the city and including the eastern spire from which the apocalyptic beasts and the twelve Apostles descend to the four corners of the world. It seemed significant to him that from the ground it was hardly possible to see these figures unless one knew of their existence.

He saw in the building mathematics, astronomy, biology, even 'evolution'. The gargoyles and other figures seemed to represent the builders' psychological teaching, 'chiefly the idea of *the complexity of the soul*'.

Again, he interpreted the carved figures as the soul of Notre Dame, as its different 'I's – 'pensive, melancholy, watching, derisive, malignant, absorbed in themselves, devouring something, looking intensely into a distance invisible to us, as does the strange woman in the headdress of a nun, which can be seen above the capitals of the column of a small turret high up on the south side of the cathedral'. It struck him that when seen beside the stone figures living people appear dead.

In the cathedral's ambience, he was struck, too, by the vainness of trying to teach people something they have no desire to know. Against this, he felt that 'perhaps the aim both of the teaching of the Apostles and of the construction of Notre Dame was not to teach *all* the people, but only to transmit *certain* ideas to a *few* men through the "space of time" '. He was envisaging a communication between schools through and across thousands of years.

In a much shorter time span, he obviously succeeded in communicating his thoughts on Notre Dame to his pupil Maurice Nicoll, who told his English group in February 1943 that the cathedral 'was built by the Fourth Way' (the discipline to which Gurdjieff would introduce Ouspensky). Dr Nicoll continued:

'A sense of humour is necessary in The Fourth Way. The gargoyles [in front of the cathedral] represent people (no longer in The Fourth Way) who have identified too much, who were too serious . . . . On the staircase and on the steeple the Apostles are descending, the top ones listening to their last instructions. The gargoyles are certain I's. [Dr Nicoll later in the talk described them as bad I's.] Unless we can see them we cannot go in through the door. To go in through the door is to begin to *Work*. . . . We have to get to the altar which communicates with higher centres. We are all outside the church. We have to enter through the seven-arched doorway into ourselves' (*Informal Work Talks and Teachings*, p. 49).

Before Ouspensky left Russia, a friend had scoffed at his hopes of finding anything new in the East, claiming he could more easily believe in finding the miraculous in Moscow's Kuznetsky Most (*A New Model of the Universe*, p. 388). A part of the traveller almost believed him, but right at the start of Ouspensky's Eastern tour, in the main street of Pera, which he said was 'the "Kuznetsky Most" of Constantinople', he found what he considered the miracle of the Mevlevi dervishes.

They showed him, if he needed persuading, that the miraculous still existed in the East. Although, as on his first time in Constantinople in 1908, he felt the presence of something real in the turning, it would not be until he visited the tekkes with Gurdjieff after the Russian Revolution that he would understand more of its meaning.

When Ouspensky called at Egypt again, his impressions of the Pyramids and the Sphinx reinforced both his belief that schools of real knowledge had existed in the past and his faith that they could be found today. Memories of his 1908 visit, when he spent two or three weeks in the area, merged with his current perceptions to help him feel a living influence projected by the monuments.

He was astonished to find that the ancient world, which he seemed to know well, ceased to be the past and became the present.

As with his sensing the soul of Notre Dame, it is possible that he was familiar with these images of the past because they were projected from his own unconscious. His pondering over the fourth dimension and eternity was no doubt essential to his reception of such vital impressions from the stone works of Egypt.

As he saw it, anyone who was himself alive could feel that the Pyramids were too. They had thoughts and feelings but existed in such a large time scale that not merely an individual but his whole life was invisible to them, because it passed too quickly.

Likewise, his preoccupation with eternity may have prepared him to see it reflected in the face of the Sphinx. Sceptics may scoff that the peculiar interests of other people might convince them of the existence of fairies or any other species or worlds. So? There is undoubtedly a basis, a grain at least, of truth in most tales and legends, man usually being incapable of creating an entirely new conception.

In Ceylon (now Sri Lanka) his attempt to understand the teaching of Buddha had most success not during his dialogue with learned monks but through an ancient statue of the Buddha with sapphire eyes in a secluded temple south of Colombo. Ouspensky was sure those eyes 'saw' him; or rather, saw what was hidden in the depths of his soul, judging him without blame.

He found it a different gaze to that of the Sphinx, but felt that both statues intimated a consciousness higher than man's. He was encouraged in his search by the conviction that these monuments were built by men who knew and could transmit through art something of that finer energy.

Ouspensky's Eastern inquiry was cut short by the outbreak of World War I. During World War II, another student of the Work, the then Lieutenant Sam Copley of the Royal Navy Volunteer Reserve, took the chance offered by leave in Colombo to inspect the Buddha with the sapphire eyes. He wrote to members of Maurice Nicoll's Work group in October 1944 that it was not difficult to find the temple 'once you know the hotel referred to is Mt Lavinia and follow O's directions'. Copley went on:

'The Guide says that only one eye of the huge Buddha is sapphire and the moonstone of the Dagoba is very large. . . I was afraid of expecting too much and certainly the colouring is rather lurid which together with the ill-smelling Temple sweeper and crowd of urchins distracts one. But there is quite clearly something about it which I have not found in any other statue of Buddha. You can stand in quite a large area and the eyes seem to be focused on you and yet go beyond you. I have never seen eyes in any figure before that had intelligence behind them.

'The face is Eastern and I was going to say expressionless but if it is expressionless it is not wooden. It is quite remarkably tranquil and might, it seems, express anything in the next moment. But once you accept the colouring and Eastern quality you feel that you have known the face for years and that it knows you almost.

'There is nothing uncanny (in the unpleasant sense) about all this at all and it is as natural as nature. Certainly it is the work of enlightened artists. The rest of the body is conventional, I think, much like other reclining Buddhas but it is stone and not plaster. The Sweeper said that the robe was added later and that the figure was 1000 years old. I fancy this is a convenient figure to express great age.

'The Sweeper's father and uncles and grandfather had the job before him and I think that it must have been his uncle who showed Ouspensky the figure. The priests don't seem to speak English very much. It is surprising how few people in Colombo know of this place and how difficult it is to find it from the Buddhists themselves.'

Another temple visitor and Work group member, Toby de Lotbinière, has reported that a temple priest in saffron robes explained to him that although Ouspensky's description of the Buddha [in *A New Model of the Universe*] became famous it did not disclose the name of the temple, so few travellers could find it. Lotbinière said that, even though he knew the temple's name, SubodKarmaya, and had the help of a Buddhist driver, it was still difficult to find, being well hidden by palm trees near the village of Dehiwela.

Although he had been prepared to be disappointed by the reclining statue, Lotbiniere says, he soon felt with a tingling shock that a faint blue light appeared in its left eye and it seemed 'something was becoming alive from far away'. Then both eyes appeared to be alive. He added, confirming or perhaps influenced by Ouspensky's description, that 'the eyes seemed to be looking from eternity deep into one – no emotion just steady communication' (*The Bridge*, No. 12, pp. 195-7).

A photograph of Ouspensky in Ceylon published in *The Work Life* by Beryl Pogson shows him attired as the typical European adventurer in the Orient, wearing a pith helmet, safari jacket and light coloured trousers, and with binoculars and a camera slung around his neck.

Ouspensky's thoughts of 'soul' on this tour culminated when he felt the emanations of India's Taj Mahal, the famous mausoleum of the seventeenth-century Empress Mumtaz-i-Mahal, near Agra. He decided immediately that the enigma of the marble monument's effect was connected with the mystery of death. To Ouspensky, this naturally denoted the birth-death cycle and, as he tried to fix in his memory all the details of the building, he passed into a psychological state new to him and realised there was nothing terrifying about death but 'infinite radiance and joy'.

A small light glimmering above the tomb represented for him the actual life we know, insignificant compared with the immense Taj Mahal, which stands for 'the future or *eternal* life'. Now, he thought, he understood the aim of the mausoleum's Sufi builders. All around the viewer, in the shape of the white Taj Mahal with its surrounding garden, towers, pavilions, fountains and mosques, was the *soul* of the empress, 'so *infinitely* great, radiant and beautiful in comparison with the little body that had lived on earth'.

Then, says Ouspensky, he 'understood that the soul is not enclosed in the body, but that the body lives and moves in the soul (*A New Model of the Universe*, p. 378).

He was gratified to suddenly grasp a meaning of an ancient mystical saying: *The soul and the future life are one and the same*. The philosopher in him saw that life is a process that has no meaning for us unless there is death also; the mathematician appreciated that everything was united in eternity, where dimensions merge.

Despite gaining many insights, when war cut short his

journey on his return to Colombo, he had to admit he felt further than ever from locating esoteric schools, preservers and transmitters of living thoughts by which he hoped to penetrate an unknown reality. He had lost his dream of a non-physical contact with schools of thought, on another plane of being, as it were, by which feat he would break the barriers of time and space.

In an analysis that was not quite a justification of his long travels, he concluded that Schools did exist, but that those he had found were devotional, philosophical or yogic in tone and not what he sought. His goal was an esoteric school that operates within everyday life (or perhaps, like the relationship between soul and body, that embraces ordinary life). Even while on his pilgrimage, he had been planning further travels, chiefly into Russian Central Asia and Persia (Iran). Leaving Colombo in August 1914 he arrived back in Russia in November after stopping at England, where he renewed an acquaintance with A.R. Orage, editor of the *New Age*, with whom he would have both a business and a Work relationship.

He did not know then that events would substantiate some truth in both the facetious prediction of his Moscow jester and his own hope. Soon he would discover what seemed the very teaching he sought right on his own doorstep, in Moscow – the miracle of Kusnetsky Most, or near enough.

Chapter 7

MEETING A MASTER

AN INVESTIGATOR OF the occult who was prepared to go a long way *In Search of the Miraculous* and who wrote seriously about subjective and objective magic, Ouspensky was bound to take notice of an advertisement for a ballet titled *The Struggle of the Magicians*, especially one said to be written by a Hindu. He did more: the Moscow journalist reported the coming attraction in his own paper, on impulse adding imaginatively that it would disclose all that travellers tried unsuccessfully to find in India.

That imaginative addendum (or hopeful prediction) seems almost an inadvertent verdict on his own attempts to discover esoteric schools in the East. Perhaps, though, it was merely a way of stimulating interest in his coming public lectures. For this happened about the beginning of 1915, when Ouspensky moved to St Petersburg, where his books were published and where in February and March he drew crowds of a thousand people to his town hall talks on his travels to India.

Soon after coming to St Petersburg, he became friendly with a young woman, Anna Ilinishna Butkovsky, whom he had met at a Theosophical Society meeting. He told her he was leaving the society because he was disillusioned by its members, who he observed behaved as sheep, producing no original thoughts. He had not been swayed from this course by an invitation to join the society's inner circle with the promise of enlightenment.

As Anna disclosed she had read *Tertium Organum* with interest, she was unlikely to have been surprised at the writer's disenchantment with theosophy. He probably told her also that he had exchanged ideas with the president, Mrs Annie Besant, at the society's headquarters at Adyar, in Madras, during his recent trip to India. He was fond of joking about the three-level caste system adopted there, with nondescript followers, hangers-on and parasites confined to the ground floor; well-to-do well-wishers entertained on the second floor; and only initiates allowed to take their place at the top.

What Ouspensky found especially worth remarking was that, although he had publicly criticised the Theosophy Society founder, Mme Blavatsky, he was immediately ushered up to the inner circle's abode.

The talk with Anna went so swimmingly that they agreed to meet the next morning at Phillipoff's cafe, which was close to both their homes; his was a flat on the Nevsky Prospect, a fashionable quarter and the centre of the artistic set, some of whom could be found at any time swapping ideas in a cafe called The Errant Dog.

The couple began to meet every day at one of the nearby cafes, Ouspensky maintaining a nervous high with bottomless cups of strong coffee. He told his new friend that even before *Tertium Organum* he had wanted to write a book on which he had bestowed the working title *The Wisdom of the Gods*, but did not feel equal to the task. She may well have agreed that a feeling of inadequacy was not surprising over such a task, or even punned on the title's verbal association with 'theosophy'. Could she have known the book would be published finally in 1931 as *A New Model of the Universe*, she may still have thought it would require a modicum of godlike wisdom.

Ouspensky confided he was also working on another book, possibly *Talks With a Devil*.

Their earnest conversations soon revealed that a big wish the pair shared was to find a teacher who could instruct them on attaining real consciousness. He confided that he detected in her an unusually strong 'will to seek'. Anna, an accomplished pianist at the Conservatoire, also possessed a rare sensitivity to what she described as a magical quality in music that expanded the mind and feelings beyond everyday affairs. This would have been a strong attraction to the artistic, Peter side of Ouspensky, who confessed he was moved emotionally when she played for him at her father's house.

After Easter in 1915, Ouspensky's lecture tour took him to Moscow, where he heard again of the man behind the *Magicians* ballet, now revealed to be a Caucasian Greek named (in Russia) Georgii Ivanovich Gurdjieff (known to his

Armenian-Greek parents as Giorgios Gurdjian, and later in the West as George Gurdjieff). Two of Gurdjieff's pupils heard one of Ouspensky's lectures and afterwards urged him to meet their teacher.

Ouspensky's reaction suggests that Gurdjieff the psychological tactician may have been too clever by half in choosing as his emissaries a musician and a sculptor, probably to appeal to the lecturer's Peter characteristics. For it seems that his artistic agents struck Ouspensky's Damian side – which was unimpressed by their talk of occult experiments and other 'self-suggested wonders'. He may have associated this with the theosophists' blandishments, and only the most persistent efforts by one of Gurdjieff's men, whom Ouspensky calls 'M.' – assumed to have been Gurdjieff's cousin, the distinguished sculptor Sergei Dmitrievich Mercourov (*Gurdjieff: The Anatomy of a Myth*, p. 72) – finally persuaded him to accept the invitation.

In arrangements worthy of a conspiratorial assignation in that troubled time of pending revolution, the initial meeting was staged in a noisy cafe in a busy Moscow street. Then, after having mutually established their credentials, as it were, they caught a carriage to a pitifully bare flat where half a dozen of Gurdjieff's pupils had gathered.

There is no indication that Ouspensky sensed that this was an important point of transition in the progress of The Fourth Way in our time, nor that it would mark an abrupt change in his personal career – but he obviously felt that there was something offering here that he had to seize in the moment.

What he perceived of Gurdjieff tallied in general with most people's first impressions, particularly the eyes' piercing quality. Actually, the impressions of different people would vary considerably, seeing that Gurdjieff showed on occasion that he was able to project what image he chose. An unusual effect in this case, however, was that Ouspensky was astonished at Gurdjieff's transparent acting. Strangely – was it planned? – this somehow helped persuade Ouspensky of his genuineness.

The character that Gurdjieff assumed to interview Ouspensky did fit the circumstances. Ouspensky perceived him – no doubt influenced by his own recent Eastern travels – as an Indian rajah or Arabian sheikh and imagined him wearing a white burnoose or a gilded turban. What he saw in fact was a man of oriental type, with those penetrating eyes and a black moustache, wearing a black overcoat with a velvet collar and a black bowler hat.

Ouspensky's surprise at his apparent disguise may be shared by others today, in view of indications that Gurdjieff had already decided to recruit the writer into the Work. Perhaps he acted in accordance with an unwritten law not to make such an offer too inviting. Or perhaps experience had shown that he should double check even his own judgments.

Once he had overcome Gurdjieff's rather off-putting speech, incorrect Russian with a strong Caucasian accent – which he associated with anything but philosophical discourse – Ouspensky was impressed by his host's superior knowledge about questions that interested him: India, secret Schools, hidden knowledge, self-growth.

That 'he put much more into each answer than I had asked for' (*In Search of the Miraculous* , p. 8) suggests he was setting an irresistible lure for this potentially useful pupil. Incidentally, it is odd that Ouspensky was struck by this trait, for Gurdjieff later poked fun at his pupil for a similar characteristic.

Ouspensky asked him about Schools, the use of narcotics, yogis. Gurdjieff's careful and precise answers, which the questioner considered had the authority of a specialist, showed the investigative writer that he had only scratched the surface of these subjects.

As Ouspensky felt new viewpoints in everything Gurdjieff said, he readily accepted an invitation to join a meeting of some of his pupils. The atmosphere of obvious bluff continued: Ouspensky had been led to believe the meeting would take place in an expensive apartment, part of the heavy expenditure that Gurdjieff said his work incurred, but it turned out to be a school teacher's rent-free flat, bare of furniture, where four men and two women had gathered (ibid., p. 9).

During conversation with these pupils, Ouspensky 'tried to

discover in what their work consisted, but they have me no direct answers'. However, he was intrigued by the reading of a story, 'Glimpses of Truth', said to have been written by one of the students. It seized his attention because 'the story began with the author coming across the same notice of the ballet "The Struggle of the Magicians" which I myself had seen ... Further – this pleased me very much because I expected it – at the first meeting the author certainly felt that G. put him as it were on the palm of his hand, weighed him, and put him back' (ibid., p. 10).

Presumably, Ouspensky was so pleased because this description of two of his own experiences in the story indicated foreknowledge on Gurdjieff's part – which perception was reinforced later when he learned that Gurdjieff had indeed proposed the idea of the tale.

Although he elicited that the Gurdjieff group's activities entailed 'work on oneself', he could not ascertain anything more definite. Despite this frustration, he sensed an uncommon quality in Gurdjieff and felt that if he did not establish a link then and there he would miss out on something valuable to his aim of gaining understanding. So he felt fortunate that Gurdjieff agreed to meet him at the same cafe the next day – it transpired that they met every day of the week Ouspensky was in Moscow.

During that week, Ouspensky asked whether it would be worthwhile for him to venture again to the East. Yes, replied Gurdjieff – if he desired a holiday. He added the serious advice that all Ouspensky sought could be found in Russia. This implied that work with him would yield the essential clues.

In this way, the teacher let it appear likely that Ouspensky would be accepted into the still, to him, mysterious group. Ouspensky said the only difficulty to his joining, seeing that some secrecy apparently cloaked the movement, was that he could not promise to refrain from publishing interesting new facts that he learned. They agreed the guiding principle would be for him to desist from writing about anything until he understood it. That he did not publish anything directly about

Gurdjieff's teaching during his life indicates that he soon grasped that to understand any one thing fully is to understand everything.

He also learned early that in Gurdjieff's view knowledge of itself did not lead to an increase in consciousness; it had to be matched by a development in a person's Being, when it was transformed into an understanding that the person could act upon.

Ouspensky asked whether any other conditions attached to a person's joining the group. The reply described succinctly The Fourth Way opinion of not just Ouspensky's but mankind's status: man, said Gurdjieff, is not – not what he could and should be; in fact, he is so lacking in consistency of will as to be incapable of making a commitment of any kind (ibid., p. 14).

This was a viewpoint that caused a serious re-think even in one who had believed he had few delusions about the ordinary man's degree of awareness. It applied to all aspects of human performance. For instance, a question about modern psychology was shown to be naive by the counter question: What sort of psychology could be applied to machines?

When Ouspensky asked if one could stop being a machine, Gurdjieff's reply sounded as though it might have been uttered by the magician in the *Osokin* story: 'If you had asked such questions more often we might, perhaps, have got somewhere in our talks.'

This may have been another surprise to Ouspensky, even though he had written *Osokin.* Doubtless he had assumed that it was Gurdjieff's secrecy that had often prevented his gaining direct answers; now the blame was being laid on his failure to ask the right questions, or to ask them in a fitting form.

It was in answer to an enquiry whether a study of occult or mystical literature would prepare a candidate for his method that Gurdjieff commented, as already related, he would beg to be taught by Ouspensky had he understood all he had written in *Tertium Organum.* But the writer, he made clear, did not understand even what the word 'understand' meant. What a person knew well was his preparation – if a man made coffee well or made boots well it would be possible to talk to him. It can be seen that Gurdjieff's meaning of 'understanding' included the ability to use knowledge practically.

Ouspensky saw that this explanation contained more than its surface meaning, one of the subtle twists that attracted him to Gurdjieff's explanations. It was eminently practical yet contained hints of a mystical insight into reality.

However, his questions soon revealed he had yet to grasp just how thoroughgoing was Gurdjieff's criticism of mankind's mechanicalness. Ouspensky asked what one must do to assimilate real teaching. This elicited a response that has reverberated ever since through the Work tradition: 'It is impossible to do anything' (*In Search of the Miraculous* , p.20).

It is a Work 'axiom', but one that can be proved for oneself, that man as he is cannot do. Things happen to him, he reacts, but cannot exercise real will. First he must rid himself, as Gurdjieff said, of thousands of false ideas and misconceptions.

In the knowledge of what he had gleaned from his study of phenomena and noumena, Ouspensky had no qualms in commenting that these false ideas were produced by the forms of our perception. Again Gurdjieff corrected him, pointing out that he was not speaking of errors within the limits of perceptions but of man's chief delusion that he could do. In order to do, it was necessary to be. He explained that 'to be' had a special meaning in the Work.

Other special words were introduced, such as 'considering'. Ouspensky records that he could not at first see any objection to considering others, but later he would understand that 'internal considering' signified an attitude that creates inner slavery to others' opinions and to one's ego. Work on this would form an important part of his own teaching.

Ouspensky was particularly interested in a talk about planetary influences on humanity and the possibility for man to choose which influences he would come under. Gurdjieff spoke of the planets as living beings, which accorded with Ouspensky's own theories, based on his mystical experiences as much as his mathematical calculations, about levels of intelligence throughout the universe.

While Ouspensky was becoming increasingly interested in Gurdjieff's ideas, he still could not see the whole picture. If he could witness 'real facts of a new and unknown character', he would be convinced the way was right for him. Gurdjieff promised there would be facts, but added that other things were necessary first.

Thus it was that the spring of 1915 in strife-strewn Russia signalled to Ouspensky the blossoming of new knowledge. He returned to St Petersburg and was still in a high state of excitement when he found Anna Butkovsky in The Errant Dog and declared that he had experienced a 'miracle'. He told her he had found the teacher they sought.

The Peter side of Ouspensky could combine with the dispassionate nature of Damian at such times. In her book *With Gurdjieff in St Petersburg and Paris*, Anna Butkovsky-Hewitt says that during one of their conversations, 'behind his face I suddenly saw another, more radiant countenance filled with a youthful happiness which perhaps no one but myself had ever witnessed. When in later years we were to meet in Berlin, in Paris and London, he had developed a hard outer shell, and I wondered why he had crushed the gentle, poetic radiance of his St Petersburg days. Possibly he thought of this side of himself as a weakness, yet it was in this happy mood that his inspiration and vision were strongest; the intellect had nothing to do with it' (ibid., pp. 22-3).

As war raged through the grim summer of 1915, and strikes by printers held up work on Ouspensky's books, probably including *Talks With a Devil*, he consoled himself with the idea he could always abandon his work in St Petersburg and join Gurdjieff in Moscow. Anna, apparently, did not quite constitute an equal consolation. However, in failing to relate his relationship with her, Ouspensky may have simply been keeping secret his personal life. It is possible that at least some aspects of the heroine of *Osokin* are based on Anna Butkovsky, seeing that she records in her book that Ouspensky had spoken of being invited to Australia, the only other reference to which is put into Zinaida's mouth in Ouspensky's novel.

In the autumn, Gurdjieff phoned that he was coming to St Petersburg for a few days. During a number of visits, he and Ouspensky resumed their talks on mankind's situation and possibilities, and the writer introduced some of his friends, including Anna, to the visitor.

When Gurdjieff brought the word 'esoteric' into discussion for the first time, Ouspensky tried to seek a definition of it but Gurdjieff said that was not important. For him, the real point was that a group of people was the essential starting point, because a single man could do nothing by himself.

He stressed that a man had to realise his real situation: he was in a 'prison' and must want to escape and to do that he had to find a man who had already escaped and learn from him.

Ouspensky was quick to grasp these ideas and was able to pass them on to others. His recruitment was paying off. Gurdjieff had formed two groups in Moscow but there is no evidence that they ever attracted a hard core of the calibre of the people Ouspensky drew together in St Petersburg.

By January 1916 the St Petersburg group had grown to about 40 and Gurdjieff came for a meeting each fortnight, sometimes bringing several of his Moscow pupils. Ouspensky soon learned a precaution he was to perpetuate in his own meetings years later. To ensure that only people who valued what he had to teach would come, Gurdjieff invariably made even the mechanics of attendance difficult. For instance, he seldom announced that a meeting would take place until shortly before it started. He also warned that he would charge a high price for group membership. During the day he treated Phillipoff's fashionable cafe as his office and conversed with a stream of people who came with psychological, business or health enquiries.

A rare pointer to Ouspensky's inner workings can be deduced from Gurdjieff's nickname for him: 'Wraps Up The Thought', awarded in rebuke for not being succinct (*With Gurdjieff in St Petersburg and Paris*, p. 75 and pp. 103-4). Gurdjieff demonstrated to the St Petersburg group that nicknames often pointed to a person's 'chief feature'; that is, the person's ingrained manner of reacting to life as a result of his or her main psychological weakness. On this, William Patrick Patterson comments:

'What Gurdjieff saw was that when Ouspensky was asked a question, he would answer so completely that there would be nothing left of the question. . . [this] pointed to a need to control; a word he used quite often. What Ouspensky was likely controlling was his emotional centre.' (*Struggle of the Magicians*)

Ouspensky says, however, that he realised from Gurdjieff's 'ingenious' description of features that not everyone's chief feature could be defined. He explains:

'With some people this feature can be so hidden beneath different formal manifestations as to be almost impossible to find. And then a man can consider himself as his chief feature just as I could call my chief feature "Ouspensky" or, as G. always called it, "Piotr Demianovich". Mistakes there cannot be because the "Piotr Demianovich" of each person forms so to speak "round his chief feature"' (*In Search of the Miraculous*, p. 267).

Ouspensky has reported in detail the discussions at group meetings in *Search*. A significant section of his book, in relation to the later separation of the two men as much as to Gurdjieff's exceptional powers, concerns the teacher's demonstration of telepathic communication to Ouspensky.

Chapter 8

FACING FATEFUL FACTS

IN THE SUMMER OF 1916 all members of the St Petersburg group, probably affected by the uncertain political situation, became impatient with their work on themselves and strove to intensify their efforts. Ouspensky again practised the 'mystical' experiments he had tried earlier, which involved fasts, altered breathing and other techniques, which kept him in what he described as a physically weak and emotionally tense state.

In hindsight he would see that this had prepared him to face the 'facts' that Gurdjieff had promised nearly eighteen months earlier. The hard facts came in August 1916 when Gurdjieff and about eight Petersburg members met at Mme E.N. Maximovich's country house. Mme Maximovich was a patient of a fellow member of the group, Dr Leonid Robertovich Stjernvall, and Gurdjieff's students had often met in her house in the then Russian grand duchy of Finland.

On such a meeting in August 1916 Ouspensky found his teacher harsh and sarcastic as his 'lazy and cowardly' pupils tried to obey an instruction to tell everything about their lives. Ouspensky reveals that he was reduced to a distinctly unpleasant state when Gurdjieff repeated to the others what Ouspensky thought about Stjernvall, an opinion he believed he had told his teacher in confidence. The hurt was particularly sharp because it was the type of talk Ouspensky always had condemned in others (*In Search of the Miraculous* , p. 261).

Later, about 10 p.m., Gurdjieff demonstrated to Ouspensky, Stjernvall and a mathematician and railway engineer, Andrei Andreyevich Zaharoff, certain physical postures that had to be made with relaxed muscles. Then he reopened the embarrassing examination of why they found it impossible to be frank about their lives. 'Everyone must show himself as he is,' was the gist of his demand. It is not reported whether they discussed the need to first know just what one was, or whether the revelation of their actions would assist them to gain self-knowledge.

Whatever else transpired during the talk was irrelevant to Ouspensky, for facts erupted during this confrontation that he regarded as another miracle. He could 'hear' thoughts that Gurdjieff sent to him alone while continuing to speak to the other two men. Their internal dialogue lasted for at least half an hour.

Some of the questions agitated Ouspensky. The reason for this still intrigues Work students. The sole important clue he revealed is that the questions were 'concerned with certain conditions which I had either to accept or *leave the work*' (ibid., p. 262).

He was given a month to decide. Ouspensky's brief report of his reply divulges little to help explain this ultimatum: 'I refused the time and said that no matter how difficult what he demanded was I would carry it out at once. But G. insisted on the month's time.'

Despite Ouspensky's assurance of his immediate compliance, he had already found he could not meet his teacher's demand to tell the others everything about himself. We do not have enough information to know whether the 'conditions' were in a completely different category. From one perspective, if it is recalled that initially Gurdjieff had told Ouspensky that an ordinary man is too mechanical to make any commitment, the mere fact that he had sought one, and a most serious one, from him could be taken as encouragement. At that time, however, Ouspensky evidently did not take his teacher's remarks as being at all complimentary – no more than anyone else can know whether they were complementary to other facets of his teaching strategy, although this lack of information has not precluded speculation in Work circles.

Something Gurdjieff said so upset Ouspensky that he rushed into the garden and then into a forest, where he walked about in the dark for a couple of hours, assailed by antagonistic thoughts and emotions. He recounts that at the 'climax of contradictions and inner turmoil' he suddenly realised

Gurdjieff was right: what he had imagined as a firm and reliable part of himself did not exist. He felt sure he had found something else within himself but could not reveal it to Gurdjieff as he would not believe it and would laugh at him.

We are left to imagine what this newly discovered quality might have been. He said later events proved it to be real, but his fear of being laughed at points to a sensitive part of Ouspensky's psychology.

In bed that night, he reports, his pulse started beating strongly and he again heard Gurdjieff's voice in his chest. He replied mentally and Gurdjieff answered him.

This experience peaked when Gurdjieff asked something that seemed to paralyse him. Ouspensky says he had wished to answer in the affirmative but could not articulate anything. He believed that Gurdjieff would not wait long for an answer. He was right. His teacher said he would leave the question for another time. In a reversal of the previous situation, now Ouspensky sought time to accustom himself to the new thought before replying, and this time Gurdjieff refused.

It may be significant that Ouspensky had experienced similar feelings during his earlier mystical experiments. During those he became fearful of infinity – in both its modes, all and nothing – and heard a warning voice, which he came to believe was his own self, more real than the usual and continually changing feeling of 'I' (*A New Model of the Universe*, pp. 320-1). Could it be that his inner memory of this might have influenced his reaction to Gurdjieff's telepathy?

The telepathic communication resumed for a short time the next morning and Ouspensky felt unusual emotions during the group's remaining three days in Finland. When he complained that this state was becoming unbearable, Gurdjieff replied that it was what Ouspensky had wanted: he was not 'asleep' at that moment.

After Gurdjieff had left for Moscow, Ouspensky experienced the final scene of this 'miraculous' drama: he not only 'conversed' with Gurdjieff in the distant train compartment but 'saw' him, too.

During the next few weeks Ouspensky was able to see 'sleeping' people, which confirmed for him that he was not asleep himself, as Gurdjieff had told him. His experiences supported one conclusion of his earlier experiments: that it is impossible to study phenomena like telepathy or clairvoyance unless one is on the appropriate emotional level.

He later inquired whether Gurdjieff had asked something that frightened him. If that was so, it meant Ouspensky was not ready, Gurdjieff answered (*In Search of the Miraculous*, p. 266).

Later still, in Moscow, Gurdjieff asked Ouspensky what was the most important thing he had learned from the Work. His experiences in August, the pupil replied. He felt that if he could evoke that emotional state at will he would be in a position to discover all he wanted to know.

Ouspensky's critics may see in this a sign that he was eager to find a theoretical system rather than a method of changing Being. But of course a desire to acquire knowledge does not preclude utilising it to gain understanding.

A more appropriate subject for speculation is the connection between the conditions, which Gurdjieff gave his pupil a month to consider, and the crucial question, which required an immediate answer. For it is possible that the telepathic exchanges in Finland contained a key to the eventual separation of the two men.

Before reviewing these confrontations, we might consider what induced the resulting unusual emotions in Ouspensky. He assures readers of *In Search of the Miraculous* that Gurdjieff used neither hypnotism ('by any known method') nor drugs in this telepathic operation. However, Gurdjieff considered that hypnotism and telepathy were closely associated. He attributed his exceptional powers of hypnotism and his ability to see through people's Personality to his ability to produce Hanbledzoin, sometimes called animal magnetism, which sustains the higher-being body Kesdjan (for an explanation of this term, see *Beelzebub's Tales to His Grandson*, pp. 568 and 727-31).

It could be that Gurdjieff used this power to make Ouspensky's Personality passive and to let a more real part of him see his level of Being and weaknesses in his make-up, and to show what qualities and effort would be needed to follow The Fourth Way.

In what may have been an attempt to sidestep the group membership conditions, Ouspensky sought to demonstrate that, as he was, he could carry out any instruction. On the other hand, the vexed question left him utterly incapable of response.

These outcomes suggest that, although the stipulated conditions perceived in the light of Gurdjieff's 'animal magnetism' (or hypnotism) may have afforded Ouspensky an objective view of any attitudes or other weaknesses in Personality, immaturity in Essence, and lack of sincerity, responsibility and trust, a strong part of him could see a way by which he could cope with all this and function efficiently.

But the question somehow brought the state induced by the ultimatum to a head, throwing Ouspensky back on himself just as, let us assume, he had become conscious of significant inadequacies in his inner development.

It may help us in analysing this situation to recall that Gurdjieff led up to the telepathic episode by reminding his pupils that they were too cowardly to reveal everything about themselves. Then he revealed the embarrassing indiscretion made by Ouspensky. It is significant that Stjernvall was the meat in the sandwich, for he and Ouspensky shared some characteristics.

Anna Butkovsky-Hewitt says that the doctor, fifty-five years old, with a younger wife, was unemotional, with a business like manner, a man used to imposing his will on others (for example, his patients) and maintaining a prestigious image. He was very interested in hypnotism, which he used in his practice (*With Gurdjieff in St Petersburg and Paris*, pp. 66-7).

Parallels are apparent with Ouspensky, the austere, authoritative lecturer, who at the time also had a younger girlfriend, Anna. Ouspensky reportedly told her with an 'arrogant smile': 'I must always feel equal to anything I tackle.' Evidently he was not using 'feel' in an emotional sense as he also said, in contrasting his type of responses with the feelings that music evoked in her, 'I never feel, I know' (ibid., pp. 18-19).

Ouspensky, too, had studied hypnotism, in Europe, India and Ceylon. The use of hypnosis might seem inappropriate in light of the Work insistence on self-effort but, as Gurdjieff had disclosed to Ouspensky, even narcotics were sanctioned in some Schools to show a student his possibilities in advance (*In Search of the Miraculous* , pp. 8-9).

In another way, Ouspensky and Stjernvall seemed to have opposite tendencies. Anna says the doctor was nicknamed 'Mean' by Gurdjieff because 'he would part with nothing he possessed, words or money' (*With Gurdjieff in St Petersburg and Paris*, p. 103). At least Ouspensky did not hoard words, seeing that Gurdjieff nicknamed him 'Wraps up the Thought' because he was over-generous in that respect.

As what Ouspensky confided to Gurdjieff about Stjernvall must have been unflattering, or he would not have been so upset when Gurdjieff relayed his opinion back to the doctor, it possibly, and ironically, referred to some of Stjernvall's just-mentioned characteristics.

Also significant in speculation about conditions attaching to the St Petersburg group is Gurdjieff's judgment on Stjernvall when at an earlier meeting the doctor had tried to recount his worst action to the group. Gurdjieff commented on his attempt: 'Another time, doctor, you will be sincere, and recall these matters accurately.' (ibid., p. 69)

The doctor's performance in that test was similar to those of his colleagues in the Petersburg Six. Ouspensky admits there were certain things he could not relate to the others. He says something within registered such a vehement protest against such disclosure that 'in speaking of certain periods of my life I tried to give only the general idea and the significance of the facts which I did not want to relate'.

'Personality hides behind essence,' G remarked, 'and essence hides behind personality and they mutually screen each other.' (*In Search of the Miraculous* , p. 248)

Ouspensky possibly saw during the episode in Finland – or more likely on reflection – that Gurdjieff had removed the screen, showing him that the weaknesses he criticised in Stjernvall existed in him, too. Certainly, Ouspensky came to realise that a main reason one reacts negatively to mechanicalness in another person is that a jagged point of one's own Personality catches on a matching flaw in the other.

Those superficial features could indicate a certain 'feeling of I' that Ouspensky had acquired – the largely fictitious character 'Piotr Demianovich', as Gurdjieff dubbed the 'chief feature' hiding Ouspensky's real self. The episode indicated that this imaginary 'I' indulged itself in requirements; in this instance that its 'confidences' be respected. The result of Gurdjieff's rejection of this wishful expectation might also have shown him whether he felt hurt and resentful (another two unnecessary negative emotions) because others would now suspect that he talked about them behind their backs.

Humiliation is known to have been one of Gurdjieff's methods of disabusing his followers of imagination that they possessed honest self-knowledge. He seems to have succeeded to a considerable extent in this with Ouspensky.

After Stjernvall's test, the Six should have been prepared for sharp lessons focusing on sincerity with oneself and others, particularly of course with their teacher. Gurdjieff had told them they did not yet understand what it meant to be sincere. When he once walked out on the Petersburg Six over insincerity, Ouspensky pleaded with him to reconsider on similar grounds to Abraham's 'righteous men' argument in defence of Sodom and Gomorrah. Gurdjieff replied sceptically the next day that if Ouspensky lumped himself with Anna and then added the other four, together they might amount to half a righteous person (*With Gurdjieff in St Petersburg and Paris*, pp. 81-2).

St Petersburg evidently was less corrupt than Gomorrah, because Gurdjieff relented and continued their instruction –

but only because they were sincerely hungry for knowledge. Perhaps this implied that self-sincerity could be attained in the development such knowledge should engender. In Finland, Gurdjieff seemed again to be allowing Ouspensky half-a-righteous-man's benefit of the doubt by granting a month's grace on his ultimatum over group membership.

The alarm that Ouspensky felt can be connected with what Gurdjieff termed the 'second barrier' (in importance after sincerity), which called for the 'conquest of fear' (*In Search of the Miraculous* , p. 230). He said man lives in an atmosphere of lies and fear, and the conquest of both is individual in form. It is the first positive work that a man can do, he said, which perhaps indicates the stage the St Petersburg group had reached in the Work.

The second barrier as described by Gurdjieff prompts a recollection of what Ouspensky regarded as the second threshold to a 'new world' of mathematical relations that he experienced in his earlier mystical experiments. As we have seen, in the first, subjective, transitional state he was suspicious of promises made by 'voices', frightened by the feeling that his development would halt if he believed them. It was his struggle against believing the voices that brought him to the second threshold. But this produced new fear, for he saw infinity swallowing the mathematical relations. He became terrified of making a wrong approach to what he saw as an infinitely varying point.

Had he experienced this state half a century later he may have compared it to that of an astronaut approaching a black hole in space-time, 'overcome with terror at the imminence of this abyss' (*A New Model of the Universe*, p. 320). Later still, this fear may have been allayed by the theory that all is not destroyed inside a black hole, although uncertainty would surely maintain a substantial degree of terror.

This allusion to space travel is not all that preposterous, seeing that Ouspensky was learning to navigate the dimensions of his own inner space; it is understandable that a threat the journey could be aborted would raise genuine fears.

The seriousness of Gurdjieff's warning in Finland indicates he judged that Ouspensky had reached a significant stage on his inner journey. He pointed out that although nothing can be expected of a person who has made no effort, so his mistakes can be forgiven, more is expected of one who has made effort. His mistakes can be wiped out only by the truth, especially in relation to his teacher but also to the others in the Work group.

Ouspensky would probably not have been surprised by a demonstration of trust being called for in the conditions. In discussions on the possibility of forming a Work group, Gurdjieff had told his Petersburg followers:

'I should have to trust you in this work and you would have to trust me and one another. . . . First of all you must understand that in a group all are responsible for one another. . . . what one acquires is acquired by all. . . . there can be no personal interests opposed to the interests of others ...' (*In Search of the Miraculous* , p. 231).

Considering that he confronted Ouspensky with a perturbing ultimatum soon after agitating him by divulging the latter's views of Stjernvall, this reciprocity principle imposed on group members could well have featured in the conditions. Today, Work people are still cautioned that if one of them leaks energy the group's presence is diminished. But when first heard by a man who considered himself independent and self-sufficient, like Ouspensky, the idea might have raised some reservation about joining a group.

Associated with that condition is the need to accept responsibility. Ouspensky was probably feeling stress in being responsible just for himself. For, despite this form of psychology being his special field of interest and aptitude, he was stretched intellectually to take in some of Gurdjieff's ideas. So it is unlikely he had great confidence in the ability of all or any of the other group members to grasp the Work principles to their leader's satisfaction.

While this indicates differences he may have perceived between himself and his colleagues, there was a similarity in his and Stjernvall's reactions to Gurdjieff's tests. Except perhaps in Anna's eyes, Ouspensky was not regarded as emotional; neither was Stjernvall. Yet during another visit to the Finnish meeting house, the quiet, well-balanced doctor had blurted out in a voice like 'subdued thunder' that he believed 'Georgi Ivanovich is not less than Christ Himself!' (*With Gurdjieff in St Petersburg and Paris*, p. 67). We are not told whether an intentional influence by Gurdjieff had produced this uncharacteristic expression of feeling, as appears to have happened in Ouspensky's case, but it seems likely.

Ouspensky, thanks to his perusal of religious texts, may well have come to regard the extremely emotional segment of his Finland experiences, when his thinking and moving centres were immobilised, as 'the dark night of the soul'. He was not privy to the changes Gurdjieff made later in his explanation of the functioning of the Law of Seven, which disharmonised the fifth stopinder, or interval, of the development octave into what Beelzebub calls the Harnel-Aoot (see The Holy Planet 'Purgatory' chapter in *All and Everything*). But students of his classic creation myth will be able to see that Ouspensky reacted as might be expected at this challenging interval.

The Harnel-Aoot is also characterised by another hazard that Gurdjieff warned his group members against, being 'between two stools'. The problem at this stage in a Work sense is that the person has learnt enough, and probably changed himself or herself sufficiently, to believe with satisfaction, and some justification, that he or she has improved their level of Being considerably. But simultaneously opposing this satisfaction is the 'terror of the situation' – an emotion that can be diagnosed from Ouspensky's intellectual paralysis – which can include the disturbing realisation that despite all one's efforts much remains to be done. Gurdjieff's pupils would have been warned that in this work it is impossible to stand still. It's either up or down – and, according to Virgil:

'Light is the descent to Avernus! Night and day the portals of gloomy Dis stand wide: but to recall thy step and issue to the upper air – there is the toil and there the task!' (*Aeneid*, vi. 126)

In practice, though, such a course is not all that light or easy on the person descending to what is in effect a lower world. And heading fears of hardships ahead is the undesirability of returning to one's previous way of life. At the Harnel-Aoot a Fourth Way follower knows too much of life's potential to welcome a return to imprisonment in a mechanical existence.

What can we imagine as the trigger that suddenly propelled Ouspensky into this stressful state? In our speculative scenario, his teacher had shaken his self-assurance about his level of Being, demonstrating shortcomings in his understanding of and commitment to truth and sincerity and a susceptibility to internal considering. But Ouspensky reports that, while accepting that his previous picture of his abilities had been inaccurate, he had found something reliable within himself.

We don't know what he considered that particular strength to be but, in the context of his activity at that time, he would have seen it as enabling him to continue studying Work ideas. Were he focused on self-study, what if Gurdjieff then intensified his insistence on the need for responsibility towards others in the group?

Ouspensky had already acted as an instructor of newcomers to the group, but how would he react if Gurdjieff now asked him to lead his own group, and be responsible for them? There would be nothing nominal about such responsibility. Gurdjieff might have conveyed to his pupil an idea of, say, the suffering of Christ who, by founding a religion, accepted responsibility for all deeds committed by its followers in His name. This suggests, even on the lower scale of a Work group, that a leader might have to bear a heavy cross.

If leadership were the issue in question, Ouspensky might well have been torn between 'yes' and 'no'. Even when part of him wished to reply in the affirmative, he says, something else kept him mute. When Gurdjieff decreed that an answer must wait until another time, Ouspensky recalls, 'I think I asked him to wait, to give me a little time to get accustomed to this thought.' But he was told to sleep.

When Gurdjieff revealed to the others Ouspensky's opinion of one of them, he may have been testing whether his pupil would deduce from this that a group leader has to be above internal considering about what his students think of his actions. Again, perhaps this was a strength that Ouspensky felt he could attain. He might also have suspected that his teacher would view it as merely a compensatory reaction by the authoritative 'I's of his Personality.

As already suggested, another ingredient in the ferment may have been the question of trust. Gurdjieff had told the original Group of Six that others would join the group, the only condition being that 'they must make the maximum effort to absorb what they hear, either from me or from one of you six' (*With Gurdjieff in St Petersburg and Paris*, p. 104). Evidently those passing on the knowledge would have to meet more conditions, for Gurdjieff later stressed that a pupil had to have complete trust in his teacher.

This did not necessarily conflict with the earlier command not to accept anything as true until proved in one's own experience. Pupils need not accept that everything their teacher said was literally accurate, but they did need to have faith that it was being conveyed to them to aid their self-development.

As his teacher's ultimate aim, the direction in which he was leading the group, became an issue that soured Ouspensky's relationship with Gurdjieff in the months ahead, it appears possible that the conflict was initiated by this condition.

Until the Finland crisis, Ouspensky had felt that he was very much an individual. But the emotions he felt during the next three weeks, when he was 'awake' for comparatively long periods, produced changes within him. He recalls:

'The first thing I could record was the weakening in me of that extreme individualism which up to that time had been the fundamental feature in my attitude to life' (*In Search of the Miraculous*, p. 266).

A second observation was that 'I understood the esoteric principle of the impossibility of violence' in attaining any aim. This also, as will be indicated later, could account in part for his opposition to some of Gurdjieff's teaching methods.

When Ouspensky expressed a wish to be able to invoke at will the emotions he experienced in those weeks of being 'awake', Gurdjieff told him that sacrifice was necessary for that. What had to be given up were fantasies, one's suffering. Ouspensky was left to ponder on what sort of suffering was meant. He would know it was not genuine, legitimate suffering and, with Gurdjieff's guidance, sacrifice and suffering became important parts of his own teaching.

Chapter 9

METHOD AMID MADNESS

SOON AFTER ANNA BUTKOVSKY met Gurdjieff, the relationship between her and Ouspensky seems to have waned. Does this signify, as J.H. Reyner suggests, the completion of an octave – a key Work concept that Ouspensky would help introduce to the world?

Whatever the reason, about this time Ouspensky formed an attachment to Sophie Grigorevna, a widow a few years his senior, a formidable lady with dark chestnut hair and flashing eyes. She had already been married twice and had a daughter, Lenochka. Although superficially they were opposites, she an extrovert and, it was said, selfish woman of the world as against Ouspensky's introverted, generous nature, there must have been some chemistry between them that inspired both partners – in the Work as well as in marriage, events were to prove.

One can only speculate on their relationship as at first they kept separate apartments and apparently it was only the threat to the customs of society posed by the imminent 1917 revolution that persuaded them to marry.

They then lived on Troitskaya Street, near Nevsky Prospect, the main street in St Petersburg. We know of this address because the musical composer Thomas de Hartmann and his wife, Olga, who were to play major roles in The Fourth Way teaching, recorded meeting Gurdjieff in the Ouspenskys' apartment there on 9 February 1917 (*Our Life with Mr Gurdjieff*, p. 9).

De Hartmann was introduced to the Work by Andrei Zaharoff. The Tsar had arranged for de Hartmann to be made a reserve officer in the Imperial Household Guards between 1908 and 1912 so he could devote his time to music, but now of course he was summoned back to active duty.

Ouspensky, too, was mobilised, temporarily. We can picture the stocky soldier in his Guards Sappers uniform with, significantly in a medical context, a pince-nez perched on his nose, setting off from his comfortable apartment each morning on a two-mile tram ride to his regimental HQ. Fortunately for the Work, the myopia that necessitated his distinctive spectacles earned his demobilisation after several months.

That de Hartmann meeting illustrated a feature of Gurdjieff's instruction: frequently, while addressing a crowd, he seemed to be speaking specifically for the benefit of an individual – at least, over the years many of his pupils felt this to be so in their personal instances.

On the night in question, someone had suggested that love could be a main impediment to self-development. Olga de Hartmann was dismayed when Gurdjieff agreed that 'love is the strongest obstacle to man's development'. She had suffered other experiences in which she and her husband would have needed to part in order to follow a particular course of purported development.

However, as though he realised this effect on her, Gurdjieff then pointed out it depended on the type of love: self-love or temporary attraction tied a person down, but real love was different. He added he was glad when a husband and a wife were both interested in his ideas, because they could help each other.

This relieved and delighted Olga. Her sensations later that night gave her an idea of Gurdjieff's telepathic power. After the meeting she went to a ball in honour of her younger sister's birthday and on entering the ballroom she felt a blow, as it were, in the chest and then realised that all the people dancing seemed to be puppets.

The meeting mentioned by the de Hartmanns took place during Gurdjieff's last visit to St Petersburg. In the closing months of 1916 some members of Ouspensky's group had seen him in Moscow and brought back Work diagrams and notes. Membership of the group grew as people found a point of security in the new way of looking at life, amid the chaos around them. Gurdjieff, meanwhile, had gone to Alexandropol in the Caucasus with his wife, Julia (nee Osipovna Ostrowska), to see his parents.

In Ouspensky's view, the turn of 1916-17 brought the last winter of St Petersburg's life (*In Search of the Miraculous*, p. 317). He expressed this feeling in a late-night stroll through the city (renamed Petrograd by then, a name Ouspensky ignored) with the editor of an artistic monthly in the summer of 1917. The editor had remarked:

'Do you know, there are idiots, even among cultured people, who feel happy in the Revolution, who believe it to be a liberation of something? They do not realise that, if it means liberation, it is liberation from the possibility of eating, drinking, working, walking, using tramways, reading books, buying newspapers, and so on.'

Ouspensky agreed:

'People don't understand that if anything exists, it does so thanks to inertia. The initial push from the past is still working but it cannot be renewed! There lies the horror. Sooner or later its energy will be exhausted and all will stop, one thing after another. . . . You will realise that the fact of our walking here and that nobody is assaulting us is abnormal. It is made possible by inertia alone. The man who very soon will be robbing and murdering on this very spot has not yet realised the fact that he can do it now without fear of punishment. In a few months it won't be possible to walk here at night-time, and some months later it will be unsafe to do it during the day.'

Later, Ouspensky commented: 'Everything, unhappily, has proved the truth of our conclusions.'

It was not only the uneducated who were gulled by Bolshevism. About a week after the revolution Ouspensky called together the main members of the St Petersburg group at Dr Sukharov's apartment and suggested they go abroad to continue the Work. He warned it would not be long before 'everything began to break up and collapse'. He found that most of the others did not realise the hazards ahead, some even thinking that 'everything that happens is for the best' (ibid., p. 328).

Many of the workers had a more self-interested view. In that same summer Ouspensky and a friend witnessed a procession of striking shop staff along the Nevsky. Asked the reason for the strike, one lad said that the shop owners had been profiteering since the beginning of the war. Ouspensky's friend suggested in jest that doubtless the strikers now wanted prices cut and unfair profits returned. The lad's answer made the position clear for Ouspensky: 'Young men and girls had for three years running witnessed a daylight plundering, and now demanded their share in the robbery.'

In that final summer Ouspensky already saw that it was the end of publication of his books in Russia. At any rate, he had neglected his writing during the previous two years to devote his time to Gurdjieff's System. And although the political climate was growing ever darker, he noted that hawkers were still selling sunflower seeds on the Nevsky, and such reminders of better days helped make it difficult to decide definitely to leave Russia while escape was possible.

Later, he realised that his unsettled frame of mind was caused, not by personal danger in a country whose affairs were running only on momentum, but by the fear of being made to look stupid by events; that is, by staying on despite his judgment that it was time to go. However, he did not wish to leave while he could stay in touch with Gurdjieff and his teaching.

Another problem was that Gurdjieff's whereabouts were unknown. When Gurdjieff finally gave him direct orders he felt as though he had been freed of a heavy responsibility. Those instructions were foreshadowed in a telegram from Alexandropol in the Caucus in June 1917: 'If you want to have rest come here to me.'

Ouspensky noted: 'That was G!' The exclamation mark presumably signifies not only that the timing was typical of Gurdjieff's behaviour but that the idea of 'rest' was received with a sense of irony.

Never mind, it was the call he had been waiting for and within two days he was on a five-day train journey to Tiflis

(Tbilisi), the capital of Georgia. In *Search* he describes his and his fellow passengers' overnight stay in the station waiting room while on the platform drunken soldiers held courts-martial over the pick-pocketing of three roubles. Three suspects were executed, two as a result of mistaken identity (ibid., p. 340).

He reached Alexandropol two days later – to find that Gurdjieff was so busy, mainly in his family's welfare in their house in the Greek quarter, that it was several days before he really spoke to him.

Ouspensky was intrigued by a portrait of Gurdjieff dressed in a frockcoat with his curly hair brushed straight back, which he said told him his profession at the time, although Gurdjieff never spoke of it. He said the picture gave him many interesting ideas but he kept them to himself as this was his personal discovery.

What seems to be a similar picture of Gurdjieff, in Tashkent in 1908, has been published and purports to show him when he was practising as a professional hypnotist. Gurdjieff himself wrote that he had studied in a Central Asian Dervish monastery a branch of science called Mehkeness, a name meaning 'taking away responsibility', part of which is known in the West as hypnotism (*The Herald of Coming Good*, p. 13). To gain practical knowledge of man's 'subconscious sphere' he presented himself as a healer of all kinds of vice and rendered 'conscientious aid to sufferers' for some five years.

We are left to wonder what Ouspensky found so interesting about this part of Gurdjieff's study of one of man's psychoses. He may have been also interested in reading in *The Herald of Coming Good* – thought by some to have been published in 1931 specifically to annoy Ouspensky – that 'theosophism', 'occultism' and 'spiritualism' are cited among the 'woeful' ideas he studied. He might also have found some significance in Gurdjieff's revelation that he needed to include among his 'Guinea-Pigs' all the 28 categories of types existing on Earth 'as they were established in ancient times' (ibid., p. 22).

Would he have taken seriously Gurdjieff's revelation that it was to facilitate the assembling of all types of guinea-pigs that it became necessary to found his Institute for Man's Harmonious Development?

When, after their reunion in Alexandropol, they did finally speak about the situation in Russia, Gurdjieff surprised Ouspensky by indicating that the unrest would soon settle and that he planned to return to see the Nevsky hawkers whom his visitor had mentioned.

To Ouspensky, it became clear over time that one subject Gurdjieff did not grasp at all fully was European politics. Ouspensky would not have realised this at that stage, however he was cautious about taking the prediction at face value because Gurdjieff also suggested it might be good to go to Persia (Iran) or to a certain, secret place in the Transcaucasian Mountains.

A fortnight later Gurdjieff announced that he and two others would accompany Ouspensky back to St Petersburg. Ouspensky remarked during the early part of the train journey that it was impossible to further the Work 'in the midst of mass madness'. He failed to understand at that stage what Gurdjieff meant by contradicting this with an assertion that it was only at such times that it was possible, and that events that now seemed to hinder them would actually prove useful.

Ouspensky, looking at the situation from the point of view of 'facts', was far from seeing that civil war and the endless lying of politics could help them. Later, however, he saw that when viewed from esoteric principles Gurdjieff's claim became comprehensible. Ouspensky posed the question of where was the need for such ideas while Europe was a comfortable place to live; and answered himself that these ideas could come only at times when most people's attention was distracted by something like war.

This solution hinges on Gurdjieff's revelation that knowledge is as material as anything else, though of course finer than most materials, so that if it is shared by many no one will receive much, but if concentrated in a few minds it is more likely to have a noticeable effect.

It is also possible that if wars are caused, as Gurdjieff claimed, by external influences acting on our planet and its inhabitants, the extra energy available at such times could also be used for positive rather than destructive ends, depending on an individual's receptive apparatus.

Esoteric possibilities aside, Gurdjieff appeared to adjust his practical assessment of the national situation after talking in Tiflis with an army general who had been in the St Petersburg group. When the train reached Mozdok, he decided that Ouspensky would continue to Moscow and St Petersburg and the others would head for Kislovodsk.

Ouspensky passed on Gurdjieff's message to group members in Moscow and St Petersburg and in twelve days was back in the Caucasus, learning that Gurdjieff was then living in a small villa on the outskirts of Essentuki, where twelve group members eventually converged.

The next six weeks, Ouspensky recalls, seemed to expand sufficiently for Gurdjieff to instruct them on what seemed to be the whole plan of the Work, as well as physical exercises connected with it (*In Search of the Miraculous*, p. 346). Of particular interest to Ouspensky were his revelations on the running of esoteric schools. One point was that a man, of his own will, could not make what he called super-efforts for long without the aid of another's will. Gurdjieff explained that it was this point about will that made Schools necessary.

An appreciation of the necessity for a School to direct self-development had a life-long influence on Ouspensky. Even when later he fell out with Gurdjieff the man, he valued what he taught and considered it came from a genuine School. He felt driven to find the original source as he did not believe Gurdjieff had disclosed the full teaching. Other members, too, would dearly have loved to know where their teacher had studied.

When questioned on this mystery a couple of decades later, Ouspensky quipped that they asked Gurdjieff about the System's origin 'about ten times a day' and he always answered differently. Asked why he gave different answers Gurdjieff replied simply that he didn't. It is likely that had his followers been able to interpret his answers they would have been seen to have a common, if disguised, element.

At any rate, he obviously operated on a strict 'need to know' basis and would have been unlikely to risk filling his students' minds with dreams of traipsing all over Central Asia – Ouspensky mentioned one location the teacher appeared to let slip out as being near Kashgar in Chinese Turkestan – in search of gurus. They had enough work to do on themselves without such distractions.

Ouspensky, of course, especially after his split from Gurdjieff, would have loved to have made contact with such an esoteric source on earth. Gurdjieff may have interested his followers in Moscow by mentioning an 'inner circle of humanity' but he never confirmed the existence of any such group in his writings, apart from referring in *All and Everything* to a Mohammedan society founded in Central Asia named the Assembly of the Enlightened, a brotherhood also known as the Assembly of all the Living Saints of the Earth (*Beelzebub's Tales to His Grandson*, pp. 1091-4, 1098).

Ouspensky remarks on the sensing exercises the group were taught because they seemed to bear out his earlier conclusion that physical states connected with his psychological experiments involving fasting and different forms of breathing began with feeling the pulse throughout the body. Gurdjieff explained that control over this depended on controlling muscular tension. Exercises on muscle relaxation gave them encouraging results, says Ouspensky.

Gurdjieff also showed them the 'stop' exercise which is connected with what was said earlier about the necessity to obey another man's will, as well as with the ability to change habitual postures, which he linked with inability to control thoughts and feelings. In practice, the exercise meant freezing their movements at the calling of a certain word. This enabled each person to observe him or herself from a new point of view. It also afforded practice in conscious obedience, as opposed to mechanical obedience such as, for instance, is drilled into soldiers.

Ouspensky found that attitudes towards this exercise showed people's attitude to the Work. Another test, fasting, showed some people the important role food played in their lives, but Ouspensky was impressed chiefly by the influence of the habit of talking. In fact, he said, the first fast resulted in everyone talking incessantly about themselves in relation to the fast.

He also notes that in answer to a suggestion that absolute silence would be a hard test, Gurdjieff brought to bear 'that wonderfully practical element which distinguished his system'. Complete silence was easier than saying only what was necessary, he pointed out. He applied the same reasoning to food, pleasure, sleep – adding that beyond what is necessary 'sin' begins. (It can be assumed that 'sin' in this context means the condition formulated by Maurice Nicoll as 'missing the mark'.)

When Ouspensky asked how people could know what was necessary, Gurdjieff again employed the Work response to such questions: they did not apply to people, only to those seeking The Fourth Way. There could be no sins for people in general, who 'are going nowhere'. Gurdjieff explained:

'Sins are what keep a man on one spot if he has decided to move and if he is able to move. . . . Sin is what puts a man to sleep when he has already decided to awaken' (ibid., p. 357).

An important lesson Ouspensky learnt from that period's theory lessons and practical exercises was the futility of dreaming about big and distant achievements. For they all reached a stage where they saw that even to begin work on oneself required many favourable inner and outer conditions, with no guarantee of future advances. The Work then did not seem worth the effort involved. Ouspensky learned that 'a man must value what he gets today without thinking of what he might get tomorrow' (ibid., p. 360).

A common question was whether people not on a way have any possibilities. Ways, said Gurdjieff, are simply aids, help given according to type. It is enough to realise that a general evolution is a possibility for people who simply live life according to conscience. His meaning of 'conscience' would become clear to them only much later, when this answer would be seen to apply to a limited number of people.

Ouspensky took a chance to ask his favourite question about repetition of lives. He did not get a direct answer. This and Gurdjieff's responses to such questions on other occasions suggest that he guarded his pupils from being distracted by the possibility of other lives, which might tempt them to work less hard in the present. Daydreams of eternal bliss are a luxury to 'machines' trying to plug into a more powerful flow of consciousness.

Chapter 10

FOUND: THE KEY TO CONSCIOUSNESS

JOURNALISTS ARE ENJOINED to record the five Ws – who, what, where, when and why – in their stories. Experienced newspaper correspondent and dedicated Time investigator Peter Ouspensky, however, omitted the precise 'when' and 'where' in reporting George Gurdjieff's revelation of the core concept that energised his self-development method. Still, that seems appropriate in view of the timeless, universal nature of that Work idea.

We do know, from Ouspensky's account in *In Search of the Miraculous*, that the disclosure came during one of Gurdjieff's talks to his St Petersburg followers before the Bolshevik revolution forced them to regroup elsewhere. It arose during a discussion on consciousness after the pupils had tried to practise their teacher's instructions on Self-observation. He had introduced that technique early in his talks because it is the starting point in personal work towards self-development. People will not wish to change their psychology unless they first discover their shortcomings. They can achieve this by observing their actions and attitudes impartially, without justifying or covering up or even trying to stop their thoughts or feelings. This exercise requires knowledge of the physical functions, or centres, persistence in controlling attention, and sincerity.

Ouspensky reports that in analysing the results of his pupils' efforts at observing themselves, Gurdjieff indicated the simple but forgotten key to gaining consciousness by announcing that 'not one of you has noticed that *you do not remember yourselves*'. He told them:

'You do not feel *yourselves*; you are not conscious of yourselves. With you, 'it observes' just as 'it speaks,' 'it thinks,' 'it laughs.' You do not feel: I observe, I notice, I see. Everything still 'is noticed,' 'is seen.' ... In order to really observe oneself one must first of all *remember oneself*. . . . Only those results will have any value that are accompanied by self-remembering' (ibid., p. 117-8).

Ouspensky says he immediately saw that these words were the key to Gurdjieff's explanations on consciousness; he soon felt that he 'stood on the threshold of a very great discovery'.

When his efforts demonstrated the difficulty of Self-remembering, showed in fact that 'we never remember ourselves', Gurdjieff told him: 'People who *know this* already know a great deal.'

This represented a major advance, because in an earlier talk Gurdjieff had made it clear that his pupil did not know very much at all about consciousness. Ouspensky relates this conversation in a way that shows the extent of the knowledge gap between a learned, extremely well-read person such as himself and his new teacher, who had studied in vastly different schools:

'On one occasion while talking with G. I asked him whether he considered it possible to attain "cosmic consciousness", not for a brief moment only but for a longer period' (ibid., p.116). As he had written about cosmic consciousness, he probably spoke as though he had an inkling of what it meant and, when asked to define what in general consciousness is, replied that it was an indefinable inner quality that one knew only in oneself.

Gurdjieff dismissed most of this as 'rubbish' but agreed that 'you *can know* consciousness only in yourself'. He said 'can know' because 'you can know it only when you have it. And when you have not got it, you can know you have not got it, not at that very moment, but afterwards. I mean that when it comes again you can see that it has been absent for a long time . . .'

He added that 'science and philosophy cannot define consciousness because they want to define it where it does not exist. . . . We have only the possibility of consciousness and rare flashes of it.'

In his struggle to Self-remember Ouspensky was confronted by a problem that, he considered, 'science and philosophy had not, so far, come across'. The exercise reminded him of his experiment in stopping thought, which he undertook after reading a description of it in Edward Carpenter's *From Adam's Peak to Elephanta.* The difference he found was that in one action the attention was aimed wholly at stopping thought 'while in self-remembering attention becomes divided, one part of it is directed towards the same effort, the other part to the feeling of self' (ibid., p. 119).

This led to one of the formulations for which Ouspensky is noted. He represented Self-remembering by a diagram of a straight line with an arrowhead at each end. 'When I observe something, my attention is directed towards what I observe – a line with one arrowhead. When at the same time, I try to remember myself, my attention is directed both towards the object observed and towards myself. A second arrowhead appears on the line.'

Although this degree of awareness was new, he felt he had experienced moments of Self-remembering since early childhood, in changed or unexpected surroundings and in emotional or dangerous moments when one 'sees and observes oneself from the outside'. The important deduction was 'that I really only remember those moments of the past in which I *remembered myself*'. That realization provoked a typically Ouspenskian question: 'Why experience so much in order to forget it afterwards?' Also typical was his afterthought: 'Besides there was something degrading in this.' He had always judged man's weak memory to be one of life's absurdities. Now the cause of this weakness had become clear: we can truly recall only moments of Self-remembering.

The results he records of early efforts to Self-remember include an awareness that houses he observed were 'quite alive, I all but spoke to them'. On the other hand, he struck times when the instant his attention was distracted he forgot all about Self-remembering.

Despite, or perhaps because of the difficulty of maintaining the desired state, he came to see Self-remembering as 'the centre of gravity of the whole system and of all work on oneself', by which 'psychology becomes an exact and at the same time a practical science' (ibid., p. 121). The concept also widened his understanding of the repeated calls on Man to awake in religious teachings.

During the exhilaration of that discovery period, he was surprised at his failure to convey what he saw as the obvious importance of Self-remembering to otherwise perceptive people outside the Work. This helped confirm Gurdjieff's comment that people in general felt no need to seek consciousness because they imagined that already they could be fully conscious at will.

Gurdjieff's elucidation of his psychological findings in the following weeks – 'I cannot help being astonished at the speed with which G. transmitted to us the principal ideas of his system' (ibid., p. 178) – convinced Ouspensky that Self-remembering is possible only if one has the right emotional approach and sufficient energy.

In one talk, Gurdjieff described Self-remembering as the third state of consciousness, self-consciousness, or consciousness of one's Being. (The first state is physical sleep and the second the so-called waking consciousness. Gurdjieff used the term 'waking' ironically, seeing that in practice it excludes wakefulness.) He explained that the fourth, the 'objective state of consciousness' where things are seen 'as they are', could be reached only after a long and difficult development of self-consciousness. Fortunately, self-consciousness is the right of man once he overcomes any delusion that he possesses it already.

At the next lecture he introduced another key concept in his teaching: ordinary man's inability 'to do'. He told his pupils: 'We want to "do", but in everything we do we are tied and limited by the amount of energy produced by our organism. Every function, every state, every action, every thought, every emotion requires a certain definite energy, a certain definite substance.' He said that we are able to remember ourselves only if we have the energy for Self-remembering. While this obviously imposes a difficulty, he added that 'every normal man has quite enough energy to *begin* work on himself', if he can avoid wasting it 'on unnecessary and unpleasant emotions, on the expectation of unpleasant things, possible and impossible, on bad moods, on unnecessary haste, nervousness, irritability, imagination, daydreaming, and so on' (ibid., p.179).

The assurance that we could preserve sufficient energy to work productively set Ouspensky on a course of study and teaching that he maintained throughout life. The task of purifying oneself of wasteful feelings, negative emotions as he called them in general, became the foundation of Ouspensky's teaching when he led his own group. So much so that some people reacted with depression to the emphasis he put on observing negative emotions, acknowledging their existence, restraining from expressing them, and eventually separating from them. A variety of tasks were devised on this basis; for instance, seeing what 'I's enjoy being negative, impartially observing one's likes and dislikes, recognising what forms of negative behaviour by other people causes negativity in us, and of course finding antidotes to these reactions.

Even today, Ouspensky's detractors find it hard to resist quoting reports that his pupils spent all their time repressing unpleasant feelings, as evidenced by their unhappy facial expressions. Although it is true that a minority of his students seemed to interpret even the Work message negatively – as of course did some of Gurdjieff's people – Ouspensky never suggested any type of repression; the whole point of his methods was to bring flaws into the light. The separation he recommended has quite a different action. As an example, if a negative 'I' is observed, the attention that lends it '*a feeling of I*' (which has become a familiar Work term) is taken from it.

Throughout his teaching, Ouspensky sought to benefit from Gurdjieff's advice on self-development: 'In beginning to struggle with all these habitual sides of his life a man saves an enormous amount of energy, and with the help of this energy he can easily begin the work of self-study and self-perfection' (ibid. p. 179). In 1939 Ouspensky was still telling his pupils they must notice that 'whatever we do, whatever we say, whatever we think, whatever we feel, we never remember ourselves' (*A Further Record*, p. 19).

He also remarked: 'You can try to remember yourself through your mind, but if you really remember yourself, even for a short time, it becomes emotional' (ibid., p. 50).

His next comment sits strangely with a criticism made by some of his ex-pupils after they had joined a Gurdjieff group: that Ouspensky's concentration on their negativity deprived them of hope. For, after noting the emotional element in Self-remembering, he gave an assurance that 'when you find yourself in the state of coming to higher emotional centre, then you will be astonished to find how much you can understand at once'. Far from denying hope to his pupils, this seems at first to have been encouraging it a mite extravagantly. However, a commitment to stating the facts apparently compelled him to add: '- and then you come back to the normal state and forget it all'. The prospect of reaching a wider understanding alludes to the Work teaching that in Higher Intellectual Centre a person can be aware simultaneously of all he or she knows of a particular subject and in Higher Emotional Centre feel all the emotions connected with it.

Usually, Ouspensky evidently focused on the states his pupils could reach at their current level of Being. Cautioning that remembering oneself with Emotional Centre takes much effort, he said that what is possible in the beginning of work is to try not to express negative emotions, adding:

'Then we must study negative emotions and learn how to struggle with them; the only way is to struggle with identification. After long work on those lines, you acquire a certain control of emotional centre, and then only will it be possible to speak of how to use it for one or another purpose.'

He also repeated Gurdjieff's at first puzzling warning against working for results, by instructing that Self-remembering 'must not be based on expectation of results, otherwise one becomes lost in thinking about one's own efforts'. Instead, the effort should be made in the realization that we don't remember ourselves but could if we tried persistently enough in the right way. Both Gurdjieff and

Ouspensky persevered throughout their lives in efforts to enable people to find the way right for them.

Apparently though, not everyone feels that Ouspensky lived up to his potential in this respect. They argue that had he not left Gurdjieff's group much more could have been done to make the System accessible to a greater number of people. Presumably this would have been enabled by Ouspensky's ability at presenting esoteric ideas in an orderly way. The argument stems from the circumstance that Gurdjieff changed or developed some of his methods after Ouspensky broke off contact with him.

All this of course remains hypothetical, seeing that it is not known whether Gurdjieff would have desired publicity for his later techniques. It is true that early on he suggested that Ouspensky write an explanation of Work ideas that would be intelligible to people at large. This might have been to ensure that the basic principles he taught his St Petersburg group were preserved; he might have judged his subsequent methods of teaching to be at the experimental stage, not ready to be included in the record.

The notion that the Ouspenskian version of the Work teaching remains frozen as at 1917 has other weaknesses. Consider the vital method of Self-remembering. It is true that Ouspensky took care not to alter the meaning Gurdjieff gave to it during those intensive sessions in Petersburg and the Caucasus, while Gurdjieff ceased to use the term, instead calling it 'red pepper' according to C.S. Nott (*Journey Through This World*, p. 96; see also *Beelzebub's Tales*, pp. 19-21). Similarly Gurdjieff designated negative emotions as the 'devil', possibly to shock people into realising they were one's denying aspect. Nott points out that Gurdjieff was constantly trying to destroy his pupils' identification by such tactics.

However, in the first paragraph of his prologue to *Life is Real Only Then, When 'I Am'*, the third series of *All and Everything*, Gurdjieff speaks of 'the full sensing of the whole of myself' in connection with 'the process of self-remembering'. This is mentioned here, not in an attempt to discredit Nott's remark about Self-remembering but to acknowledge that Ouspensky did not elaborate on 'sensing' to the same extent in his lectures as Gurdjieff did in his talks and exercises. Not surprisingly, this led to a perception in some 'G. groups' that those who followed what might be called the Ouspenskian tradition lacked practical work. Just as inevitably, some of those so judged reacted by assuming that such an opinion could be held only by people who imagined that the physical side of the Work is pre-eminent, whereas they focused on a struggle against negative emotions.

Fortunately, by the present time those on both sides of the Gurdjieff-Ouspensky divide have managed to resist adopting the easy, blinkered view. Gurdjieff clarified that both sensing and feeling, as well as thought, were necessary for Self-remembering. In a 1923 talk on Self-remembering he explained:

'We shall call "feeling" the one whose place of origin is what we call the emotional centre; while "sensations" are those so-called feelings whose place of origin is in what we call the moving centre. Now, of course, each one must understand and examine his sensations and feelings and learn approximately the difference between them.

'For primary exercises in self-remembering the participation of all three centres is necessary, and we began to speak of the difference between feelings and sensations because it is necessary to have simultaneously both feeling and sensation.

'We can come to this exercise only with the participation of thought. . . . We desire, we wish; therefore our thoughts can be more or less easily adapted to this work, because we have already had practical experience of them.

'At the beginning all three need to be evoked artificially [by talking, reading, arguing, etc.] ... artificial things are necessary only in the beginning. The fullness of what we desire cannot be attained artificially, but, for beginning, this way is necessary' (*Views From the Real World*, pp.231-2).

When he had addressed a meeting in London in 1922 he indicated that 'Self-remembering' was not the only description of this state and exercise. Explaining the different levels of consciousness possible for man, he said:

'There are moments when you become aware not only of what you are doing but also of yourself doing it. You see both 'I' and the 'here' of 'I am here' – both the anger and the 'I' that is angry. Call this self-remembering, if you like' (ibid., pp. 79-80).

Let's see if we can put ourselves in the place of Ouspensky's pupils listening to this lecture. It might seem to them as though Gurdjieff was recognising that Ouspensky still called this state 'Self-remembering', and acknowledging that it was acceptable, the implication of 'if you like' being that it could also be described differently. To Ouspensky the implication might well have been that it would be *better* described differently to the term he used – another hint of the coming clash that would harden him against his old teacher's apparent change in attitude.

On the other hand, Gurdjieff seems never to have changed the precept he issued in Russia that 'the only right way to objective consciousness is through the development of self-consciousness' (*In Search of the Miraculous* , pp. 141-2). With that in mind, it hardly seems accidental that he sent out into the world a steadfast drill sergeant who would discipline selected recruits to perform training aimed at achieving self-consciousness in strict accordance with Moscow/Petersburg rules.

Although Ouspensky's lectures might well have seemed carved in stone by comparison with the ingeniously expressed hints and prods that Gurdjieff gave to his pupils, it appears likely that the two men's methods stemmed from different motives. We can assume that Ouspensky's aim was to develop his understanding so as to help preserve and spread the Work teaching and also to free himself from having to repeat life exactly as before. No one knows Gurdjieff's aim but it appears to have been connected with, at the beginning, finding by experiment an efficient method of enabling people to see reality, then, late in his life, recruiting a number of people who could continue, possibly organise and perhaps even develop, his teaching.

Another point needs to be made in rebuttal of the charge that Ouspensky hindered development of Fourth Way teaching. Despite his adherence to the principles revealed by Gurdjieff in Russia, Ouspensky did say that every point in the teaching could be developed. He evidently did not mean by this that the basic meaning was to be altered. What he intended is illustrated by the outcome of his suggestion at a lecture in the United States about 1944 that his group members try to develop a new classification of the sciences based on what cosmoses they investigated. A notable outcome of this is Rodney Collin's 'theory of celestial influence' and his reflections on Self-remembering, a memorable example of how the understanding of a Work method can be developed without debasing the traditional teaching.

Gurdjieff had told his pupils in St Petersburg that without Self-remembering 'you yourselves do not exist in your observations' (*In Search of the Miraculous*, p. 118). Ouspensky reports that he was then led to 'a certain, possibly a very incomplete, definition of "self-remembering" which nevertheless proved to be very useful in practice' by the idea of dividing attention, which he illustrated in his diagram of a line with two arrowheads pointing in opposite directions (as mentioned above).

Collin found that while it was extraordinarily difficult to remember oneself and the environment simultaneously 'it was much more possible to remember oneself and one's surroundings *in the presence of something else*'. He explains this with the help of the Work teaching on the fundamental Law of Three, which attests that every manifestation is the result of the action of three forces. When this is borne in mind during observation the attention recognises 'one's own organism, the subject of the experiment; the situation to which this organism is exposed in the moment; and something permanent which stands on a higher level than both and which alone can resolve the relation between the two' (*The Theory of Celestial Influence*, pp. 214-5).

He adapts Ouspensky's diagram of a base line pointing in

two directions by adding the third, higher force, represented by a Sun symbol and connected to the other two end points, making a triangle, the triad of the Law of Three. This introduces another task for, as he says, each person must find his own form of the third factor – 'his school, his teacher, his purpose, the principle he has learned, the Sun, some higher power in the universe, God'.

Remembering the cosmological flavour of the project set by Ouspensky, Collin adds that if one is 'occupied with some inner task, then it is necessary to remember *three worlds in oneself, three places in oneself*'. He means that by dividing the attention into three, one part of the force is directed towards action in the outer world, one part towards connecting with higher powers, and the third part retained in oneself.

Another of Ouspensky's pupils, Maurice Nicoll, developed down-to-earth ways of explaining Work ideas, as can be seen in his five-volume *Psychological Commentaries on the Teaching of G.I. Gurdjieff and P.D. Ouspensky*, in which his papers on Self-remembering fill many pages. He observes that the *act* of Self-remembering 'is the most important thing in the Work and the least attempted' (ibid., p. 1250). He says that in the early days of Ouspensky's teaching a constant cry was 'What have I to do?' The answer was always: 'All you have to do is to remember yourself.'

Nicoll comments: 'Now if you think that this is a giving up of yourself you are quite wrong. It is finding yourself and losing what you took as yourself – all this mess one is' (ibid., p. 927). This poses the paradox that real Self-remembering 'is to try to remember something that you are not'. Remembering something that you are at present, such as your misery, was called negative Self-remembering, he says. It leads nowhere useful.

To illustrate true Self-remembering he quotes Ouspensky as having said that it 'means having an element of will-control. It is an act of *doing*. It is not dreaming of doing, but an action. At first it takes force because it is using something we are not accustomed to use. But later on it gives force' (ibid., p. 1183).

Nicoll commented on this energy in one of his early talks on how to Self-remember:

'The first sign that you are doing it rightly is that you have a distinct feeling of force entering you, as if something had opened in you. Immediately you feel this, stop. You must stop instantly, and forget about the whole thing' (ibid., p. 38).

This instruction to stop may be connected with Gurdjieff's disclosure that initial success in Self-remembering will be artificial, so that further effort would lead to identification.

Nicoll says that 'all self-observation should be accompanied by some degree of self-remembering. Remembering why you are observing yourself and feeling the presence of the work in your mind while observing yourself is a degree of self-remembering' (ibid., p. 39). He also includes 'inner stop' made in connection with Self-observation as a form of Self-remembering. It might be made 'when you observe that you are beginning to talk in a certain mechanical way, or that you are getting annoyed with somebody, etc.'.

He concludes another talk with this observation:

'Self-Remembering comes down from above and full Self-Remembering is a state of consciousness in which the Personality and all its pretences almost cease to exist and you are, so to speak, nobody, and yet the fullness of this state, which is really bliss, makes you, for the first time, somebody' (ibid., p. 533).

One of Nicoll's students developed the Ouspensky form of teaching as an interpretation of the Gospel message, as told in the large, anonymously written book *A Point in the Work*, which records talks to a group in England over 16 years. In a passage about Self-remembering the group leader advises:

'So much in the Work can be taken in several ways. We all take it as we see, this must necessarily be so, but while this is so remember that there are meanings that you have not seen but that are there for you to see through self-observation; this, worked on for a while, will show you all things. I only hasten the showing by my elucidation of perhaps one thing, but do not forget that there are many, just as there are many kinds of

Self-Remembering, not one' (ibid., p. 132, vol. 1, Eureka Editions; p. 92, Work Books edition).

The writer says that in The Fourth Way

'We see that we must not expect God to lift our burdens by some magical new patent process, or because we lead what we believe to be good lives; no, we see that we ourselves must raise ourselves, bear our own burdens which in the main we have fashioned for ourselves, and so strive to raise ourselves, to know ourselves. We ask for God's help, yes, that is so, and help is given, but it is given by our seeing, our understanding of the casting of our burdens in an intelligent way, and it is only by learning to know ourselves that we can even think of casting our burdens in the right way.' (ibid., p. 19/12-13).

A starting point towards this is given as Self-observation. After some years

'we are prone, I believe, to think we understand self-observation ... but then comes real self-observation ... then we must commence deeper down, on what I will call the more secret self-observation; for as we have truly observed our more surface phases, so the secret, deeper ones will have come a little nearer the surface, and so it will not be impossible to see those also . . . they must be brought up into the light of our understanding' (ibid., pp.19-20/13).

Seeing into our depths means 'trying to take something, no matter what, without an "I" in it. . . . There are many kinds of Self-Remembering and none can be taken on the surface [of our minds, our lives] or we are not Self-Remembering, only thinking we are'.

'It is said we need food, manna, for strength to see the way through 'the mass of falsity that we are'. We obtain it 'by seeking the Light, by observing what we really are. One ray of truth gives us the food we need . . . so what of many rays? And they are within our reach. We have only to put out our hand and commence to climb the Octave, and the way to take the first step is by Self-Remembering. If we Self-Remember more often we shall find the way to have the strength to climb it . . .' (ibid., pp. 20-21/13).

A Point in the Work stresses that 'it is through the initial self-observation that all Work truths come' (ibid., p. 47 EE; p. 32 WB). It also tries to show that we must 'broaden out and take our truth also from those who have thought and studied wisely and widely'. That shows the goal: 'to remember yourselves that you may, through being awake to yourselves, be awake to others' (p. 49/33-4).

The group leader asks: 'Have you noticed how unmanageable your emotions are? . . . It is only when they are quite steady, when they have opened up to their Higher Centres, that Self-Remembering begins.'

Yet another of Ouspensky's pupils, John G. Bennett, analysed the principles of Gurdjieff's teaching in a brilliant intellectual light that revealed their sound basis under rigorous examination. His study of energies puts the idea of Self-remembering, or Self-consciousness, or intense sensing, or 'red pepper pods' in a new perspective. He describes energy as 'the means whereby nature passes from a state of potentiality to actual being', that is, the 'vehicle of the will'. What he terms sensitive energy is presented as the highest of the life energies. 'It has a remarkable property of self-awareness', makes choice possible (to a limited extent), and 'is the source of the power of recall' (*The Dramatic Universe*, vol. 2, p. 229).

The next highest degree, consciousness, is the lowest of the cosmic energies in Bennett's grading of qualities. 'Consciousness is the link that connects individual existence with universal being,' he says (ibid., p. 231). 'It is experienced by man as the direct awareness of a power that is both within and beyond his own presence.'

In Bennett's categories, creative, unitive and transcendent energies are on a progressively finer scale than consciousness, the passive content of the cosmic energies. Thus, he says, conscious energy 'does not transmit a creative or dominating power in the world, but rather makes it possible for the universe to be itself – a whole with interrelated parts'. It is 'the link that connects individual existence with universal being'.

In both the Work and spiritual writings, an analogy is

frequently made between consciousness and light. Bennett's description can help us to see the validity of this, for he shows that although consciousness is not an active force it enables us to see a situation as it really is.

He says that the power of consciousness is to make connections – 'If it is doing its proper work it connects us to ourselves – that is what Gurdjieff calls self-remembering' (*A Spiritual Psychology*, p. 113). To have the dual awareness of 'looking on at what one is doing' both sensitive and conscious energy are needed, one to throw an image of what is observed on the mental screen, the other to give it a previously unimagined, 'beautiful clarity' (see ibid., pp. 129-30).

Ouspensky was adept at detecting descriptions of Self-remembering, under other names, in ancient teachings. In *Notes on St John's Gospel* he recorded his feeling that 'Saint John is a poet. He gives new meaning to ordinary words; when he speaks of Wine, Bread, Light, Flesh, Blood, he means Foods – New Powers. Food is a key. It is a new force which starts machinery. Food is another name for Power. If we stop for an instant feeding, we die'.

He continues: 'Innumerable keys turn the wheels which control the circulation of our blood and feed our brain and keep up movement in us continually, which we call life. *Our* food is light, air, vision, sound, and every impression of feeling and sensation drawn from our surroundings. We have an illusion of being active. In reality we depend entirely on our foods and have no more power in ourselves than a windmill without wind.

'Self-remembering is an effort to make new power which will be Food for new faculties which otherwise are starved.'

Chapter 11

GROUP WORK SUSPENDED

ANY FANCY THAT LIFE with George Gurdjieff would be 'just roses, roses' was dispelled by events in the late Caucasian summer and winter of 1917, although Ouspensky had felt reservations about the direction the Work was taking him before that. The group's first big shock came in late August when Gurdjieff told those living in the Essentuki house that he was stopping all work. He announced he would go to the Black Sea coast with Andrei Zaharoff alone, then later agreed that any others who wished could follow him – but in the knowledge there would be no Work instruction.

For Ouspensky, this reinforced doubts about his continued presence in the group. He considered this an inappropriate time for acting, even if their teacher had created the crisis to test his pupils. Ouspensky seems to have found difficulty in isolating precisely what 'provoked' him. If the apparent abandonment of the group was a trial, well, outwardly he demonstrated his determination by following his erstwhile leader to Tuapse. In his thoughts and feelings, by contrast, he began to separate Gurdjieff the man from the System, 'of which I had no doubts'.

He did not find this division easy to accept, in inner or outer life, as he had forsaken his writing and sacrificed the opportunity to flee the Russian troubles in order to learn all that he could from Gurdjieff.

Perhaps he would have time to think about his position while he returned to St Petersburg to try to put his affairs in order. His book collection was Ouspensky's most treasured possession; so much so that he did not risk attempting to take it with him to the Caucasus. He left an extremely tense St Petersburg on his return journey on October 15, 1917, just a week before the Bolshevik Revolution – and the consequent loss of his books.

Ouspensky and his family joined Gurdjieff at Uch Dere, on

the Black Sea about 16 miles north-east of Sochi. He saw their group of houses was in a delightful position, the sea on one side and snow-capped mountains on the other – but the atmosphere among those sheltering there was far from congenial.

Even Zaharoff, who had seemed to be in an envious position – hypothetically, of course, envy being recognised as a severe handicap to, and thus not to be entertained by, those trying to raise their level of being – as Gurdjieff's selected companion shortly earlier, was depressed. Ouspensky learned he was preparing to quit and return to St Petersburg because his revered teacher was refusing to speak to him after having expressed displeasure at something Zaharoff said during a quarrel between Gurdjieff and neighbouring Latts.

Ouspensky's opinion of Gurdjieff the man did not improve when he rejected conciliatory overtures that Ouspensky had urged Zaharoff to make, effectively forcing him to return to St Petersburg, which at that time was wracked by famine and lawlessness.

Although he could not understand Gurdjieff's purpose in this incident, Ouspensky wrote later that he found the next two months 'interesting'. That was to put in mildly, unless he was impervious to physical hardships, for they had many adventures in travelling about the war-ravaged countryside, seeking security and food for themselves and fodder for their horses.

The party moved back to Essentuki after hearing rumours that the Caucasian army was marching along the Black Sea shore. In yet another switch, in February 1918 Gurdjieff sent a letter, signed by Ouspensky, to the group members still in Moscow and St Petersburg, inviting them to live and work with him. Among those who answered the summons was Zaharoff. Ouspensky's opinion of the dismissal incident darkened further when he saw how ill his colleague had become.

By March, work which Ouspensky described as being of the most varied kind began, including, in addition to housework, gymnastics, lectures, rhythmic exercises carried out to music (which progressed in time to dervish dances), mental exercises, breathing techniques and even many fake ways of imitating psychic phenomena. Gurdjieff explained that study of these trick methods was obligatory in Schools as a preliminary to learning techniques for performing genuine super-normal actions.

Public lectures were also held in the house twice a week. It would seem that the Work was continuing in the former way – but not for Ouspensky. For the past year his doubts about Gurdjieff as his leader had mounted, and now he felt he would have to leave the group. The reason he gives is that a student in such an organisation must not disagree with his teacher, whom he has to obey in everything.

Gurdjieff had told the group the approach to this strict obedience was via the stop exercise, as practised by all esoteric Schools. He had also told Ouspensky, during their first talks in Moscow, that there were no general Schools; each was led by a specialist, say a musician or an astronomer, and it was necessary for the pupils to master that particular field. But that was only a beginning; to round off their 'second education' it would then become necessary for the students to find other specialist gurus.

If this were so, Ouspensky wondered, how had Gurdjieff amassed his knowledge? He would reveal only that he had been among a number of 'specialists' who pooled what they had learned. When asked what had happened to his companions, Gurdjieff replied: 'Some have died, some are working, some have gone into seclusion.'

Two points in Ouspensky's recollection of this conversation appear significant. He detected a degree of acting by Gurdjieff, who seemed to be occasionally throwing in a word that would make him prick up his inner ear and 'think in a definite direction'. He also reports that the word 'seclusion', which he associated with a monastic language incongruous to his expectations at the time, gave him 'a strange and uncomfortable feeling' (*In Search of the Miraculous* , pp. 15-6).

This uncomfortable feeling appears to have surfaced again in Essentuki, because he suspected then that Gurdjieff was leading them towards a religious way. This, he argued to himself, was a different direction to that indicated when he joined the group, and one he could not follow, even if his teacher were a specialist in that way.

Was he justified in reaching this conclusion? While we cannot pretend to fathom the thinking of a man on as high a mental plane as Ouspensky, much less understand Gurdjieff, it is possible to make certain deductions by reading between the lines of the written record of their exchange of ideas.

Ouspensky, eager to locate a source of real knowledge, may at first have been puzzled by Gurdjieff's dismissal of any reasonable chance of finding specialist esoteric schools. Gurdjieff had claimed that for ages in Schools, India had offered only philosophy, Egypt theory, and Persia (Iran), Mesopotamia and Turkestan practice. And these were subdivided according to the special subjects studied in each. So, to attend a succession of specialist Schools to complete the work on himself might well take a seeker a thousand years.

Gurdjieff's explanation that he and his companions had shared what they understood implied that he himself could be the source of the knowledge Ouspensky sought, without replicating their individual odysseys. At first, that seemed an opportunity beyond Ouspensky's dreams; later he was less certain . . .

From what he learned about the traditional 'ways' to truth, designated by Gurdjieff as the Way of the Fakir, the Way of the Monk and the Way of the Yogi, Ouspensky's imagination was fired by the 'quick' method Gurdjieff introduced: The Fourth Way. In this – a surprisingly simple method but one which seems miraculous because no one ever manages to conceive of it by his own power of thought – the seeker lives an inner life attuned to elements of all the other ways, and at the same time carries on his ordinary outer life.

Gurdjieff assured his pupils that this 'sly man's' method was surer than the others – for those who could grasp and stick to it

– because its time span was conceivable. This was possible because it developed all the relevant centres of a person, intellectual, emotional and physical, simultaneously. In the traditional ways, fakirs concentrated on the body, monks on the emotions and yogis on the brain. Gurdjieff pointed out that when a fakir, for instance, had finally won control over his body, he was unlikely to be in a favourable condition to begin developing emotional and intellectual potentials.

In Essentuki, Ouspensky apparently decided that Gurdjieff had veered from what he for one understood as The Fourth Way.

A point that cannot be ignored is that, as a number of Gurdjieff group leaders have stressed, Ouspensky's disenchantment coincided with the teaching's sharp transition from theory to physical practice. That is to say, it seems as though Ouspensky the thinker was eager to absorb the ideas that Gurdjieff seemed able and willing to supply indefinitely, but was dismayed when the flow of new knowledge was suddenly cut off. He was noted to have made but a perfunctory effort to perform the Movements and obviously could not see that physical exercises held any advantage for him. Indeed, Frank Pinder, whom as we shall see helped him survive this Turkestan period, said Ouspensky had 'had a perfunctory fling at the movements; and even confessed to being lazy' (*Journey Through This World*, p. 90).

The reasons Ouspensky divulges for his self-expulsion raise further curious questions when viewed in the light of what he had written in *Osokin*. It seems to be more an expression of faith than fiction when the magician demands that Osokin 'must do everything I tell you without evasions or excuses'.

As was noted earlier, such words sound very much as though they could have been spoken by Gurdjieff. In real life, Ouspensky objected to an identical condition, although, of course, he could rationalise that it appeared to contradict Gurdjieff's initial instruction not to take anything on faith; and, as a corollary, not to act unless one understood what one was doing; or, as the pupil now saw it, not to follow a strange course unless one knew the planned destination.

On his objection that the 'new' course Gurdjieff was piloting was taking a religious direction, it cannot be imagined that Ouspensky had any opposition to spirituality per se, judging by his studies of the Gospels and other religious traditions. He was certainly critical of modern institutionalised forms of religion, but would surely judge Gurdjieff to be the last to adopt any exoteric system.

Maybe he was anxious not to be steered towards the Way of the Monk because, although convinced of the need to develop emotions, he was more interested in the Way of the Yogi, if not that of a Superman. He must have dismissed any possibility that the 'religious' instruction by Gurdjieff could readily form part of a wider Fourth Way that he could follow.

Two other factors, which we must leave for a while, are Gurdjieff's warning that he had his own aim in the Work, which might be different to those of his pupils, and Ouspensky's refusal during the crucial trial by telepathy in Finland – when 'everyone must show himself as he is' – to accept a certain unreported condition to remain a group member.

The immediate outcome of this internal debate was that Ouspensky rented a separate house for his family and resumed work on *The Wisdom of the Gods*.

When Cossacks began raiding Essentuki in August 1918, Gurdjieff and most of his followers evacuated the town on foot and after many hardships and adventures crossed the North Caucasus mountains and reached the Black Sea town of Sochi a month later. There, Gurdjieff again announced that the expedition had ended. Only a Moscow group member named Zhukov, Dr Leonid Stjernvall and his wife and the de Hartmanns chose to stay with their leader. In January 1919 Gurdjieff and his core group moved to Poti and then toTiflis.

By June 1919 Ouspensky managed to leave Essentuki for Ekaterinodar, which he says was at that time the capital of Russia. There he met friends from St Petersburg, one of whom asked about practical results of the work on himself. He replied he had acquired a 'strange confidence' in the insignificance of his ordinary self but a confidence that if something terrible happened to him it would be met, not by 'this ordinary I, but another I within that would be equal to the occasion' (*In Search of the Miraculous*, p. 380).

He also thought at that stage that it would be possible for him to continue the Work, even in Russia. 'The ideas of the System found a response and obviously answered the needs of people who wanted to understand what was taking place both in them and around them,' he says. He formed a small group there, and later in Rostov, and gave lectures relating Gurdjieff's System and the experiences of ordinary life which led people to it.

The near destitute Ouspensky family, which included his wife Sophie, stepdaughter Lenochka Savitsky and her son, Leonidas ('Lonya'), lived for a time in Ekaterinodar, from where Ouspensky somehow managed to dispatch a series of 'letters' about life in Russia to *The New Age* in London. The weekly's editor, A.R. Orage, whom the writer had met on his journey to the East, sent urgent messages to Major Frank Pinder, then in Ekaterinodar as head of the British Economic Mission to General Anton Ivanovich Denikin's Volunteer Army, to assist Ouspensky. Pinder employed Ouspensky to write press releases, paying his salary himself, on War Office instructions.

Zaharoff, whose path crossed Ouspensky's several times, also found work in the mission's propaganda section.

Ouspensky's letters to London paint a graphic picture of the stark situation in South Russia and also present a well-founded prediction of the outcome of the civil war and the future effect of the Soviet Revolution on Europe. They also give an idea of Ouspensky's sense of humour in the way in which he describes the appalling conditions.

In his first letter, dated July 25, 1919, he professed pity for everybody not living there, 'everybody who is living in the old way, everybody who is ignorant of what we now know'. For outsiders did not have 'the necessary perspective; you cannot get away from yourselves and look at yourselves from another point of view'.

For Russians, the question 'Shall we ever live again in the old way?' did not mean restoration of the old regime or oppression of the working classes but: 'When shall we be able to buy shoe-leather again, or shaving-soap, or a box of matches?'

'We know too much to be able to speak to you on equal terms,' Ouspensky told the English. Russians knew that 'war' and 'politics' and 'economic life' had no points of contact with the lives of individual men and women, 'except when (the former) does not allow the latter to live'.

'We are able to understand without difficulty that a Nation is a creature standing on a far lower stage of development than individual men and women; it is about on the level of zoophytes, slowly moving in one direction or the other and consuming one another.'

In the Russia of the day, everything acted 'according to one general rule, which I may call the Law of Opposite Aims and Results'. He illustrated this law: 'When a "war upon speculation" is declared, we all begin to groan and cry out. For it means that some article of necessity – milk, butter or eggs – will disappear altogether from the market, and when afterwards it comes back it will cost three or four times what it cost before.'

To show how much more interesting life in Russia was over that in England, Ouspensky reported something he had obviously experienced:

'The scene is Rostov station about a month ago. The night train for Ekaterinodar is about to leave. There are no tickets to be had. This means that you must pay a porter 140 or more roubles for a third-class ticket costing 40 roubles. For this you get a ticket for a numbered seat. But when the passengers get into the train it appears that for every seat four tickets have been sold. Then even we begin to be irritated. An official appears, something like an old-time gendarme, and invites anyone who wishes to remain behind and make a complaint. When he is given the number of the porters who sold the tickets, and is told to fetch the stationmaster and the booking clerk, he merely smiles at the naivete of the questions and says that these gentlemen are busy.'

The pre-eminent topic of people's conversation was 'the strangeness of our all being alive (not all, of course, but we who survive), and the reflection that we may all perhaps be alive for a little while longer'. The next favourite topic was the high price of everything, with necessities having risen by up to six hundred times while workmen's wages increased perhaps a hundred times, and that of a 'brain-worker', a teacher or a doctor, say, a maximum of three times.

On the psychological side of these prices, he said:

'In some people they create panic, in others complete prostration, in others a kind of mystic fatalism. In primitive people they evoke a thirst for profits, because never in any place were profits made so simply and easily as now in Russia. The prices are different in every place. To carry something from one town to another is to make money.'

The train stations were 'crowded with people with bags and baskets; they carry typhus and cholera, and regulate commercial relations between the States of the Don, Terek and Kuban' (*Letters From Russia 1919*, Letter 1).

Ouspensky assured his readers that even if they had seen Bolsheviks in England they were not the real thing. He gave them an idea of the genuine article in four following letters, including this observation:

'The original cause of the destruction of Russia, what led to the Revolution, was robbery – i.e., what you as a polite and cultured people call profiteering. . . . (Bolshevism) assimilated itself to robbery. The masses wanted to have their share in the general plundering of Russia. Bolshevism sanctioned this plundering and gave it the name of Socialism.'

The letters prompted a *New Age* journalist, Carl E. Bechhofer, who had met Ouspensky in pre-Revolution Russia, in England and in India and who admired his books on India and Indian philosophy, to seek another interview with the writer in South Russia. The intrepid journalist describes in his *In Denikin's Russia and the Caucasus, 1919-1920* how he met Ouspensky again at Rostov-on-the-Don in the middle of the 1919-20 winter.

As all available rooms in Rostov had been requisitioned by the govenment or army officers, Ouspensky put Bechhofer up in his room, which he had been lent by an officer who was returning the next day. 'Then we must look for a new room, if we can find one.'

The visitor was concerned they might have to spend the night on the freezing streets. Ouspensky smiled and said nobody who lived under the Bolsheviks worried about what might happen so far ahead. 'Fancy thinking about what will happen tomorrow! What a strange idea!'

Bechhofer reported that Ouspensky's possessions 'consisted of the clothes he was wearing (principally a rather ragged frock-coat, a remnant of former fortunes), a couple of extra shirts and pairs of socks, one blanket, a shabby overcoat, an extra pair of boots, a tin of coffee, a razor, a file and whetstone, and a towel. He assured me that he considered himself exceptionally fortunate to have so much left'.

The next day they moved to share two small rooms over a barn in the courtyard of a large house. An officer ordered up-country for a fortnight had lent them to Ouspensky's friend Zaharoff. The landlord tried to turn them out so he could rent the rooms to a rich refugee from the Bolsheviks, but Ouspensky schemed a way to forestall him. He sent Bechhofer, as a visiting journalist, to the army commandant who wearily told him he could requisition a room if he could find one empty. Bechhofer said he knew of one and an officer was sent with him to inspect the house. All the rooms seemed to be taken, but the army response ensured the landlord did not dare try again to toss them out.

Bechhofer's aplomb also served to pull off another Ouspensky scheme, this time to get coal, which was almost unobtainable, to warm the icy rooms. First, Zaharoff by unexplained means got hold of an engineer's fuel permit for a ton and a half of coal at a cut price from the government stores. Ouspensky and the Englishman queued for three hours at the Don Treasury to pay for the coal and collect a receipt. Then Bechhofer was sent to the engineer's office for a ticket to exchange for the coal. A clerk tried to avoid serving him that day, so the bold foreigner marched into the chief engineer's office – who, being delighted to talk with an Englishman, instructed the clerk to make out the ticket. At the coal depot it transpired the clerk had filled in the ticket incorrectly and Bechhofer had to exercise all his powers of persuasion to break through the red tape.

Eventually, he was walking brightly back to their rooms beside a cart of coal. The porter had confided he had loaded on quite a bit extra and asked permission to add a little for himself. No objection at all, my dear chap. Along the way the carter sold two large lumps to a private coal store for 200 roubles.

Bechhofer wrote that when living as they were from hour to hour, a good fire was something to make a fuss about. They had also found a quantity of alcohol in the barn and by adding orange peel Ouspensky transformed it into vodka.

Zaharoff had protested against taking the alcohol but Ouspensky told him if they did not drink it the Bolsheviks would before its owner returned. (A convenient excuse, but one that proved prophetic in the timing of the Bolshevist capture of the town.)

It may be of interest to connoisseurs that Ouspensky remarked that throughout history nothing better than salted cucumber had been found to go with vodka. Of more general fascination are the reminiscences of his life in Moscow that this tipple triggered. He recalled brewing vodka for a party thrown by a cousin and thought its quality was well illustrated by its effect on one guest, a young man with long hair, beard and moustaches and a sad distant look in his eyes. After one glass of their concoction he stood up and walked straight to a hairdresser's, where he had his head clipped and shaved as bare as an egg, then went home to bed.

When relating his wide acquaintanceship with the Moscow police through his peace-making ability induced by alcohol, Ouspensky mentioned the mystery of his arriving home one night with a sleeve of his overcoat missing. 'How I lost it, and where, I never discovered, although I have given the matter very careful thought. Indeed, I once thought of writing a book about it.'

Ouspensky also told a yarn about the local police chief just after the outbreak of revolution two years earlier. Sitting in his office, scratching his head in perplexity over the contents of a pile of newspapers and proclamations, he was heard to mutter, 'I can understand that the proletariat of the world ought to unite, but why must they unite in Rostov-on-the-Don?'

Zaharoff remarked that thanks to the fire they would have hot water that night, adding: 'We shall be able to wash our faces, clean our teeth and indulge in all sorts of unaccustomed amusements.'

At one point, Bechhofer wondered where they would be in a month, at which the two Russians commented that clearly he had never lived under Bolshevism. 'If you had you wouldn't ask that sort of question. You would acquire the sort of psychology that does not admit reflections of that kind,' was the gist of their collective response.

'And yet,' said Ouspensky, 'when I was under the Bolshevists last year, I did once consider the future. I was in Essentuki in the North Caucasus. The Bolshevists had requisitioned all the books in the place and taken them to the school there. I went to the Commissar and asked him to make me librarian.

'I had been schoolmaster there previously. You didn't know I had been a schoolmaster since the revolution, did you?' he asked his English colleague. 'Yes, I've been a house porter, too. (This remark had relevance to his companions, the porter of their current lodging having caused them much inconvenience, as he had to open the gate for their comings and goings, after chasing two fierce dogs to their kennels, a process that sometimes left them standing in the snow for a quarter of an hour, especially when he was drunk.)

'Well, the Commissar didn't quite know what a librarian was, but I explained it to him. He was a simple man and began to be almost frightened of me when I told him I had written books of my own. So he made me librarian and I put up a big notice on the door, saying that this was the Essentuki Soviet Library. My idea was to keep the books safe, without mixing them up, so that when the Bolshevists went away they could be given back to their owners.' The books were returned after Cossacks drove out the Bolsheviks, he added.

Zaharoff commented that Bechhofer's earlier question had a certain theoretical interest and he too wondered where they would be in a month's time. 'You may wonder as much as you like, but you will never find better vodka than this,' interjected Ouspensky.

A month later the English journalist was able to answer his own question. He was in Novorossisk writing about the spirited Rostov barn encounter, Ouspensky was at Ekaterinodar trying to move his family to safety, and Zaharoff had died three days earlier of smallpox, contracted about the time he had expressed a theoretical interest in his future whereabouts. (The preceding extract from Bechhofer's writing appears as an epilogue to *Letters From Russia 1919*.)

Zaharoff understandably had been in a negative state about the Work but Ouspensky believed he showed him that his original evaluation of the System was right, regardless of his relationship with Gurdjieff. Zaharoff had decided to rejoin Gurdjieff and was on his way to Tiflis when he died.

They had learned about Gurdjieff's recent activities from Alexander Nikanorovich Petrov, like Zaharoff a mathematician and engineer, who also had been driven away from the group. He became director of a state school in Maikop and when visiting Essentuki to see his mother told them that Gurdjieff and his wife and the other four followers had gone to Tiflis and were concentrating on music, dance and rhythmic exercises.

Later, Gurdjieff wrote to Ouspensky that he had opened an Institute for the Harmonious Development of Man in Tiflis and enclosed a prospectus in which he and Petrov were listed as specialist teachers. Apart from the physical difficulties in the way of either 'specialist' going to Tiflis, Ouspensky rejected

Gurdjieff's offer to work with him because he still believed he could see through his motives.

He may have thought that the obstacles to his continuing with Gurdjieff were too fundamental to have been contrived as a test. But one episode while Gurdjieff and his small band were at Tiflis gives an idea how tough he could be in setting challenges by means of which his followers could develop new powers in themselves.

Olga de Hartmann was a beautiful aristocratic lady who even in peacetime had never stepped onto a St Petersburg street without an escort. She was the obvious choice then, to Gurdjieff's way of thinking, when he needed someone to travel alone on decidedly hazardous routes from Tiflis to Essentuki to retrieve what remained of their 'hidden' possessions after they had been unearthed by soldiers. She also carried letters to Ouspensky and to Gurdjieff's sister in Essentuki.

In contrast to his customary manner of ordering such tasks, Gurdjieff did not deceive her that this would be a pleasure excursion; and he gave her a suicide pill, just in case. . .

Despite seemingly impossible obstacles, and with great courage, she succeeded in obtaining visas and tickets and in travelling by train, boat – the vessel was blown off course temporarily to Turkey and she was forced to seek refuge in the captain's cabin to escape from a lecherous Greek – and more trains to locate a few valuables.

Zhukov escorted her from the port of Novorossiisk to Essentuki, then controlled by the White Russians. When she called at the Ouspenskys' house, 'I saw Mr Ouspensky walking back and forth carrying in his arms a little baby, who was crying lustily. It was Lonya Savitsky, the son of Mme Ouspensky's daughter.'

Although little remained of the valuables they had hidden, Mme de Hartmann recovered from the army eight priceless Persian miniatures and a good astrakhan coat, which later helped Gurdjieff's party escape to Turkey.

Their belongings, however, were not the essential point of her trip. She viewed her task as a pretext 'to have me thrown alone into life, to see how I could manage in conditions far more difficult than anyone, even Mr Gurdjieff, could imagine in advance. And most important of all was to see whether we both [she included her husband, Thomas] could accept such a task and deal with it' (*Our Life with Mr Gurdjieff*, p. 130).

Olga de Hartmann was a notable example of the transformation of a person's psychology thanks to Gurdjieff's teaching. One incident in which this is illustrated involved a clash with the same Zhukov who helped her during her hazardous treasure hunt. Thomas de Hartmann explains that Zhukov, 'a hard-working, practical man . . . was a native of Moscow, and for some reason Muscovites were not fond of Petersburgers, who were, for the most part, civil servants, Guards officers and the like' (ibid., p. 98).

Olga reports that one evening (before her journey to Essentuki)

'when Zhukov and I were unloading the horses the friction that had been smouldering between us burst into the open. Unable any longer to contain his ill-feeling, for some reason or other he threw a small satchel right in my face. In the exchange that followed I was lucky enough not to identify with the offence and succeeded in remaining free in myself. Gently, but without holding anything back, I was able to get across to him the incorrectness of his attitude and conduct towards me as a fellow pupil. . . . The result was remarkable. Almost overnight Zhukov became a different man. . . . our former hostility was transformed into conscious friendship – which never hindered us on occasion from giving each other a rap on the knuckles' (ibid., p. 100).

Thomas de Hartmann, too, survived all manner of contrived dangerous, awkward or humiliating positions; his invaluable service as the musician largely responsible for making Gurdjieff's music known to the world often seemed incidental in his daily life as a Fourth Way pupil.

Ouspensky was another who coped with the physical privations of their years in the Caucasus, whether designed by

Gurdjieff or occurring fortuitously as a result of the chaotic life around them. Psychologically, however, he still harboured an attitude he could not change, perhaps connected with his perception of a beckoning Monk's Way, perhaps something quite different.

On a practical level, despite his earlier optimism for the future of the Work in Russia, it eventually became apparent that a philosophy that put the rights of the individual over those of the state would be illegal in the new nation. So, though a patriot of the old Russia, Ouspensky planned to escape to England to organise lectures and groups and publish his book.

Rostov fell to the Bolsheviks on 8 January 1920. Major Frank Pinder escaped to Essentuki where he met Gurdjieff, on Ouspensky's recommendation, and later became one of his leading disciples. He urged Gurdjieff to leave Russia before the counter-revolution failed completely.

Chapter 12

CONSTANTINOPLE: BRIEF REUNION

WHEN THE WHITE ARMY was forced out of Ekaterinodar, Ouspensky and his family sailed to Constantinople, to where the defeated troops were also evacuated from the Crimea. In a brief account in his 'Autobiographical Fragment', Ouspensky summarises his flight and refuge from the civil war in these sparse words:

'. . . in January 1920 I left Russia for Constantinople and stayed there for about a year and a half. Constantinople then was full of Russians. I began lectures there on psychology, on my travels, etc., and in the summer of 1920 I met G. who had come there from Tiflis. I tried to work with him again but soon found it impossible for the same reasons as before' (*A Further Record*, p. 302).

In an almost equally succinct note in *In Search of the Miraculous*, Ouspensky reports he met acquaintances from St Petersburg who helped him arrange lectures in the offices of the Russki Miyak, the Russian YMCA or 'Lighthouse'. In the talks, which drew fairly large audiences, mostly of young men, he connected 'general ideas of psychology and philosophy with ideas of esotericism' (ibid., p. 382).

Gurdjieff and his party sailed into Constantinople harbour about six months after Ouspensky's arrival. After a separation of nearly two years, the two met again at the Black Rose cafe in June 1920. To Ouspensky this signalled that they were approaching the period, which he had foreseen during the darkest days in Russia, when they would establish their system of ideas in Europe.

On the eve of this new era, and in the interests of the Work, Ouspensky resolved to forget their differences, so handed over to Gurdjieff's leadership all those who had been attending his lectures on the System. Gurdjieff's work was now concentrated on *The Struggle of the Magicians*, his ballet, which he hoped could develop into the basis of a School. A core curriculum of ballet may seem to hold out the prospect of an excessively specialist 'School', but Ouspensky saw that the people being trained to perform its dervish-based dances would have to study long and strenuously to control their attention, discovering in the process a way to higher consciousness.

Gurdjieff repeatedly showed that the training was in fact the whole purpose of the operation, by abandoning the project just when script, scenery and dancers were ready for a public performance, pointing out that the exercisers had achieved the objectives he had set, so did not need to go on stage.

Ouspensky relates that one night when they translated a Dervish song for the ballet he saw Gurdjieff the poet and artist, sides of him that he usually kept hidden (*In Search of the Miraculous* , p. 383).

He also saw again the genuine Mehlevi dervishes. On this second visit to Constantinople, he was relieved to discover that, although the city in general was losing its colour by adopting Western 'drabness and hideousness', the tekke of the dervishes at Pera remained as fascinating as before.

He could appreciate the turning better now thanks to his admittedly elementary experience with Gurdjieff's Movements. And Gurdjieff explained how the whirling was performed to a mental exercise based on counting.

Ouspensky's subsequent writing about the turning facilitated the export of the whirling technique and teaching to England, as will be explained in due course.

While Ouspensky and Gurdjieff were in Constantinople, the head of the British Military Intelligence office there was John Bennett, a circumstance that proved of vital assistance to both Fourth Way teachers.

Like Ouspensky, Bennett was interested in higher dimensions. Just before meeting the Russian, the Englishman had been intrigued by Albert Einstein's scientific paper on the lumeniferous ether. Einstein demonstrated that if this was material it must have the apparently impossible property of travelling in every direction simultaneously at the speed of light. Struck by the possible geometrical implications, Bennett had a vision of a new world.

What he saw as the solution to the geometrical hypothesis 'struck me like an electric shock':

'If there is a fifth dimension not like space but like time, and if it is orthogonal to the space-time we know, then it would have the required property. Any matter existing in that direction would appear from our standpoint to be travelling with the speed of light. And moreover it would travel in all directions at once. This must be the solution to Einstein's riddle. If so, the fifth dimension must be as real as the space and time we know. But the extra degree of freedom given by the fifth dimension opens all kinds of possibilities. It means that time itself is not unique, and if there is more than one time, there is more than one future. If there are many times, there should be the possibility of choosing between them. In each line of time there can be a strict causality but by changing from one line to another we can be free' (*Witness*, pp. 56).

The similarity to Ouspensky's conclusions about time suggest that at that stage he and Bennett would have had much in common in their world viewpoint. Bennett also writes of his consequent vision of eternity, which was a vision of 'freedom and determinism', for the idea of a fifth dimension seemed to resolve the conflict he had felt between free will and determinism.

In another parallel with Ouspensky's methods, Bennett thought of 'exploring' the fifth dimension by inducing a higher degree of consciousness – by smoking hashish, of which there was no shortage in Constantinople. This proved to be a disappointment, and he accepted the advice of a friend, Prince Mehmet Sabaheddin, not to pursue this method as it could injure the astral body, which he described as a quasi-material organ linking the physical and higher parts of the self (ibid., p. 57).

Oddly though, Ouspensky never showed interest in Bennett's mathematical deductions – in some respects rather like the Royal Society in England, which accepted and published Bennett and two co-workers' Unified Field Theory in 1949 without comment. Bennett reflected on that occasion that Ouspensky had predicted it would be 'just another physical theory'. (The Unified Field Theory is published as an appendix to *The Dramatic Universe*, vol. 1, pp. 499-505.)

Bennett met Ouspensky through another Russian, Mikhail Alexandrovich Lvow, a former Imperial Horse Guards colonel who forsook his aristocratic life to follow the ideals of Leo Nikolayevich Tolstoy at Yasnaya Polyana, where he supported himself by making shoes. Forced to flee the revolution, in 1920 he was existing in poverty in Constantinople, sleeping under a staircase in the Russki Miyak.

Winifred Beaumont, later Mrs Bennett, let him have a spare room in her flat at Matchka, where he did his own housework, mended boots for other poor Russian refugees, and spent hours in meditation. One day he hesitatingly told them that a friend, one Peter Ouspensky, wished to lecture weekly in Pera but could not afford a meeting room. Mrs Beaumont agreed to let Ouspensky use her drawing room on Wednesday afternoons.

Bennett recalls in *Witness* that these meetings sounded like pandemonium, with everyone shouting at once. One imagines that an unimpressed Ouspensky would have remained detached from all this excitement. Bennett also writes that, although the Russian's English was hard to understand, he and Mrs Beaumont tried to make friends with him.

Though not eloquent in English, Ouspensky earned a little money by teaching that language to other Russian refugees who knew even less of it. He also taught mathematics, in which he was certainly no novice, to children.

Asked about his lectures, he told Bennett they were connected with 'the transformation of man', explaining: 'You suppose all men are on the same level, but in reality one man can be more different from another than a sheep is from a cabbage.'

He drew a diagram of seven categories of men, which Bennett remembered as: 1, Instinct Man; 2, Feeling Man; 3, Thought Man; 4, Transitional Man; 5, Integrated Man; 6, Conscious Man; 7, Perfected Man. The first four categories were drawn on a horizontal level, with Men 5 to 7 ascending vertically from Man 4.

Ouspensky explained further that 'if any man aspires to transformation, he must first acquire balance and harmony of his instincts, his emotions and his thoughts. . . The transformed man acquires powers that are incomprehensible to ordinary people. Even man No. 5 is for us a superman'.

Bennett confesses in his autobiography that the scheme struck him as artificial and not nearly as interesting as his notion of the fifth dimension, which, however, he did not mention. As he did not respond to this idea of transformation, Ouspensky did not mention it to him again during their acquaintance in Constantinople.

Despite this initial dead-end, in time Bennett was to become one of the main promulgators of the Work message of transformation, incorporating a remarkable degree of original development.

Also despite the lack of communication in some respects, Bennett and Mrs Beaumont remained friends with Ouspensky and occasionally visited his family at their lodgings on the island of Prinkipo.

As an organiser of music concerts in Pera, Bennett met the conductor Thomas de Hartmann and his opera singer wife, Olga. Bennett gained the impression that Hartmann possessed some secret knowledge but attributed this to his friendship with the Russian pianist and composer Alexander Skriabin, who had a mystical belief that music could awaken man's higher faculties, and who died in Siberia in 1915.

Bennett's third introduction to The Fourth Way followers then concentrated in Constantinople came when Prince Sabaheddin invited to their regular Wednesday meeting a man he had not seen since 1912, and whom he described as one of the few who had penetrated into the hidden brotherhoods of Central Asia. The surprise guest, who arrived completely unruffled one and three quarters hours late, was of course Gurdjieff.

Speaking in Turkish, Gurdjieff explained he had come two

months earlier from Tiflis where he had founded an institute to make his research findings public. He said he planned to go to Europe and had been invited by Jaques-Dalcroze, the founder of eurhythmics, to take over his headquarters at Hellerau, Germany.

When the Prince spoke of hypnotism studies currently engaging him and Bennett, Gurdjieff intrigued them by explaining with the understanding of a specialist various levels of experience and energies involved in its practice.

Bennett mentioned his ideas of a fifth dimension, to which Gurdjieff gave a typical reply:

'Your guess is right. There are higher dimensions or higher worlds where the higher faculties of man have free play. But what is the use of studying these worlds theoretically? Suppose that you could prove mathematically that the fifth dimension really does exist, what use would that be to you as long as you remain here? . . . If you wish to ascend into the world of freedom, then you must do so in this present life. Afterwards, it will be too late. . . Neither your knowledge nor all your activity will give you freedom' (ibid., pp. 66-7).

(Bennett reviews studies into 'Five-dimensional physics' in an appendix to *The Dramatic Universe*, vol. 1, pp. 490-8.)

The intelligence agent replied to Gurdjieff that he realised knowledge was not enough, but what could one do but study?

Without answering directly, Gurdjieff discussed with the Prince the importance of temple dances for the study of ancient wisdom. He invited them to a demonstration of such dances by a group of his pupils from Tiflis. At the demonstration a few days later, Bennett and Mrs Beaumont were surprised to see de Hartmann at the piano and Ouspensky among the spectators. They were fascinated by the exercises, including one representing the initiation of a priestess in a Hindu Kush temple.

What Bennett remembered from Gurdjieff's talk on dimensions was that 'it is not enough to know that another world exists: one must be able to enter it at will'. Gurdjieff may have been showing him, as he is believed to have tried to indicate to Ouspensky, that the dances and Movements demonstrated the necessary practical side of the teaching.

After several months, the same old difficulties emerged between Ouspensky and Gurdjieff. When the Institute for the Harmonious Development of Man opened in October, Ouspensky felt unable to join it. Two months later he restarted his own lectures, which continued for another six months. He and Gurdjieff, who appear to have related more amicably when working apart, occasionally exchanged visits and in the spring Ouspensky gave lectures, assisted by his teacher, in the Institute.

Ouspensky revealed that he planned to write a book to expound Gurdjieff's Russian talks and Gurdjieff authorised him to publish it. As we know, he did complete the book, *In Search of the Miraculous: Fragments of an Unknown Teaching*, but it was not printed until after his death. The book shows that, despite his differences with Gurdjieff, Ouspensky always credited him with revealing the secret of how to attain higher states of consciousness. And Gurdjieff's authorisation of the proposed book indicates that he valued Ouspensky's contribution to the Work.

In 1921, it was an earlier book by Ouspensky that was to play a major role in the introduction of the Work to Europe.

Chapter 13

PARTING OF THE WAYS

MOMENTUM FOR A SECOND major impact of *Tertium Organum* on Ouspensky's life – the first was his admission to the Work following Gurdjieff's interest in the book – began to build up early in 1918. That was when one of Ouspensky's countrymen, Nicholas Alexandrovich Bessaraboff, a Russian edition of the book in hand, turned up on the doorstep of American writer Claude Bragdon. An enthusiastic Bessaraboff soon infected Bragdon with his conviction that the book should be published in English.

Bessaraboff made a literal translation of the text and Bragdon, who had already written a book on the fourth dimension, turned it, as he later explained, into the simplest English he could and published it under his own imprint. The book generated such a demand that he turned it over to the publisher Knopf.

The translators wished the original writer to receive his share of the profit, but they did not know his whereabouts, or even if he had survived the Russian Revolution. Hindu dramatist Gopal Mukerji told them of the 'letters' from Russia Ouspensky had written for *The New Age* in London but its editor, A.R. Orage, could advise only that the writer had left the war-ravaged Caucasus for an unknown destination.

Ironically, the Theosophical Society, which Ouspensky had put down even while acknowledging that it had set him on the track of life's deeper meaning, indirectly came to their aid. An American traveller, Spencer Kellogg, of Buffalo, visited the society's English headquarters during the summer of 1920 in the hope of buying a copy of *Tertium Organum*. There he met a Russian woman who knew Ouspensky and who told him he and his family were refugees in Constantinople.

With this information, Bessaraboff was able to write to Ouspensky, enclosing copies of the book and a royalty cheque. A grateful Ouspensky replied in a letter dated 17 November

1920, that events had confirmed 'the conviction I arrived at during my trip to India, that there is in the world a small number of men united by something, although they may not themselves know it, and may not know one another yet'.

Bragdon recounted later that, although he was not in a position to help Ouspensky any further financially, he felt 'sure that it was in the pattern of his [Ouspensky's] life to come actively in contact with those English-speaking people who had been spiritually awakened by his book'. He wrote to him that he was convinced help would be forthcoming.

About the time Ouspensky read his letter, Bragdon, at his home in Rochester, received a telegram from Washington:

'Tertium Organum interests me passionately. Desire very much to meet you if possible. Leaving for England end of month. – Viscountess Rothermere.'

(The above account is from Bragdon's 'The Romance and Mystery of Ouspensky's *Tertium Organum*', reprinted in the *Gurdjieff International Review*, vol. II, No. 2.)

As soon as she received Ouspensky's address, Lady Rothermere cabled him, in mid-May 1921, offering to pay his travel to England. Ouspensky was delighted to accept the invitation, the only proviso being that he and his family must first obtain visas and travel permits. John Bennett encouraged Ouspensky by disclosing that Viscount Rothermere was said to have influence with the English Prime Minister, Lloyd George, but privately the intelligence officer realised that even such clout could not always overcome bureaucratic bias and torpidity. Money for the fare arrived but when, after some weeks, no travel documents eventuated, Bennett petitioned his service's Russian Section, and four visas were issued: for Ouspensky and his wife and Lenochka Savitsky and her husband.

No doubt Ouspensky had believed the rest of his extended family would have been as eager as he to exchange their precarious existence in Turkey for what seemed to be an assured livelihood in England. Mme Ouspensky, however, considered Gurdjieff to be her teacher, and now she demonstrated she had the courage of her convictions. She and the others of her family stayed with Gurdjieff.

This surely would have had a considerable effect on Ouspensky but of course he does not comment on their domestic situation. All he notes is that before his departure Gurdjieff proposed that he go with him to Germany where he intended to open his Institute and prepare his ballet. 'But in the first place I did not believe it was possible to organise work in Germany and secondly I did not believe I could work with G.' (*In Search of the Miraculous*, p.384)

Ouspensky, who knew more or guessed more accurately about current European affairs than his teacher, despite the latter's best efforts at sounding out knowledgeable friends like Prince Sabahedden, left for London not long before Gurdjieff, the Hartmanns and others in his party started a rail trip to Germany.

Gurdjieff ever played his cards close to his chest; those in his group seldom knew of his next move much in advance of its happening, and even then rarely were quite sure of the reasons behind it. But they knew why they left South Russia, and the exit from Constantinople fell into a similar category. With memories of Turkish massacres in Armenia fresh in his memory, Gurdjieff was anxious to quit Turkey before the outbreak of a new round of attacks on foreigners, a threat he detected because 'the wiseacring of the Young Turks began to have a particular smell' (*Meetings with Remarkable Men*, p. 283).

Unlike Ouspensky, he and his followers had neither invitations nor visas to England, nor a wealthy benefactress. Gurdjieff did have an invitation from Emile Jaques-Dalcroze, who had moved to Geneva, to base his Work activities at the centre for La Méthode Rhythmique at Hellerau, near Dresden. So he decided, ostensibly for cultural and perhaps scientific reasons, to try Germany. Dalcroze was keen to sell his grand human movements centre.

To raise cash to support his followers, Gurdjieff says that 'once gain I plunged into feverish activity, continuing to make money by every possible means in Constantinople itself, as well as in Kadiköy on the opposite side of the Bosphorus . . .' (ibid., p. 283). He also discloses: 'I participated in the sale of a certain ship.' Bennett expands that he helped in this 'amazing' deal. He says Gurdjieff 'had cured a Greek youth of drunkenness and drug addiction, in return for which he received a half-interest in a ship that had been requisitioned by the British Navy.' Bennett was able to get the ship released 'and Gurdjieff sold his share for a large sum of money that he used to get his group away to Germany' (*Gurdjieff: Making a New World*, pp. 130-1).

In London, Ouspensky, after a lavish welcome, stepped straight into a comfortable little flat at Gwendwr Rd, South Kensington. In Germany, as inflation rocketed, Gurdjieff and some of the others spent many fruitless hours seeking suitable accommodation for a dance troupe.

Ouspensky had an immediate success in attracting many of the cultural elite to his lectures. Men like A.R. Orage and Maurice Nicoll immediately saw much of the significance of the system of ideas propounded by Ouspensky. Some in the audiences had money, too, a useful attribute that would not have escaped Gurdjieff's attention. As well as Lady Rothermere, these included a north country millionaire coal miner, Ralph Philipson, and some leading professional people.

In Germany, Mme Ouspensky could inform Gurdjieff from her husband's letters that Ouspensky was riding a steady wave of success in London. Gurdjieff's leading pupils did not realise for some time why he was now instructing them to learn English. He himself was learning this tongue from Olga de Hartmann – although he had claimed it was good 'only for discussing in "smoking rooms", while sitting on an easy chair with legs outstretched on another, the topic of Australian frozen meat or, sometimes, the Indian question' (*Beelzebub's Tales to His Grandson*, p. 10).

The postal lines of communication worked both ways. Frank Pinder, for one, was writing enthusiastically to friends in England about Gurdjieff's teaching, and of the teacher's present close proximity to them. As well, Ouspensky's Rostov drinking companion Carl Bechhofer's first-hand account, *In Denikin's Russi and the Caucasus*, put Gurdjieff firmly at the head of the school of knowledge now being expounded by his former disciple. Not that Ouspensky made an outright secret of the origin of the system of ideas he was making known to Western minds. Still, he possibly found it convenient as well as practical to emphasise the teaching itself rather than personalities.

Ouspensky had never stood in Gurdjieff's way – in fact, as he had shown in Constantinople, he was even prepared to hand over his pupils to him. All the same, Ouspensky must have felt inner reservations when numbers of his followers, including his patrons and patroness, pressed him to invite Gurdjieff to England. For he wrote later that the old problems posed by Gurdjieff had resurfaced "even before he arrived".

Ouspensky would have foreseen that with the unsettled state in Germany, Gurdjieff would surely find England a much more suitable place for his Institute. Georgivanch tested the waters for himself on 13 February 1922, on Ouspensky's stamping ground, the Theosophical Hall at 38 Warwick Gardens, South Kensington. The hall, to which Ouspensky could walk in minutes from his Gwendwr Road home, was the venue of Ouspensky's main meetings, where he had grown accustomed to lecturing a selection of London's intellectual and establishment elite. It was, however, a rare opportunity for Gurdjieff – who, as his once principal pupil knew, was able to present his own ideas in a much more dramatic fashion than could Ouspensky – to have in his magnetic presence some sixty susceptible listeners constituting a cross-section of the Bloomsbury artistic and intellectual set.

They included Maurice and Catherine Nicoll, Orage, Lady Rothermere, Philipson, Dr James Carruthers Young, Dr Mary Bell and Clifford Sharp, editor of *New Statesman*. Sharing the platform with Gurdjieff and Ouspensky were Frank Pinder and Olga de Hartmann, both qualified to act as interpreters of Gurdjieff's Russian – not as well, of course as Ouspensky himself, but he had the distinct feeling that this was not his party.

Gurdjieff spoke of man as 'a plural being' and his listeners may have been impressed by the added force his words gave to what Ouspensky had already revealed about man's lack of a unified 'I'.

The more attuned to Gurdjieff's cryptic style of exposition would have gathered something of his lateral meaning when he criticised the West as being not as congenial for him as the East, but revealed that this very irritability of Western life facilitated his Work. Ouspensky, however, would have been inwardly alarmed when he referred specifically in this context to the dispiriting weather of London. He would read in this a broad hint that Gurdjieff could bear to reside in such an irritating place for the sake of the Work.

Worse was to come. 'You must find a teacher,' Gurdjieff told this guidance-seeking gathering of Ouspensky's pupils (*Views From the Real World*, p. 81). This advice was not directed explicitly against Ouspensky's leadership. In a lecture on man's plurality of being, Gurdjieff had said that to change this 'you will have to make a choice, to decide – to seek either to become completely mechanical or completely conscious'. Asked if there were no other ways, he said:

'In England, no. In the East, it is different. There are different methods for different men. But you must find a teacher. You alone can decide what it is that you wish to do.'

The message may have been implicit, but it had the effect Ouspensky least desired. A significant number, including Orage and Nicoll, two of the most likely Fourth Way adepts, were sure they could recognise the teacher of their choice. As Orage explained:

'Ouspensky for me represented knowledge, great knowledge: Gurdjieff, understanding – though of course Gurdjieff had all the knowledge, too.'

In a private talk after the meeting, Gurdjieff is said to have told Ouspensky that he was working wrongly, too intellectually, and that consequently his pupils were not on a useful line of work.

Gurdjieff's final visit to London came a month later. There is some discrepancy in accounts of the, for Ouspensky, painful meeting that ensued. Some recollections do not mention any external sign of friction between the main protagonists. At least one other claims that Ouspensky protested that Pinder was translating Gurdjieff's comments wrongly and that Gurdjieff admonished Ouspensky, in front of his pupils, for the interruption. The second version is similar to a report of a heated exchange later in Gurdjieff's headquarters at the Prieuré.

C.S. Nott quotes Pinder as claiming that once 'when Ouspensky came to the Prieuré, Gurdjieff refused to let him interpret for him to a crowded Study House of English and Russians and visitors. Ouspensky, an educated Russian, was of course a more suitable person than myself, an Englishman, but Gurdjieff said that as I had done it all along I had better continue. Ouspensky interrupted several times, objecting to my translation, and Gurdjieff retorted, "Pinder is interpreting for me – not you. . ." '

'Ouspensky apparently thought that he understood Gurdjieff and his inner teaching – which he did not, and Gurdjieff had to make him choose whether to stay with him and submit to discipline, or break away. The episode was painful but according to law. Ouspensky knew the theory, better than anyone possibly – he had the knowledge, but he did not understand. . . .

'Ouspensky could never forget Gurdjieff's attacking him in front of his pupils. Ouspensky had set out, in the Theosophical tradition in old St Petersburg, in a role in which he saw himself as a successful religious teacher – though he may not have been of this' (*Journey Through This World*, p. 91).

The idea that Ouspensky entertained a self-image of being a religious teacher would surely have given that critic of orthodox religion some amusement. However, Pinder's theory of Ouspensky's relation to Theosophy is included in the passage quoted above not as light relief but to help position his analysis of Ouspensky's power of understanding on a reliability scale. To facilitate this estimate, it can be added that at the same time Pinder also linked Maurice Nicoll and Ouspensky as mere 'plagiarists of "mystical" writings'. Readers of those two writers will realise that, if they had failings, passing off others' work as their own was patently not among them.

One of Maurice Nicoll's recollections of Gurdjieff's lectures at the Prieuré also has a bearing on the interpretation dispute. Nicoll's secretary Beryl Pogson relates:

'Dr Nicoll told us that he used to sit beside Mr Pinder who would often have a whispered conversation with him when the Russian proved unfit for English ears. Listening to a talk through an interpreter used to be very tantalising, Dr Nicoll told us, because whereas Gurdjieff would pour out a torrent of words which lasted for several minutes, Mr Pinder would give a laconic interpretation, just a sentence or two, whereupon Gurdjieff would look at him and shrug his shoulders, smiling sardonically' (*Maurice Nicoll: A Portrait*, p. 82).

Light is thrown on Gurdjieff's motives by a remark he reportedly made to Pinder after casting doubt on Ouspensky's qualification as a group leader: 'Now they [Ouspensky's pupils] will have to choose a teacher' (*Journey Through This World*, p. 99).

This can be seen as a bid for pupils: a more generous interpretation is that the master devised the ultimatum to illustrate what it means to make a real choice.

Regardless of what transpired on the London meeting platform, it does seem that privately at least Gurdjieff managed to convey that he had less than full confidence in Ouspensky's ability to transmit Fourth Way teaching. Perhaps he even suggested that, like his wife, Sophie Grigorievna, Peter Demianovich should re-enroll as his pupil. Judging by his record of forcing away his best pupils, in hindsight it is obvious that Gurdjieff would not for a moment have expected Ouspensky to heed this advice.

At the final meeting in Warwick Gardens most in the audience were too awed by Gurdjieff's presence to open their months. Orage at last asked how to attain a radical transformation of Being. The answer came in the form of a lecture on Essence and Personality, during which Gurdjieff said it is not normal for a grown-up man to have the Essence of a child. Someone also asked what it would be like to be conscious in Essence. 'Everything more vivid,' was Gurdjieff's succinct and subsequently much reported reply.

Most of those who heard Gurdjieff – and who had previously been appraised by Ouspensky of their guest's unique powers – were excited at the prospect of having him permanently in London. Lady Rothermere offered to let him use her studio in St John's Wood. Nicoll joined a delegation to urge Home Secretary Edward Shortt to allow Gurdjieff to settle in England. A subscription was raised among those interested and an Institute formed in London.

Ouspensky was equally moved by all this – in the opposite direction; he decided that he would transfer his operations to Paris or the United States if the plans worked out.

He need not have worried. The India Office dusted off its files on Tibet and apparently decided that 'the very dangerous Russian agent, George Gurdjieff' could still be considered a risk to British policy. (Even though Gurdjieff was more diplomatic than to repeat just then his belief that the Francis Younghusband 'Expedition' against the mountain nation in 1903-4 had resulted in the accidental death of the one man who could have averted eventual world war. (For this 'precursor of disaster' see *Gurdjieff: Making a New World*, p. 262.)

The British bureaucrats decided on what they saw as a compromise between the wishes of Gurdjieff's supporters and his Foreign Office opponents: Gurdjieff would be allowed visits, but his Russian followers were barred. It is no surprise that the group's leader and life support found this condition unacceptable.

The London Institute was thus stillborn. Then in June 1922 Gurdjieff lost a court action in Dresden over rights to Dalcroze's Hillerau property. Germany joined England, Turkey, Georgia and Russia on the reject list of possible

Institute sites. Suddenly it suited Gurdjieff to recall that Paris was the centre of Western culture, and thus surely a fitting venue for his Institute. With twenty to thirty pupils, he entered Paris on Bastille Day, 14 July 1922.

Quickly, to maintain momentum, a meeting of the key players – including Gurdjieff, Ouspensky, Philipson and Lady Rothermere – was arranged in Paris to map out the future, particularly the financial needs, of the proposed Institute for the Harmonious Development of Man. For people of means, it would not, after all, be far from London.

It is likely that Ouspensky would not have been averse to the agreed flow of money from England to France, considering that it would leave him to conduct his groups in London without interference. There was more to his support for Gurdjieff than that. When Gurdjieff had set his sights on England, Ouspensky said:

'I still expected a very great deal more from his work and I decided to do everything I could to help him organise his Institute and the preparation of his ballet. But I did not believe it was possible for me to work with him' (*In Search of the Miraculous*, p. 384).

There is no doubt that sentiment still applied. He wished Gurdjieff well, but did not regret that the English Channel separated them.

The Dalcroze Institute in the Rue de Vaugirard in Paris was taken as a temporary venue for Gurdjieff's work and in August a number of English pupils joined up to learn the exercises. Among the first pupils was one of several psychologists who were to give up their Jungian therapy practices to learn the Work, James Carruthers Young.

He later reported (in an article, 'An Experiment at Fontainebleau', in the September 1927 issue of London's *The New Adelphi* magazine) that the exercises 'certainly fulfilled expectation in that they were directed towards overcoming the inertia or limitation of body habit . . . some of them required the combination of four different movements, each of which had its own distinct rhythm. To attempt these exercises involved a great strain, and to continue for any length of time was very fatiguing. One became intensely aware of the inertia of a body, perhaps otherwise well-disciplined (as by athletics), when called upon to make these unaccustomed combinations of movements. The struggle against this inertia, then, was one of the means to be employed in order to 'wake-up'.'

The other main activity in Paris was making costumes to be worn during public exhibitions of the exercises and dances. Says Young:

'The keynote was "Overcome difficulties – Make effort – Work". There was little time for meals during the day, but at night there was a fairly substantial meal. You may imagine that this kind of communal work, together with misunder-standings that arose from language difficulties, called upon one's exercise of the virtues of self-remembering, non-identifying and non-considering to the utmost. [Gurdjieff's group at that time included Russians, Armenians, Poles, Georgians and one Syrian.] My impressions were very mixed. The people fell short of the standard of culture which Ouspensky had led me to expect. However, I tried to reassure myself with the thought that we were all "machines", and that one machine is as good as another so far as "mechanical" life is concerned.'

It is interesting at this point to consider what Ouspensky apparently led his pupils to expect. Young relates:

'During the period of the lectures and meetings in London, Mr Ouspensky had spoken of a remarkable man called Gurdjieff whom he had known in Moscow as the composer of an original kind of ballet, and whom he had met again in Constantinople after the Revolution. He averred that Gurdjieff had travelled widely in the East, in Turkestan, Mongolia, Thibet and India, that he had an intimate acquaintance with monastic life in those countries, that he had acquired an unrivalled knowledge and repertoire of their religious exercises and dances, and a profound understanding of their application to psychological development, and that he wished to found a school in which his knowledge would be incorporated in accordance with the psychological system which Mr Ouspensky was expounding. The latter also stated that Gurdjieff, who was then in Dresden, had a trained staff of instructors in physical exercises and all sorts of handicrafts, and counted among his entourage a number of distinguished artists, musicians, doctors and philosophers, most of whom were refugees from the Bolshevik regime, and who had already formed the nucleus of an institute in Dresden.'

There is a slight suggestion in this that some of Ouspensky's pupils may have gained the impression that the System was as much his as Gurdjieff's. However, the likelihood that this was merely an individual interpretation is indicated by Young's other apparent understanding that Ouspensky had stated as a fact that Gurdjieff already had a staff of various specialists. In reality, of course, Ouspensky was as bemused as anyone by Gurdjieff's fictions, especially as his own name was wont to appear in such 'prospectuses' even during his periods of separation, geographically and personally, from his teacher.

While Thomas de Hartmann was charged with locating a flat in Paris for Gurdjieff, his versatile wife, Olga, was tasked with finding a country house for the Institute. When she phoned him details of Le Prieuré des Basses Loges, a chateau at Avon, near Fontainebleau, forty-four miles south-east of Paris, Gurdjieff approved a bid to secure it, sight unseen (unless he made use of his undoubted power of clairvoyance). After some sly psychological manoeuvres instigated by her teacher, Mme de Hartmann negotiated an acceptable leasing arrangement.

Mme Ouspensky's authoritative, sometimes aggressive manner stood her in good stead in organising the Prieuré kitchen. She cooked for the advance guard of workers and prepared for an influx of visitors to the Institute. Those who came as pupils were mainly from England. The French tolerated the strange new colony in their country, but at that time showed no interest in the philosophy it expounded, although they did relish a serial scandal in the press about 'the Forest Philosophers'.

Gurdjieff arrived at the Prieuré on 1 October 1922. He recounted later that the first inhabitant to greet him was Mrs

Serious Problem, one of the common symptoms he was fond of humanising, such as in Mr Pride and Mrs Vanity. Economically, the ever pressing problem, needless to say, was that of obtaining enough funds to put his ideas into practice on a decidedly larger scale than to date. That, however, is to say nothing of the even more daunting task of finding sufficient candidates capable of meeting his psychological – and, it would seem to the newcomers, physical – demands.

He had plenty of choice. People of all types visited the Prieuré that summer. Some, like Lady Rothermere, who stayed for only a couple of days, were feted and not expected to perform hard labour – they met the Institute's needs in a different way. Ouspensky's former girlfriend, Anna Butkovsky, turned up for a short visit, probably for old times' sake. Others, whose unsuitability for The Fourth Way was apparent to Gurdjieff, were sent off without ceremony and often in high dudgeon.

The Institute attracted most notoriety in reaction to false rumours over New Zealand writer Katherine Mansfield's death there from tuberculosis after a short stay. She had gained an introduction to Gurdjieff from Ouspensky who, despite being at odds with his old teacher at the time, was foremost in ridiculing any attacks on Gurdjieff's integrity in the affair. Ouspensky saw her at the Prieuré in November, when he finally accepted Gurdjieff's invitation to the chateau. Talking to Ouspensky in a salon one evening, she said of the teaching at Avon: 'I know that this is true and that there is no other truth.'

Commented Ouspensky: 'G. was very good to her, he did not insist upon her going although it was clear that she could not live. For this in the course of time he received the due amount of lies and slander' (*In Search of the Miraculous*, pp. 385-6).

Olga de Hartmann later revealed that at first Gurdjieff did ask Miss Mansfield to leave because of the risk of infecting others, but relented and arranged for one of the young women to care for her.

Ouspensky's verdict on Institute life: 'the atmosphere on the whole was very right and left a strong impression'.

He was interested to learn how his former pupils were faring among the 'motley company assembled' at the Prieuré. The brilliant intellectual Alfred Richard Orage had been reduced to despair by the rough work, both physical and psychological, but was determined to make a super-effort. Even the usually unflappable and outgoing Dr Maurice Nicoll occasionally isolated himself in perplexity over the whole situation, his own inner condition in particular, and was for once unable to help others remedy their similar attacks of incomprehension. Nicoll's London colleague Dr Young reckoned the labour at the Prieuré more exhausting than confinement in the trenches of Flanders five winters earlier.

Ouspensky was present when building of the Turkish bath was completed, however it is difficult to imagine his revelling in gatherings of naked men telling ribald stories. Not necessarily to avoid that weekly method of segregated bathing, he returned to West Kensington shortly after the bath's opening and resumed his bachelor existence, which was centred of course on his writing and lecturing.

Not a man to make a fetish of meals, Ouspensky was occasionally seen working in his flat with an empty sardine tin on the mantelshelf, its contents evidently having sufficed as a repast. This contrasted with the banquets Gurdjieff regularly organised, and sometimes helped prepare. Mme Ouspensky and Gurdjieff's wife, Mme Ostrowska, prepared one such feast on 12 January 1923 to inaugurate the Study House. Anywhere else it would have been surprising that this celebration followed Katherine Mansfield's funeral at Avon earlier the same day; Gurdjieff did not regard such transitions of Being as deserving only grief.

(It might be noted, Ouspensky's casual eating habits at home having been remarked upon, that he was considered an expert in the preparation of some foods and drinks. For instance, he was one of a select group that Twinings consulted annually for an opinion on their latest blends of tea. As for

Gurdjieff's banquets, the host was seldom observed to consume his due portion.)

Whatever his menu of victuals as he continued to run his groups in London, Ouspensky found many impressions hard to digest. When pupils asked if it would be an advantage to go to France, he believed some of them had already made up their minds.

'I feared they would meet with disappointment because G's work seemed to me not sufficiently rightly organised and therefore to be unstable. But at the same time I could not be sure of my own opinions and did not want to interfere with them because if everything went right and my fears proved to be false then they would undoubtedly have gained by their decision.'

He conceded that others had been unable to get along with him as a teacher and now thought they would find a 'short cut' with Gurdjieff. 'I of course advised them to go to Fontainebleau and work with G.' Other pupils were undecided whether to 'give up everything' and follow the exodus to France as the only way to continue the Work. 'To this I said they should wait until I was there' (ibid., p. 385).

Perhaps at that stage Ouspensky expected he would visit the Institute for extended periods. This did not eventuate. However, it was at Ouspensky's suggestion that one of his brightest students, John Bennett, joined the Institute in July 1923. This appears to confirm that Ouspensky was genuine in saying that he would help form the Institute.

During that summer, after someone had complained about the food, Gurdjieff seized on this as an opportunity to declare that the kitchen overseers, Mme Ostrowska and Mme Ouspensky, were no good at all as cooks – and passed on their role to a startled Thomas de Hartmann. In his amusing account of this period, de Hartmann confesses that in fact Mme Ouspensky stayed in the background throughout, directing operations. At the conclusion of his term in the extremely demanding and time consuming job, which did not excuse him from his duties as director of music, she brought him breakfast in bed – 'a most tasty ragout, the final chord of my existence as a cook' (*Our Life with Mr Gurdjieff*, pp. 196–201).

Bennett was present in August 1923 when Gurdjieff announced: 'For one section of the people here, their stay has become completely useless.'

Bennett wrote later that he left the Prieuré at the beginning of September. Gurdjieff had asked him to stay on and learn Russian so he could act as his interpreter and accompany him to America, but he felt he had to work in life to pay off his debts. Consequently, he did not see Gurdjieff again for twenty-five years. This parting in a way throws a glimmer of light on Ouspensky's situation. From one viewpoint, it might seem that Bennett had thrown away his best chance to learn from the man he recognised as a supreme teacher. Much later, however, it transpired that one of the lessons Gurdjieff was teaching him was to stop being so much of a "yes" man; he had to learn how to say "no" to demands he was unable to fulfil. This time, Gurdjieff had put him in a situation where it was impossible to say 'yes'.

'It was much rather as if Gurdjieff himself had withdrawn from me, and would not let me follow him' (*Witness*, p. 134)>

Ouspensky's course likewise was near inevitable.

Maurice and Catherine Nicoll also understood the Institute was closing in the autumn of 1923. It was suggested that Nicoll should go with Orage to America and teach the System, but Nicoll was doubtful he could do that. Orage went alone, followed by Gurdjieff and a troupe of dancers.

The Nicolls never saw Gurdjieff again. They returned to London, where Dr Nicoll rebuilt his Harley Street practice and where they both resumed going to Ouspensky's meetings in Warwick Gardens. They introduced to the group another medical man who was also to become a Work leader and writer, Kenneth Walker.

Ouspensky was at the Prieuré in January 1924 when Gurdjieff and a party of his pupils left for America for lectures and Movements demonstrations. He concludes *In Search of the Miraculous* with these thoughts:

'And this departure reminded me very much of his departure from Essentuki in 1918 and all that was connected with it. On returning to London I announced to those who came to my lectures that my work in the future would proceed quite independently *in the way it had been begun in London in 1921.*'

A hint of how at one stage Ouspensky viewed Gurdjieff's teaching is given by a 1925 draft of his *Fragments of an Unknown Teaching* (published as *In Search of the Miraculous*) which has been preserved in the Yale University archives. Ouspensky writes that since 1922 Gurdjieff's work had been chiefly dedicated to 'perfecting methods of the study of rhythm and plastic art'. In criticising a 'demonstration of eastern dances and rhythmic movements at the Theatre des Champs Elysees in Paris in 1923' as uneven and, in the case of whirling dervish routines, 'a superficial imitation', he appears to belittle the value of the Movements.

He also says the 'interesting' program of the Institute for the Harmonious Development of Man at Fontainebleau was never realised, mainly because of Gurdjieff's choice of students.

As already indicated, Ouspensky admitted to being lazy when it came to physical exercises. It is unlikely, however, that this characteristic would prejudice him against the potential benefits of the Movements for suitable students, even though he obviously did not regard it as an essential method of achieving self-awareness. He focused instead on combating negative emotions as a step towards experiencing real feeling. Ouspensky devised many tasks, based on Gurdjieff's early teaching, aimed at preparing people to reach this state.

Likewise Gurdjieff, while awarding a high degree of importance to the Movements, made clear that the exercises were a means, not an end. It takes a personal trial to discover whether their results can be obtained by other methods, including those Ouspensky preferred. At this point, lest the foregoing remarks appear to be an attempt to gloss over an omission in Ouspensky's learning and teaching by underrating the Movements' role, let us consider their benefits.

First, Gurdjieff observed that they can be useful in both a healthy everyday life and in work for inner development, provided mind, body and feeling combine in their performance. Dances, he said, are for the mind: the soul does not need them. The overall aim is to develop something that cannot be developed automatically. Certain movements, he explained, contain definite knowledge. Each position of the body corresponds to an inner state; unaccustomed postures enable a different self-observation, which is particularly noticeable when outer and inner movements are frozen on a 'Stop!' command. (*See* Gurdjieff's *Views From the Real World*.)

An idea of the Movements' effects on those performing them may emerge from this amalgam of comments by half a dozen Work writers:

They were Gurdjieff's form of art. In doing them it is the attention that gives energy, created when one goes against oneself. They constitute a precise means of self-study based on ancient principles and knowledge; an organic experience of self-remembering. The obligatories, six fundamental dances that create a practical tool for working on Gurdjieff's ideas, require a sincere effort to master physical, mental and emotional challenges.

Movements are considered necessary for self-study because man in repose, who knows where he is (e.g., in thinking, planning, art), loses contact with himself in motion. Some moves occupy a particular part of a centre so as to free energy for other centres, enhancing the quality of thought, feeling or sensation. Other movements entail a specific requirement; e.g., remembering one's parents with remorse for what one has not done for them. All the moves lead through stages of growing awareness, moments of sensation and inner observation to a taste of paying attention.

As a prayer made by three centres, the Movements develop a freeing of attention and control of the body, feeling and thought and when perfected alter the circulation, breathing rhythm and oxygenation to the brain. Advanced dance levels enable the experiencing of refined feelings and avoidance of identification, which help the development of will, one's Real I.

And here is a speculative addition by J.G. Bennett with which even Ouspensky, whose interest is seen by his detractors as limited to theory, may well have agreed:

'If it had not been for his accident in 1924 [after which the Institute group was disbanded], Gurdjieff would no doubt have begun to use the movements in the traditional way as they were used in the ancient temples, for the principal purpose of transmission of knowledge directly to the higher centres without passing through the mind' (*Gurdjieff: Making a New World*, pp. 228-9).

There seems to be general agreement with Bennett's next comment, that the Movements' main use now is the 'the inner development of those who directly participate in them'.

In London in 1924 the Nicolls found that Ouspensky continued to teach the System in the same way as before, but their experiences at the Institute made the ideas alive for them practically as well as intellectually. They attended Ouspensky's meetings for the next seven years. Their presence was a tonic as much for their teacher as themselves. Nicoll's biographer, Beryl Pogson, writes:

'Dr Nicoll gained increasing insight into the psychological state of his patients through his own self-knowledge gained from the System. A very deep personal relationship developed between himself and Ouspensky. Other members of the group have told me that Dr Nicoll was apparently the only one of the group with whom Ouspensky could really relax, and, more than anyone else, Dr Nicoll could make him laugh. Ouspensky told him later that this relationship developed because Dr Nicoll was the only one of his group who would really speak to him emotionally of what he had said at a meeting. He and Mrs Nicoll would attend these meetings on three nights a week, and he used to start the meetings for Ouspensky before he came in, asking for questions. . . . often most of the questions were dismissed summarily by Ouspensky as theoretical, not real, until perhaps a question based on psychological experience would evoke an unforgettable answer from the depth of the Master's being – in fact, it might be the preliminary to an hour's talk. If there were no questions at the beginning of a meeting, Ouspensky would leave, and the group would be obliged to disperse. Dr Nicoll thought it was a Russian characteristic that made it possible for Ouspensky to put up his deaf ear and say, 'What?' to all questions that he did not want to answer' (*Maurice Nicoll: A Portrait*, pp. 94-5).

Beryl Pogson says that one of the Nicoll group's tasks was to help with the revision and preparation for publication of *A New Model of the Universe*, the original draft of which was written before Ouspensky met Gurdjieff. Dr Nicoll's diary describes Ouspensky's method of working on the *New Testament* in preparation for a chapter of the book:

'O. has the New Testament in German, French, Russian and English, and when he is speaking of a verse he looks at the translation in each of them and in the Greek version. He has a number of dictionaries in his room. He is fond of pencils sharpened to very fine points and always has several on his table. His mantelpiece is covered with old photographs, prints and packets of toning paper. He sits on a small uncomfortable chair' (ibid., p. 95).

While Ouspensky's lectures opened the way to a new life for people such as the Nicolls, they did not have universal appeal. A well known writer stamped out of an early meeting declaring: 'This system has no love.'

It is true that Ouspensky did not speak of love in his introductory lectures, knowing that his audience was unaware of the distinctions between mechanical, self-, physical, emotional and conscious love. It would be more beneficial to their inner growth if they could first see and deal with their likes and dislikes before aspiring to attract or transmit the very fine energy of love.

One of the more prepared students, Maurice Nicoll, could see from his training under Carl Jung that 'what we call love is simply the projection of ourselves into someone else'.

Ouspensky concentrated his pupils' efforts on self-observation and the non-expression and eventual transformation of negative emotions. Even after many years not all his students realised the full extent of their mechanicalness, but he never ceased reminding them of the necessity to try to do so.

Bennett records that about July 1924 Ouspensky invited him to a meeting of about ten people at Ralph Philipson's flat in Portland Place, when he announced:

'I have asked you to come because I must tell you that I have decided to break off all relations with Mr Gurdjieff. This means that you have to choose. Either you can go and work with him, or you can work with me: but if you remain with me, you must give an undertaking that you will not communicate in any way with Mr Gurdjieff or his pupils.'

Only blunt north-country man Philipson dared ask what they were all thinking: Why? Ouspensky, choosing his words carefully, replied:

'Mr Gurdjieff is a very extraordinary man. His possibilities are much greater than those of people like ourselves. But he can also go in the wrong way. I believe that he is now passing through a crisis, the outcome of which no one can foresee. Most people have many 'I's. . . But with Mr Gurdjieff there are only two 'I's; one very good and one very bad. I believe that in the end the good 'I' will conquer. But meanwhile it is very dangerous to be near him. We cannot be of any help to him, and in his present situation he cannot be of any help to us. Therefore I have decided to break off all contact. But this does not mean that I am against him, or that I consider that what he is doing is bad.'

Asked what could happen if Gurdjieff went the wrong way, Ouspensky replied:

'He could go mad. Or else he could attract to himself some disaster in which all those around him would be involved' (*Witness*, pp. 133-4).

Shortly before this, on July 8, Gurdjieff's speeding car had crashed into tree at a crossroads in the hamlet of Chailly on a straight stretch of the Paris-Fontainebleau road. He was concussed when the steering column broke on hitting a low stone embankment and he jumped or was thrown out of the car before it hit the tree. For weeks he seemed to hover between life and death.

When he learned of Gurdjieff's accident, Ouspensky is reported to have responded with dismay that his Institute was set up to help people escape from the Law of Accident. 'Has he gone too far? I tell you, I'm terribly afraid,' he said.

During his convalescence Gurdjieff seemed to draw force from gazing into bonfires made from old poplar trees that had lined one of the Prieuré vegetable gardens. No one really knew his real condition, but, as Olga de Hartmann writes, 'We were not prepared for what happened next.'

On August 26 Gurdjieff dictated to Mme de Hartmann a speech which, after dinner, he started to read to all those present at the Prieuré and then had Olga complete the reading. In it, he said he did not remember the accident. 'In principle, I had to die, but accidentally I stayed alive.'

He said his memory had returned only a few days earlier and 'I decided to close the Institute for many reasons.

'First of all, there are very few people who understand. I gave all my life for my Work, but the result from other people in general was not good and that is why I think it is not necessary for those few to sacrifice their lives here. And I don't wish to continue as I have done until now. . . .

'I will liquidate this house. There are many people here; they can live here as guests. I always received guests for two weeks, and now my house is also open for two weeks, but later I will ask everyone to leave. All the same I cannot throw away all my Work. . . .

'In two weeks I will begin a new work. The names of those who may stay will be posted. . . .

'I repeat that the Institute is closed. I died. The reason is that I was disenchanted with people after all that I have done for them and I have seen how 'well' they have paid me for it. Now, inside of me everything is empty. . . .

'I have to rest and use all the time for myself. . . . From today the Institute will be nothing. My Work will be different and those who are not invited cannot come to this Work' (*Our Life with Mr Gurdjieff*, pp. 233-5).

The speech seemed in line with Ouspensky's perception that during this crisis Gurdjieff's pupils could do nothing to help him and he could not help them – not, at any rate, as far as their inner lives were concerned. On the mundane level of simply obtaining sufficient food to sustain their physical bodies, some of the dozen or so remaining group members sought various jobs to raise cash. De Hartmann records that in those critical days meals were reduced to bread and soup with pieces of beef, lentil soup being a highlight on the menu. The hard times were eased when Orage arranged for a woman well-wisher in America to send $10,000.

The number staying at the house gradually increased again but not to the same level as before. Mme Ouspensky had been among those sent from the Institute. But she did not go to her husband in London. She settled in Asnières, just three miles north-west of Paris. About this time she wrote to Bennett:

'I do not pretend to understand Georgivanch. For me he is X. All that I know is that he is my teacher and it is not right for me to judge him, nor is it necessary for me to understand him. No one knows who is the real Georgy Ivanovitch, for he hides himself from all of us. It is useless for us to try to know him, and I refuse to enter into any discussion about him' (*Witness*, p. 166).

Incidentally, Mme Ouspensky's daughter, Lenochka Savitsky, had a daughter at the Prieuré. Madame's grandson, Leonidas, also lived at the Institute at the time, and later events suggest that his early education did not produce the most manageable of boys.

Mme Ouspensky proved extremely resilient during Gurdjieff's efforts to send away his most devoted pupils. However, she could not expect to dodge forever playing her role in the fulfilling of a solemn vow he had made during his 'Great Illness' when sympathizers 'came, sucked me out like vampires and went away':

'In the future, under the pretext of different worthy reasons, to remove from my eyesight all those who by this or that make my life too comfortable' (*Life is Real Only Then, When 'I Am'*, p. 45).

As his physical life at that point permitted little chance of comfort, presumably he referred to his inner life and purpose.

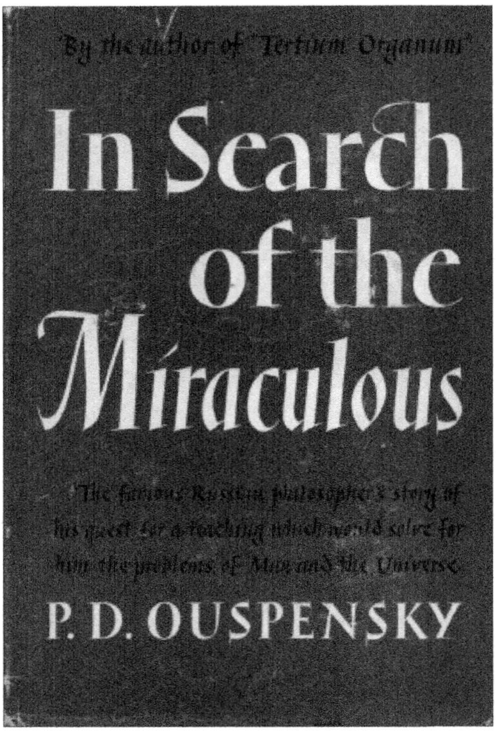

Chapter 14

POLES APART

WITH HIS ATTEMPT TO form the Institute for the Harmonious Development of Man in France collapsing around him, Gurdjieff's new tactics for implementing his grand strategy helped start another Fourth Way School in England. His methods were devious but over time they worked.

Gurdjieff reveals in his Third Series of writing, *Life is Real Only Then, When 'I Am'*, that he had not been able when in full strength to introduce into the life of people the truths he had elucidated for them, so in severe illness he had to do this in theory.

This sits oddly with the familiar criticism that Ouspensky was more interested in theory than practice. It is ironic that Gurdjieff, after the road accident that left him facing a crossroads also on his inner journey, should decide that failure to complete the practical aspect of his experiment meant that he must start afresh to ensure the theory survived for future generations.

This 'failure' is in itself not surprising; all the great attempts to make mankind conscious of a higher level of life have been destined to 'fail' from our exoteric viewpoint. So, if Gurdjieff's writing implies any personal shortcoming this impression might indicate that he was following 'the way of blame,' among his other disciplines.

An impartial observer is more likely to gain the view that it was his 'guinea pigs', despite their representing a wide spectrum of the species, who had been found wanting, being still under the influence of the vestigial organ Kundabuffer (the former organ supposed by Gurdjieff in *Beelzebub's Tales to His Grandson* to have induced human mechanicalness).

Early in the summer of 1928, one of the important but unsuspecting agents in his urgent scheme, Sophie Grigorievna Ouspensky, was still living at Asnieres. From there she could easily travel to see Gurdjieff in his apartment at the Boulevard

Péreire in Paris or at his table-sized 'office' at the Café de la Paix. Through her, as earlier in Germany, he was able to review Ouspensky's progress – or stagnation, according to some critics – in London.

In view of his latest objective, Gurdjieff was possibly amused to learn that Ouspensky appeared to be driven largely by the hope of contacting a 'Higher Source' of the teaching. Ouspensky made no secret of this wish to receive help from a representative of Conscious Humanity. He confided to several of his closest disciples that he did not hold out hope of being able to search the world for such a miraculous source of knowledge, although he believed such Schools must exist in the Middle East or in Europe. His best hope was that conscious men, possessing powers unknown to ordinary mortals, would be aware of finer energy being transformed by a group who had raised their level of consciousness. The Source would then, he anticipated, come to him.

He told Stanley Nott and John Bennett, among others, that this expectation was his main reason for keeping his London organisation active. True, he did keep the Work as he knew it alive, but the manner in which he ran his groups brought criticism he was not allowing the teaching to develop. It was, after all, part of his own understanding that the Work could not stand still; it must either go up or down.

Clearly, his main motive was to avoid adulterating the teaching with personal views or parts of other systems. Maintaining this safeguard requires a nice sense of discrimination seeing that the Work is practised not by following any cut-and-dried dogma but through response to request.

Ouspensky, of course, realised this but, despite the tempting and gratifying freedom that an individual approach might offer, was careful to transmit The Fourth Way ideas essentially as he had received them from Gurdjieff, sometimes formulating them to make them clearer. As he saw his role, it was enough that he was presenting the principles in a way that Westerners could understand, if they were prepared to work.

As for the objection that he did not proceed to the 'practical' work that Gurdjieff supervised in France, his critics did not appear to appreciate that this was no more a final stage than the intellectual work that they saw only as 'theory'.

At any rate, Madame Ouspensky had made a surprise visit in the summer of 1928 and was applying Gurdjieff-type methods at the group house, 'The Dell', in Sevenoaks, Kent. So Ouspensky probably thought he was doing about all that could be expected. His main frustration stemmed from his belief that Gurdjieff had lost contact with his Source, possibly before he had understood the complete teaching.

Might he also have considered the possibility that the System appeared fragmentary because Gurdjieff had not chosen to pass on all his knowledge, or because he himself had not grasped some vital points that Gurdjieff had disguised to test his understanding, or stimulate his self-development?

These questions are prompted by Ouspensky's persistent perception of the teaching as fragmentary. It is well known that *Fragments of an Unknown Teaching* was his preferred main title for his seminal account of Gurdjieff's teaching, published posthumously as *In Search of the Miraculous*, with the 'Fragments' description surviving although relegated to the subtitle. It seems certain that he meant the word to imply that only part of the System had been disclosed.

Beryl Pogson, Dr Nicoll's successor as a group leader and unmistakably a teacher in the Ouspenskian tradition, was struck by an alternative idea: that the term merely means the teaching is *presented* in a fragmentary form. She told one of her groups why she thought this:

'Certain ideas are given so that . . . we may use the ideas, as enough is given for us to go on thinking from; the clues are there. Even if you have been studying the System for thirty years, yet it is ever new, because there are such depths of meaning. These fragments are ancient truths which have been handed down orally from the beginning and have been preserved in the Schools. What we speak about is very ancient teaching. It is the teaching behind all the great religions. The

Source is always the same, but when it becomes exoteric with rule and outward form, it falls into multiplicity and gets further from the Source. It is purposely given in the form of fragments so that we have to assemble the fragments into our understanding' (*Centenary Fragments*, p. vii).

This raises the question of whether we can ever expect to receive more than fragments of knowledge in the search for truth and reality. Certainly there seem to be only parts of disciplines in the records of the great religions.

Ravi Ravindra says something that touches on this subject, in connection with his question to a senior group member about a puzzling statement by their teacher, Mme Jeanne de Salzmann, to whom Gurdjieff had passed on responsibility for his teaching. Ravindra did not fully understand what she meant by saying it was necessary to work, otherwise 'the Earth will fall'. The man from whom he sought help replied he did not know what it meant and 'as far as he was concerned such statements are for the apostles or the abbots'.

Ravindra laments that the unsatisfactory answer did not lead to an exploration of the question. He contrasts this with the attitude prevailing in the original Moscow and St Petersburg groups, when Ouspensky and others would talk for hours in trying to understand something that Gurdjieff had told them. Ravindra asks:

'Were the early students of the Work more serious? Or do we now have too easy an access to the ideas?' (*Heart without Measure*, pp. 180)

This bears on the weakness of feeling frustrated by a partial supply of information, for were students presented with the full System, laid out in orderly fashion for easy comprehension, this surely would constitute 'too easy an access to the ideas'. Experience teaches that seekers are more likely to glimpse reality now and then if put in the position of the early Russian groups, obliged to use their wits and intuition to piece together the fragments their teacher tossed to them.

It is likely that Gurdjieff understood perfectly well why his former pupil stuck so religiously to the teaching as given to the groups in Russia. And, despite any outbursts he may have made to suggest the contrary, this consistency could not have displeased him, for (as already suggested) it provided a carbon copy, a back-up, of the Work that would be invaluable should anything happen to him – more than a remote possibility considering his painful experiences with bullets and cars.

At the same time, he evidently felt that a little practical tuition of the type that the plain-speaking Mme Ouspensky could inject would spur the straitlaced English more quickly up the steps to the beginning of The Fourth Way.

It was Ouspensky who formulated the step diagram, a salutary sign of just how far aspirants to higher Being have to go before they can be said to be *working*. He told his pupils that Gurdjieff had said the first step begins when a person seeking the way meets one who knows it. It is then necessary to climb a metaphorical stairway before reaching the path, which is on a different level to ordinary life.

Gurdjieff had added that The Fourth Way differs from other paths in that a man cannot ascend to a higher step until he has brought another man to the level he occupies. He pointed out that the level of the teacher corresponds to the pupil's level. This means, for instance, that only a person on the level of an Apostle could really follow Jesus Christ. In The Fourth Way the 'elder' in understanding is considered the teacher.

When Gurdjieff had been asked what sort of person could climb this stairway, he introduced the term 'Householder'. Since Ouspensky began to disseminate the System the more definitive 'Good Householder' has become a familiar term in the Work, signifying a person who is able to fulfil his role in life without being deceived by appearances and as such has reached the basic standard needed to be able to grasp the Work. In practice, it is found that a candidate, as well as being a Good Householder, needs to have a 'magnetic centre' that attracts or seeks the type of ideas on which The Fourth Way is built.

Ouspensky's pupil Maurice Nicoll drew a simple step diagram for his group, marking Life on the bottom level and X at the threshold to the Work path starting at the top of the stairs. He commented:

'We have none of us got so far yet as to *work*; and no one counts for anything in this Work till he has got to the point X where he really enters the path. The Work henceforth is the only thing that matters to him: he is never negative about it again.'

Nicoll, following Ouspensky's example, also used the step diagram to illustrate that the universe was created according to the Law of Three and the Law of Seven. He said the diagram 'represents the universe as a strange kind of psycho-physical digestive tube in which everything eats and is eaten' (*Psychological Commentaries* vol. 3, p.1104). This stairway shows the Ray of Creation in the form of three octaves, proceeding in triads from the Absolute down to 'matter lacking Third Force'.

During 1924 Nicoll shared with John Bennett the answering of questions at group meetings when Ouspensky was absent. The busy Bennett also assisted Ouspensky with the translation of his books from Russian into English and, when he saw Mme Ouspensky, helped her with her English; she reciprocated by improving his Russian.

When Bennett received a tempting career offer abroad, he sought Ouspensky's advice on his future, as taking the job would mean separating from his Work teacher for months or years. By way of reply, Ouspensky, peering through his pince-nez while standing with his back to the gas fire in his Gwendwr Road sitting-room, related a Russian fairytale about a knight who is on a great adventure but uncertain which of three roads to take. A wise old man tells him if he goes right he will lose his horse, if left he will lose himself, while on the centre road he will lose both. Ouspensky told Bennett he was in just that position – offering the rather obscure hint that whatever road he chose it would be the same in the end, the point apparently being that the only necessity was that he should 'persist and never give up'.

The decoded fairytale apparently gave Bennett a fair idea of what he must sacrifice to find his true course, yet also provoked him to remark that, although he was sure the Work could lead to consciousness and immortality, 'I am not sure if I can reach it myself'.

Ouspensky retorted that he, on the contrary, was *sure* of nothing. Unsure he may have been, but he made clear that he *knew* that 'we' (by which he seemed to include the people in his groups) had nothing and therefore did not risk losing anything. He seemed to go a fair way towards contradicting himself by disclaiming hope or faith in anything but in the next breath declaring he would never give up the struggle, a perseverance which certainly denoted a strong faith in something. These contrasting expressions were more or less reconciled by an explanation that he believed in the *possibility* that Fourth Way groups would attain what they sought but thought they had yet to find 'the way'.

That was why, being sure that Gurdjieff had gained knowledge from a 'Higher Source', he thought it essential to gain more enlightenment from the same source.

Be that as it may, Bennett found that Ouspensky's confession that he was unsure gave him more confidence, presumably in his own and the group's potential to develop, than any positive affirmation would have done (*Witness*, p.137).

Another student who had great confidence in Ouspensky in that period was the writer 'Diogenes', who contributed articles to *Time and Tide* magazine and London's *Evening Standard* newspaper in the nineteen-fifties. It is believed that Diogenes may have been the pen-name of W.J. Brown, who had been an Independent Member of Parliament for Rugby and also a student of Ouspensky and Nicoll. In one article he wrote of the time he had studied in a London group:

'It was fascinating and sometimes awe-inspiring, to watch that powerful, meticulous mind at work. . . . Ouspensky seems to have been sublimely indifferent to the fate of his lectures. Once, when asked whether he intended to publish his lectures, he replied, "What is the use? The most important is not the lectures, but the questions and answers.". . .

'Ouspensky's great work was to systematise the raw material provided by the brain of that genius G.I. Gurdjieff. . . . . Ouspensky propounds, after the teaching of Gurdjieff, a "Fourth Way", which does not involve, as some other ways do, withdrawal from the world. But it is a hard way. Its basis is that Knowledge is a function of Being. If you want to know more about Truth you must become, in your Being, other than you are. At some levels of Being we become accessible to knowledge which at other levels of Being is utterly beyond our conception or our comprehension.

'Knowledge is auxiliary to Being. The Fourth Way is concerned with Being. The System begins with assertions which are calculated to destroy all pride and vanity. Man as we know him, the System declares, is not really "conscious" at all. Until he is awakened, he is a machine, responding to external circumstances quite automatically.

'He is not a unity. He has no self. He is a multiplicity of 'I's, one of which is in control of him at one moment and another at the next. His name is Legion and his nature is anarchy. And he lies, or his multiplicity of selves lies, to himself and to everybody else, all the time. 'The psychology of lying,' says Ouspensky 'is the most important part of the study of the human being. If man could be described as a zoological type, he would be described as a lying animal.'

That extract is from a literary review by Diogenes of Ouspensky's book *The Fourth Way*, which he warns the prospective reader 'will start you on a "high, austere, and lonely way". Which is precisely what you need, whether you know it or not'.

Diogenes was also an avid reader of Maurice Nicoll's books, in which he saw a kind of evolution of the Work teaching. Ouspensky, he said, 'wrote for the highly literate and educated. To make Gurdjieff's teachings available to a wider audience another commentator was needed and Dr Nicoll filled that gap'.

He added that

'it should be emphasised that the teaching of Gurdjieff and

Ouspensky is not a "new religion" – least of all of the Californian variety. Sometimes both men referred to it as "esoteric Christianity". It is a system designed to enable men to get out of the condition of "waking sleep", the condition of hypnosis in which most of them pass their lives.'

Rare stuff to read in a popular newspaper.

Throughout the nineteen-twenties Ouspensky concentrated on building up a core of people who could understand the System. A condition of their attending meetings was that they not talk about the ideas with anyone outside the system, unless it was someone who might be worth introducing to him. They were not even to discuss the Work among themselves unless they were in an appropriate state of mind; it was explained that chatting idly about the principles would devalue them.

While there can be no argument against these restrictions on the question of value, Ouspensky's insistence on secrecy was seen to border on obsession. This was certainly John Bennett's impression when he returned to London in the autumn of 1929 after working in Greece and found that his teacher would not talk to him and had forbidden his pupils to see him. He discovered that this stemmed from his arrest on what he claimed were false charges in Greece, when police found several letters in his flat bearing Ouspensky's name. As it was Russian, they handed the letters to the British Embassy on the suspicion they might have indicated a communist affiliation. Ouspensky had been called to the Home Office and questioned about his connection with – the Bolsheviks! He was so angered, said Bennett, that he could not easily forgive him (*Witness*, p. 157).

Ouspensky's experience with the Russian authorities apparently had made him deeply suspicious of police. This fear evidently stayed with him in England. His reaction was in contrast to his first response to news of Bennett's arrest, when he 'had sent me a friendly telegram saying: "Sympathy to Bennett under ninety-six laws." This was a reference to Gurdjieff's doctrine that man lives on earth under forty-eight kinds of limitations or restrictions upon his freedom of action. By his own folly and weakness he can fall under more and more limitations. The limit is reached when he comes under ninety-six laws.' (ibid.)

Dismayed over this treatment, Bennett contemplated returning to Gurdjieff, but the master was in America. Bennett's wife, taking a charitable view, told him later: 'If Ouspensky has turned you out, it may be because he knows that you should be working on your own' (ibid., p. 159). Although this reasoning is in accord with the supposition that Gurdjieff did exactly this in Ouspensky's case, Ouspensky did not seem to be acting from such high principles at that time, although he may well have held the view in general that Bennett should take on more responsibility in the Work.

In fact he did, forming his own small study group in London in 1930, after initial recruiting by his wife. Well aware of his separated teacher's strict rules about transmission of the Work, he sent a full report of each meeting to Ouspensky, saying that if he disapproved the group would disband. He heard nothing from Ouspensky until months later his Russian secretary, Madame Eugenic Kadloubovsky, phoned that he and several others of his group were invited to Ouspensky's next lecture at Warwick Gardens (ibid., pp.160-1).

This might suggest that Bennett had passed some test, or that his group, as shown by the content of their meeting notes, had proved their worth. It is more likely, though, that their preparation for work suited Ouspensky's plan to expand his groups. After working almost furtively for the past seven years with forty or fifty pupils, building a nucleus that might come to the notice of a Higher Source, Ouspensky had decided it was time to take his lectures to a wider audience, to scatter the Work seeds farther afield.

Ignoring past differences, he soon gave Bennett the task of reading lectures aloud in his presence, before asking for questions. Several meetings a week were needed to cater for a rush of new members. Bennett recalls that a series of lectures on 'The Search for Objective Consciousness' attracted much interest in London. Ouspensky would have hoped that the subject would also have attracted the Higher Source

Bennett also resumed visiting his teacher at his Gwendwr Road flat. In one of their talks, Ouspensky implied that he had kept a steady course for the past decade because he 'wanted to see what Mr Gurdjieff would do'. He still believed Gurdjieff had not achieved the results he sought and had not been able to find a key element of the System. Ouspensky's hope was still that a Higher Source would seek out his group, if it showed it could be useful. That was the purpose of his lectures, he revealed (ibid., pp. 161-2).

In this dream of a distant Higher Source of knowledge, it is easy to detect a reflection of Ouspensky's earlier failure to see that what he had sought in Egypt and India was waiting to be discovered on his own doorstep. However, the visitor he had received in the summer of 1928 was not – to his thinking just then, at any rate – the representative of Higher Source but his own Sophie Grigorievna, forced to England by the Institute's closure and Gurdjieff's departure for America.

The family reunion did not run smoothly. Mme Ouspensky evidently did not feel inclined to acclimatise to the English atmosphere – that formed by the populace rather than the weather – for she returned to France in the autumn. This was to little avail because Gurdjieff, concentrating on the writing that he now considered important towards humanity's redemption, was unavailable for tete-a-tetes.

Consequently, in accordance with her teacher's undisclosed plan to remove those closest to him, by early summer 1929 she was again boarding the boat-train for England, probably not feeling that she had been expelled or victimised, however, because Gurdjieff was finding 'vital' missions, well away from himself, for his principal pupils. (Gurdjieff later explained that at this stage he resolved to rid himself of all the people who contributed towards easing his suffering and discomfort because this muffled the key reminding factor that helped him to Self-remember continuously, and at that time he needed to maintain a high level of consciousness to carry out his final work.)

Back in her English home, 'The Dell', at Sevenoaks, Madame agreed, with a number of conditions, to work with some of Ouspensky's pupils. She insisted, however, she was not a teacher in the mould of her husband. Like Gurdjieff, although she would not have presumed to make that actual comparison, she could create conditions for practical work. This meant putting the Work principles into practice psychologically and emotionally, usually by the trusty method of treading on 'pet corns'; in her case by being clinically frank about her pupils' major weaknesses, advice which was invariably surprising and seldom painless at the receiving end..

In 'The Dell' and its gardens she had scope to supervise only a small number of pupils. She had reserved the right to choose whom she would instruct, and interpreted this as power to reject unceremoniously any who did not meet her requirements.

Without her presence, Ouspensky most likely would have been content to continue living in his 'bachelor' flat as in the previous decade. He proved able to live in his mind, enjoying immunity to his surroundings.

His friend Maurice Nicoll had noted in his diary an impression of the unremarkable decor of Ouspensky's living room: 'The walls are covered with a miscellaneous collection of pictures belonging to the landlord, all of which I have stared at many times without being able to remember any of them' (*Maurice Nicoll: A Portrait*, p. 95). This despite the fact that Ouspensky was a connoisseur and collector of fine prints, particularly of old Russia.

Mme Ouspensky needed more space than a writing room to exercise her particular talents, but she did not make immediate demands in the realm of real estate as she had not yet committed herself to a leading role in the group.

One move, or precaution, remained before Ouspensky began expanding his influence in England. In 1931, for an unexplained reason, he went to see Gurdjieff, but was not invited into the Prieuré. In a rebuff not calculated to close the rift between them, Gurdjieff met him instead at the Cafe

Henri IV in Fontainebleau, where it can be assumed 'Gurdjieff pressed heavily on Ouspensky's pet corn' (*Gurdjieff: The Anatomy of a Myth*, p. 241).

If Ouspensky had been hoping to hear that his old master had made fresh contact with Higher Source, or even to pick up tips on the most effective way of running a School, it seems he was disappointed.

Probably, as in Finland in 1916, Gurdjieff employed some sure way of again alienating his former star pupil. His reason for doing so poses a greater puzzle than Ouspensky's motive in calling on him. Gurdjieff was desperately in need of money at that time and, on past experience, he could have relied on assistance from Ouspensky's rich supporters had he asked for it. It seems to have been more important to him to keep Ouspensky separated from him than to accept outside help to save the Prieuré.

If that was his plan, it worked remarkably well. After that midsummer meeting of 1931, Ouspensky in private conversation over a few bottles of wine occasionally spoke of Gurdjieff as mad or criminal.

This was quite a turnabout. Back in 1923, after a visit to the Prieuré of the usual mystifying kind, Mrs Winifred Beaumont, later Mrs J.G. Bennett, asked Ouspensky for the truth about Gurdjief. She said she could see he was an extraordinary man, 'but I cannot tell if he is very good or very bad'. Ouspensky, despite his history of differences with the master, had answered: 'I can assure you that Gurdjieff is a good man.' At the same time, Ouspensky said that Bennett had been right to leave the Prieuré because 'he is not yet ready for that work' (*Witness*, p. 131).

This could be construed as an unintentional indication that Ouspensky felt that Gurdjieff sent him away because he, too, was not yet ready for the intensity of work that was engaging his former teacher. On the other hand, Gurdjieff could have maintained a break in relations precisely because Ouspensky was doing the job expected of him in England.

The apparent conflict, as might be expected, generated

much speculation about exactly what pressure Gurdjieff had brought to bear on Ouspensky. C.S. Nott, quotes with obvious approval French occult writer Denis Saurat's opinion that Gurdjieff had tried to break down Ouspensky's 'particular form of vanity' (*Journey Through This World*, p. 47). Given Gurdjieff's frequent warning that vanity is one of the chief obstructions to *everyone's* inner growth, this does little to explain the separation.

In what does seem to be an accurate appreciation of the outcome of the confrontation, James Moore says that yet another 'final' estrangement had polarised the Work, 'imbuing it for decades with a priceless and painful vitality' (*Gurdjieff: The Anatomy of a Myth*, p. 241).

His perception of polarity is worth noting, for the relationship of Gurdjieff and Ouspensky can be likened, and probably has been before this, to that of the positive and negative poles of an accumulator cell battery, both of which are necessary for an electric current to flow. This analogy tends to make irrelevant the opinions of those who criticise Ouspensky's style of teaching because it differed from Gurdjieff's. The energy that flowed may have been priceless, as Moore judges, yet there was a price to pay, perhaps it was what he alludes to as 'painful'.

It is said that the Work, in exchange for a person's self-development, demands payment in advance. In that case, could it be that Ouspensky, and his followers through the effort of practising what he taught, had already paid for a step or two up the stairway to The Fourth Way? As though in reward for this application of Work principles, there was now an enthusiastic surge in the English groups.

The confirmation of Ouspensky's peculiar polar isolation (even though he is unlikely to have seen it in that light), his current desire to extend his teaching, and the growing support of Mme Ouspensky – and maybe also some painful spurring from Paris by a past-master of that form of encouragement – all combined to foster the idea of organising a group more resembling a Fourth Way School in England.

Before the passing of the prep-School days, however, Ouspensky acted towards the man who was possibly his closest student effectively in much the way Gurdjieff previously had treated him. On 9 September 1931 Ouspensky had a short conversation with the good doctor: 'Nicoll,' he said, 'you had better go away.' Then, after a long pause, he added, 'Go away – and teach the System' (*Maurice Nicoll: A Portrait*, p. 109).

Hardly a sledge-hammer blow such as Gurdjieff could have been relied upon to deliver in such circumstances, but it stunned Nicoll. Naturally it would, seeing that their parting of the ways meant his starting from scratch, finding his own pupils, relying on what he understood of the system, unaided by books or official instruction sheets, save unauthorised notes he had jotted down after lectures.

Ouspensky had employed a piece of Gurdjieff-like psychology on Nicoll quite early in their association, when he asked his promising student to open a forthcoming meeting by himself. Nicoll prepared thoroughly for this and when he turned up at the meeting hall – found he was not needed (*Ouspensky: the Unsung Genius*, p. 86). He realised Ouspensky had just wanted him to observe how he related innerly to the event; whether subsequently he had resisted reacting with negative emotion, and to see in retrospect whether he had prepared for the test from Personality, from internal considering, or from a real place in himself.

Now, however, Nicoll was to run his own group; and eventually his own Prieuré-like country houses.

The Ouspenskys, however, were the first to put such a program into action. A few years after Mme Ouspensky's final return to England she and her husband (and their financial backers) agreed that a rural property should be acquired both as their residence and for practical work by the group. They chose 'Gadsden' in Hayes, Kent, a large Victorian mansion on seven acres. About ten people moved in permanently and many others in the group came down at weekends to join in activities devised by Madame, as she was usually addressed.

Peter Ouspensky in particular had relished a taste of English country life before that. In 1926 Maurice and Catherine Nicoll had rented for six years Alley Cottage as a weekend retreat at Sidlesham on the Sussex sea marshes. Nearly every other weekend Ouspensky would join them there. Here Nicoll records in his diary his teacher's first visit:

'We took him down to the sea. He walked a little in his overcoat, carrying a great number of glasses and cameras. He looked at a smack for a long time. He said his eyes improved as he grew older and pointed out that the binoculars he used did not have to be corrected for his vision as before' (*Maurice Nicoll: A Portrait*, p. 97).

The diary entry describes Ouspensky's first evening at Sidlesham:

'O. ate lobster, fresh caught, and cucumber, and good Southdown mutton at supper. "This is really good food," he said. He looked intently round the cottage room. "One can almost feel the world turning here," he said.'

Ouspensky said that the old cottage was an extraordinary place. He enjoyed standing in the garden by the sea-wall, looking over the marshes at the sand bay lit up by the setting sun at low tide. One afternoon he sat reading a novel for a long time. When Nicoll asked how he read, he said he was usually thinking of something else. Nicoll noted that he was sometimes silent, preoccupied, nearly all day.

'Sitting in the Crab and Lobster Inn at night among the farm hands, he said he liked the sound of a tavern and that he thought his liking for it was in his very bones. They were talking in broad Sussex and somebody was playing a concertina and the place was dimly lit with a swinging oil lamp. He said I should paint a sign for the inn – which had none – illustrating a crab and lobster toasting one another. I observed that the conversation going on around us was boasting in one form or another. "All over the world," he said, "everyone is boasting."'

Standing beside a friend's car about ten at night before driving back to London, Ouspensky reminisced about travelling long distances with horses in Russia. He estimated that driving with four horses he could reach London (70 miles away) about two or three the next day.

While driving Mr and Mme Ouspensky down to the cottage one day, Nicoll recommended steak and kidney pie at a hotel, 'but it turned out poor stuff'. Later, Ouspensky said the Nicolls' dog Pushti was ill because they fed it meat; in Russia 'the borzois are only fed on very coarse porridge'.

His own cat, Ouspensky revealed, was growing longer and broader. 'It becomes a cat. It eats only fish. It likes asparagus and olives very much.' Nicoll saw that his hands were not covered with scratches from 'this fierce beast' as formerly.

The next day they lunched on the lawn at the Crab and Lobster.

'We ate a great many crabs and lobsters, drank chablis and watched the big liners passing up and down Southhampton Water. . . . There were many small sailing vessels and seaplanes and all very lively and fresh. O. was pleased and Madame O. seemed to enjoy it. We went to tea at Bosham. We returned by the marsh road past Dell Quay and so home to Sidlesham. I said to him that one could experience two quite different sorts of feeling alive – one when you went out of London into the country in air and sun; and one when suddenly after the mind had been stopped for days it awoke and thought flowed. He looked at me for some time and then said: "But people have their minds shut all the time. They only know the first feeling." That evening he was himself. By this I mean that he looked well; he seemed bigger, his eye was bright, he smiled a little at times and spoke in a lucid rich way about anything that came up' (ibid., pp.100-01).

That was the night he spoke of Ouspensky Mountain in the Caucasus, named after an ancestor, an army general. During a discussion about drinking alcohol, which he said was like 'borrowing from the morrow', he said he had never been able to overcome a dislike of milk. Gurdjieff had once told him he must drink milk, but he could not.

Driving down to Sidlesham before dawn one day they

stopped on the way and ate bread and raw bacon and drank wine 'which tasted good in the chill air'. Nicoll wrote:

'I reminded O. of the drive to Chamonix with the roasted goat, and G. and the precipice. He laughed and said: 'The Suicide Club . . .' (ibid., pp. 102-3).

Nicoll's description of that 'suicidal' drive, which Gurdjieff occasioned to satisfy a sudden wish to sleep at high altitude, is related by Beryl Pogson. The trip was memorable for Nicoll because while they ate roast goat by the roadside, he was reproved by Gurdjieff 'for letting his attention be diverted from the feast by the sight of a beautiful view' (ibid., p. 87). Mention of a precipice possibly was a reminder of the terrifying nature of Gurdjieff's driving. The tone of the reminiscence suggests that Ouspensky might have been one of the passengers, but this is unlikely.

At another time Nicoll was driving Ouspensky to Bournemouth and planned to stay overnight at a hotel in Romsey. He thought the town had grown – it turned out to be Southampton. They stayed at a hotel there and discovered good hock in half-bottles and very courteous waitresses. Nicoll commented that, like Gurdjieff, Ouspensky appreciated courteous servants, and detested people who were rude to waiters.

At Bournemouth, crowded with people recovering from influenza, the tables in their hotel dining room featured flagons of Australian wine, which Nicoll explained was recommended by doctors, mainly to English aunts. 'Doctors have much to account for on the last day,' Ouspensky replied.

During a talk with Nicoll, Ouspensky confided that he felt that in one sense the Institute in France had been made possible by his work in England. Financially, of course, there is no doubt about this. It is likely that Ouspensky meant more than this, for he also considered that Gurdjieff had shown approval of his work by inspecting his group in London (ibid., p. 104). The English group supplied most pupils to the Institute, but Ouspensky may have meant more than that, too.

Perhaps it was a dividend from this investment that, while Gurdjieff was losing his Prieuré mortgage in 1933, enabled

Ouspensky and Madame – who could now be regarded as having been his proxy at the Institute – to open their own version of such a School at the small Kentish village of Gadsden, on the edge of greater London.

There, Ouspensky remained working in his study for much of the time, leaving to Madame the task of applying the type of friction that makes a pearl.

One of the group people who came to Gadsden at weekends was the surgeon Kenneth Walker, who says that Madame had the bearing and presence of a grand dame and, when she sat at the head of the long dining room table, he pictured her receiving party guests at a great house in czarist Russia. He remembers her chiefly, however, for her ability to strip off the masks of Personality (*Venture with Ideas*, p. 104).

Bennett apparently had supervised too few English lessons, for, says Walker, it was difficult sometimes to understand her words, although her eloquent gestures usually made her meaning clear. If not, she could call on a Russian-speaking member of the group to clarify her message. In such a case it might well happen that

'after an awful pause there would be hurled into the quiet of the hushed room the comment that had previously been mercifully blanketed: "Madame says that you only repeat Mr Ouspensky's words and that a clever parrot can be trained to do that," or "Madame says that you are a warning to us all and are quite useless" ' (ibid., p. 105).

The 'useless' soon received their marching orders. 'You come here because you think this a country club but Madame has no time for idle people who show no desire to work. You not come again,' was a typical appraisal and dismissal.

Walker likes her description of the False Personality as 'a huge hot-air pie which the owner carried about with him on a tray in order to exhibit it to his friends and have it admired'. The pie's thin crust meant it 'had to be guarded very carefully for otherwise this pretentious thing crumbled at the slightest touch and revealed to the world its emptiness'.

Madame, on the other hand, was interested only in what

was real. Walker says of a typical drawing room scene at Gadsden:

'How dumbfounded my friends would be if they were suddenly transported here! . . . How puzzled they would be to explain that we, reasonably intelligent people, were sitting here at the close of a hard day's work at the feet of a woman who seemingly did nothing but insult us. She had just referred to one of us as "a piece of meat" and to another as a person "completely devoid of mind" . . . What was happening here ran counter to everything else in life. It was "the work" and entailed a struggle against the whole current of mechanical existence. It was an heroic attempt on the part of a few people to oppose the mighty forces of nature. . . . But whether this venture ended successfully or in failure, whether it was reasonable or irrational, I realised that I no longer had any choice. I must go on with it (ibid., pp. 105-7).

During the summer, meals were often taken on four tiers of seats built in a natural amphitheatre near the kitchen garden. Four or five small tables and chairs were placed in front of the seats for Madame, visitors from London and Ouspensky – 'should he elect to join us instead of eating as usual in his study'. For any guests in the know, sitting in full view of Madame would be no small ordeal, for it was virtually impossible to prevent their Personalities being revealed by their every gesture and facial expression.

Walker says he often tried 'to assume the external demeanour of a person who was in a good state' as he walked up the drive to the house, but Madame 'always penetrated the pose'.

Although the more dramatic teaching usually is attributed to Madame, it was not unknown for her husband, too, to employ shock tactics. One of his senior pupils, Dr Francis Roles, recalls that in June 1933 he and Ouspensky were sitting in the drawing room at Gadsden when, about midnight, Roles raised one of his pet subjects, 'how everything would be different if we could love our enemies'.

He was told he did not know what 'loving enemies' meant. Did he really have a serious enemy, someone he would shoot?

Roles thought of one woman, but added that 'our relations change all the time'.

Such changeability, Ouspensky declared, was the problem: 'We cannot even have enemies. One minute we like, next minute we hate.' For an hour or two Ouspensky refused to continue this subject, then he appeared to grow into a temper and would not let Roles have any more wine but made him drink beer. To one question he said Roles had no understanding and had better amuse himself some other way.

When Roles became furious at this badgering, Ouspensky advised him that now he had an enemy – so now they could talk about the strange expression 'love your enemies'. It only had meaning in School life, Ouspensky said, adding:

'Much has to come first. But what can you try to do? You can try to reason with yourself, to prepare yourself. Then when I speak to you, you can try not to express your feelings and you can keep thoughts from turning about it. But you will not for a long time be able to love (*The Bridge*, No. 12, pp. 231-2).

Some people commented that Ouspensky seemed to become even more aloof than usual after his close friend Nicoll left to form his own group. Not that they were completely separated. Some of Nicoll's people occasionally were invited to attend Ouspensky's meetings in Warwick Gardens where they were in great awe of the master, although he answered their questions kindly. Sometimes, too, Ouspensky took one of Nicoll's meetings, which was a telling test of the new group leader's ability to maintain his equilibrium.

In some ways, Nicoll seemed to be working in parallel to his teacher for about the same time he, too, built a meeting house in the country, Tyeponds, at Lakes Farm, near Braintree in Essex. However, it was not used residentially by the group until the outbreak of war, when evacuees poured in – then it was taken over by the military and the group moved to another house in Gloucestershire, where they lived communally.

Oddly enough, Nicoll is reported to have been critical of Ouspensky for allowing Madame to take so much control of the practical work of the group. James Webb writes that in a drinking session with Ouspensky and a senior member of his group at Gadsden, Nicoll accused his teacher of 'going soft' and of being too much under his wife's influence (*The Harmonious Circle*, p. 411). Webb allows, however, that Nicoll may have been acting a part, devised by Ouspensky himself, particularly as he tried to persuade the 'senior member' in the drinking trio to start a group of his own.

Whatever the actual circumstances, it is unlikely that John Bennett would have shared this view of Madame's role. One of her husband's most remarkable pupils, he says of his relationship with her:

'Her influence upon me has been one of the chief factors in my development, and it has been altogether good; so that I owe her an extraordinary debt of gratitude' (*Witness*, p. 166).

That debt had begun to accumulate at Bennett's first visit to the Prieuré in 1923 when, despite his scientific brilliance, Mme Ouspensky had to show him how to mop up water when his enthusiastic floor washing flooded the kitchen. He said this brought home to him his mental arrogance but practical ignorance.

He described the work at Gadsden as 'the nearest approach to what we had at the Prieuré: hard physical effort and disturbing psychological conditions'. One of the things she taught him was to 'try to be yourself'. She had asked:

'Why do you imitate Mr Ouspensky in everything? You even copy his mistakes in speaking English. Why? You have your own way of working. You can never succeed in work by imitating others. Remember the saying in the *Bhagavad Gita* which I made you read this afternoon' (ibid., p. 175).

The Gita verse is:

'Better one's own way of life – *dharma* – even if it lacks merit, than that of another, even if one well performed. The way of another is fraught with danger: salvation comes only by following one's own way.'

That it was read during Work instruction underlined one of the differences between the methods of Ouspensky and his wife. Although he constantly studied *The New Testament*, she made much greater use of quotations from various religious works in her talks with students. She even had one of the Russians translate the *Philokalia* into English so that she could show how the holy fathers' key to the Scriptures was very close to the System.

While he was established in England, and nearing the peak of his teaching career, Ouspensky did not forget his origins. For several years he had wished to start a group for Russian emigres. Nicolai Rabeneck tells (in *The Bridge* No. 12, pp. 145-8) how one such group was organised late in 1932. He quickly learned that Ouspensky was still imposing his demand that members should not talk about the Work to outsiders. He may, at any rate, have found that difficult to do for a while. When, at their first interview, Ouspensky explained that man consisted of Essence, Personality, body and soul, he confessed he had 'no place to put Essence and Personality into my thinking'. Nevertheless, he was invited to study and also to visit the Ouspenskys in their country residence.

This group's initial meeting was held in Ouspensky's London apartment, when his secretary read the first chapter of *Fragments of an Unknown Teaching* and its author answered the ensuing questions 'in a colloquial tone'. Rabeneck reports that in the relaxed atmosphere the Russians had no hesitation in asking questions and the answers were short but precise. He asked whether any demands would be put on people taking part in School work. 'Not to argue' was the reply.

At about the sixth meeting they were surprised to find the table laden with bread, cheese, glasses and beer. After the repast, Ouspensky spoke of recurrence and memory – and reminisced with the others about Moscow.

The Russian woman who organised the group also held interim meetings at her house where they discussed the new ideas and prepared questions. She arranged for a Russian actor to read them *Strange Life of Ivan Osokin*. 'These readings naturally stirred us up, but we had to hold our breath, for discussion was not permitted as the reader did not belong to our group,' says Rabeneck.

To what Rabeneck describes as 'naive' questions, such as how a pupil could find him earlier in Moscow 'next time', Ouspensky answered with only a smile. This corresponds to an exchange at a meeting of the main London group, when 'a pupil asked in tones of awe, "Are you a Number 6 Man?" to which he replied with a twinkle in his eye, "Why so low?" (*Ouspensky: the Unsung Genius*, p. 48) [On this Work scale of categories of man from one to seven, the overwhelming majority of people are on the one-to-three level.]

Suddenly, at a day's notice, the Russian group was told to visit Gadsden. At the first meeting there they learned a repetition exercise. It was suggested they repeat the Lord's Prayer, preferably in Latin or Greek instead of their habitual Church Slavonic. Speaking of his own experience of repeating the prayer in two or three languages simultaneously, Ouspensky said this demanded great, prolonged and even exhaustive efforts.

At the next meeting Ouspensky outlined the group work under Gurdjieff in the Caucasus and demonstrated some of the few exercises that were within their – and Ouspensky's if truth be known – physical ability. Ouspensky insisted on questions at the third meeting, to ascertain what they had learned, and on the fourth they met Mme Ouspensky and were treated to dinner.

Madame made it clear that these were not social visits; they were there to help with the farm, and to learn. Rabeneck for one learned very quickly what she meant, for she ordered the roast meat to be placed before him for carving. His hesitant handling of the knife and fork prompted her to remark – humorously, he says – that she could already see what type he was. The roast was taken away and carved in the kitchen.

When the Russian meetings with Ouspensky ended, the members joined the regular meetings at Warwick Gardens, and also continued to gather for discussions at the group leader's house.

Thomas and Olga de Hartmann, who came to London in the spring of 1935 to arrange for the publication of some of

Thomas's music, visited the Ouspenskys at Gadsden. They then took a message to Stanley and Rosemary Nott from Ouspensky that Orage's death (on 5 November 1934) had changed the situation in which various Work groups were incommunicado and that he would like to see them.

Nott felt that the Gadsden drawing room, full of beautiful Russian prints, ornaments and icons, might have been in old Russia; also that Ouspensky 'was not the cold, severe intellectual I expected to find, though this was one aspect of him; he was warm and friendly and easy to talk to'.

He might, however, have agreed with Nicoll's apocryphal opinion that Madame exerted too great an influence.

'During tea Madame Ouspensky did most of the talking, asking me many questions about how I understood this and that. Then, after a long pause, she said, "Ah! I see gaps in your understanding; many things you do not understand!" I replied, "I know that I don't understand many things. In fact I am beginning to realize that I understand very little, in spite of, or perhaps because of my work with Orage and Gurdjieff," and I went on to say something about the group in New York, but she interrupted me with, "There were many things that Mr Orage did not understand or understood wrongly. Mr Orage was too formatory for one thing." "I'm sure Orage would have agreed with you but you had not seen him for ten years, and he had changed very much in that time. And you know, Gurdjieff himself once said that Mr Ouspensky was too formatory." . . . We got a little heated and I said, "Madame Ouspensky, I didn't come here to be put through a catechism but to have a friendly talk." Out of the corner of my eye I saw Ouspensky making a signal to her as if to pipe down' (*Journey Through This World*, pp. 95-6).

Something he heard from Nott that day may have contributed to Ouspensky's reported diagnosis that Gurdjieff never recovered mentally from his car accident. When he asked Nott how he understood the Work terms 'considering', 'Self-remembering', 'self-observation' and 'negative emotions', Nott replied that he never heard Gurdjieff use those terms.

Instead, he called Self-remembering 'red pepper' and the negative emotion, the denying part, was 'the devil'.

Nott pointed out that groups tended to become identified with expressions. Ouspensky, always precise in his Work syntax, is unlikely to have accepted this as valid criticism of the terminology he had maintained.

In exchange for lending him a copy of Gurdjieff's *Beelzebub's Tales to His Grandson*, Ouspensky allowed the Notts to attend his newest group – when the offer was made, Nott had requested they join the youngest group. The Notts had to agree, however, not to mention Gurdjieff's book to Ouspensky's pupils.

They found the atmosphere at the meeting hall in Warwick Gardens tense and expectant when they arrived before 8pm on the appointed day. One of the older pupils came in and asked for questions, which were recorded by a woman secretary. He replied to some and left others for Ouspensky to answer. Fifteen minutes later four other men and Ouspensky came in and took seats facing the audience. As Ouspensky answered questions, Nott was impressed with the breadth and clarity of his 'powerful mind – so far as *knowledge* was concerned'.

The Notts found that the questions followed a pattern they had noticed in Orage's early groups in New York; that is, they were 'according to types'. The answers, too, were 'strikingly similar' but all the same Nott was stimulated by Ouspensky's replies and the general atmosphere. What he learned from Ouspensky, he says, was training of the mind to formulate thoughts and feelings.

When the meeting concluded about ten-thirty, the thirty or so pupils were asked not to loiter outside. The hush-hush precautions reminded Nott of a Russian secret society, and he felt they had little to do with the Work (*Journey Through This World*, pp. 102-3).

Actually, even Nott, who faulted Ouspensky for an alleged failure to apply the Work practically, by which he meant emotionally and physically, either to himself or his pupils, felt closer to him than to Madame. He noted:

'She was always the Grand Duchess, keeping you at a distance, and I never felt the warmth that Ouspensky, in his mellow moods, radiated' (ibid., p.107).

Curiously, Nott found himself in the position of defending Gurdjieff from attack by Ouspensky and vice versa. He recounts:

'Some time after meeting Ouspensky I was in Paris with Gurdjieff and at lunch told him about my contact with him and about our going to his group. He listened, and made an unflattering remark about Ouspensky. 'Mr Gurdjieff,' I said, 'I like Ouspensky and I enjoy talking to him.' 'Oh yes, Ouspensky very nice man to talk to and drink vodka with, but he is weak man' (ibid.).

It is impossible of course to know why Gurdjieff said this, whether he was serious or whether his object was to influence Nott in some way. Nott did in fact wonder about Gurdjieff's meaning in calling Ouspensky weak, knowing that everyone has weaknesses. He concluded Ouspensky's particular feature was that he was undeveloped emotionally. Nott says this thought led him to see that he could trust no one emotionally, 'least of all myself', because ordinary emotions could change from hour to hour.

Even a realisation like this, if it was significant in Nott's own psychological work, could have been what Gurdjieff wanted him to see, and in that case would have had little to do with Ouspensky's real character.

Nott's interpretation of the exchange of opinions also demonstrates the logic of a condition that Ouspensky applied whenever comments he had made at previous meetings were thrown in his face. 'In what context did I say that?' he would ask, indicating that the words could have various implications depending on the circumstances surrounding their utterance.

Whether or not he was justified in finding fault with Ouspensky, Nott seems to be an honest and accurate reporter of opinions expressed in his hearing. He writes that about 1934-35 after a few glasses of red wine, Ouspensky told him that Gurdjieff had been 'difficult' at Esssentuki and

Constantinople but had changed for the worse at Fontainebleau, doing things that Ouspensky did not like, and in a 'stupid way'. That was one occasion when he expressed his belief that Gurdjieff's mind did not recover from his car accident.

Ouspensky also left no doubt that Gurdjieff's actions in London had been very unpleasant to him.

'After this I saw that I must break with him, and I told my pupils that they would have to choose between going to Fontainebleau or working with me' (ibid., p. 97).

If Gurdjieff's remark to Pinder after the 1922 London lectures is recalled, it can be seen that Ouspensky had unintentionally helped further Gurdjieff's objective.

In 1936 the Ouspensky group moved to a larger house, Lyne Place, at Lyne village, situated between the railway stations of Virginia Water and Chertsey in Surrey. The mansion stood amid 65 acres of farmland, sweeping lawns, woods, lakes, and a fine rose garden. (In 1968 its name was changed to Lyne Place Manor by a developer who divided the mansion into eleven apartments and sold off the lodge and stables, the lakes and most of the woods, leaving some eight acres. The farm had been sold earlier.)

Nott now suggested that his wife and Mrs Jessmin Howarth, a former choreographer at the Paris Opera, could show the group some of the sacred dances and Movements that Gurdjieff had taught. Ouspensky agreed, and some of the pupils were taught the Obligatories, first at the Notts' flat in Hampstead and later at Lyne Place. Stanley Nott, because of Ouspensky's ban on any mention of Gurdjieff or *Beelzebub's Tales*, had declined to join in the activities at Lyne Place, so when a big demonstration of the Movements was put on there Mme Ouspensky refused him permission to view it.

The Movements were also introduced to Maurice Nicoll's group in London. Nicoll – a chorister as a schoolboy – recollected what he could of Gurdjieff's music and a pianist in the group, Miss Marjorie Stalker, harmonised his hummed tunes. He recalled the Obligatories, the March and the

Counting Exercise. In the autumn Mrs Howarth and Mrs Nott taught them a few Movements in the basement of the Finchley Road house where they held meetings.

Ouspensky repeated his call to Nott to join the work at Lyne Place, but he, with memories of the Prieuré still vivid in his memory, felt that it lacked the strenuous tasks and shocks that Gurdjieff's Institute provided. His summing up of Lyne Place: It was a well-run philosophical school, unique in our time perhaps, with nearly a thousand pupils; and no breath of scandal ever touched it' (*Journey Through This World*, p. 104).

To put the influence of The Fourth Way in perspective at this time, compared with Ouspensky's thousand followers, Nicoll had a group of more than a hundred in London and the country, Nott had a dozen people in London, Gurdjieff a few Americans, English and Russians in Paris and about twenty of Orage's old group met in New York.

These figures perhaps indicate why Ouspensky, who once said he had been surprised to find he had the beginnings of a School on his hands, was casting around for help from an elevated level. At Lyne Place, Nott says, Ouspensky told him: 'It is necessary that we get in touch with an esoteric School. There must be Schools, either in Europe or the Near East.'

He did not accept Nott's contention that Gurdjieff's was an esoteric School, saying there was a 'missing link'.

Nott regularly suggested that Ouspensky let his people read *Beelzebub's Tales*, but the latter argued that the book needed a lot of mental preparation. Nott retorted that what was needed was an ability to read between the lines, patience, and perseverance; many simple people could see more in it than intellectuals. Pressed further, Ouspensky claimed he had not read it himself because 'it sticks in my throat' (ibid., p. 107). It is hard to believe that Ouspensky would not really have read every word of anything written by Gurdjieff. It seems more to the point that he probably doubted the writing style would win many converts.

Later he gave Nott the *Fragments of an Unknown Teaching* typescript and asked his opinion. Nott, a publisher, told him 'it was wonderful stuff; it was in a different vein from *A New Model of the Universe*, much higher in the scale of ideas; it was a verbatim report of Gurdjieff's talks'.

After three glasses of wine, as recommended by Gurdjieff, Nott opened up and talked freely and gradually 'the liking for Ouspensky warmed into a real affection, for here I saw quite another side of him; not the somewhat forbidding philosopher, but a warm and sympathetic man'.

Ouspensky in turn confided in him:

'I tried many times to come to an understanding with Gurdjieff, but it was not possible, and when he came to London and tried to break up my group I had to sever my connection with him (*Journey Through This World*, p. 105).

Nott comments it was not possible to come to an 'understanding' with Gurdjieff. 'You either accepted him as a teacher or you did not.'

One reason for the necessity of this approach is suggested by a resolution psychologist Maurice Nicoll made after his training at the Prieuré:

'never to forget that G. is circular – not to take one point in that circle and criticise it (*Maurice Nicoll: A Portrait*, p. 89).

Chapter 15

EXPANSION TO SCHOOL

THE SEARCH FOR AN esoteric School or, failing that, the hope that such a Higher Source of knowledge would contact him dominated Ouspensky's for most of his life. That he began looking in the wrong place became evident when he discovered in Moscow the sort of wisdom he had sought in the Orient. To certain people, that situation recurred in the nineteen-thirties when he agonised over the 'missing link' to School at the very time he was creating his own. He himself conceded he had been surprised to find he had the 'beginnings' of a School on his hands. The period in England leading up to World War II can easily be viewed as his personal 'Camelot', as far as his relations with his pupils goes. And, as Nott says, it was achieved without any of the scandal generated by Gurdjieff's method of teaching, and of choosing students.

In an 'Autobiographical Fragment' – allusions to fragmentation occur frequently in his and his followers' musings – written in 1935 Ouspensky says:

'In 1931 I published *A New Model of the Universe* in English. It was a very long work. The correction of the translation took about two years. After 1931 my work was chiefly connected with the development of a psychological system based on the study of 'self-consciousness' and 'objective consciousness'. These terms need explanations. I am preparing a book on this system and it may be published in a year or two.'

The book then in preparation was to be the most important of his 'fragments' and it is apparent that in 1935 he expected to release it soon to the public. Later, when he learned Gurdjieff was contemplating publishing *Beelzebub's Tales to His Grandson* first, he told Stanley Nott he would not in that case go public with *Fragments of an Unknown Teaching* (*Journey Through This World*, p. 106). He would not give his reason for this, but as it turned out fate did not allow him the final say.

The main drive of his expansion program was a series of

'preliminary' lectures which began in September 1934. The basis of these were six, later condensed to five, 'Psychological Lectures', which he had written to outline how he and his associates were working. A senior pupil usually read them to new people, after which Ouspensky would answer their questions on these new ideas.

Many of the new people had been attracted by his books. Those who wrote to him seeking more knowledge he invited to take part in the introductory course. He reasoned that 'only five, or better ten, lectures could give an idea of the direction of my work'. The lectures were continually revised over the years and are available now in the book *The Psychology of Man's Possible Evolution*. In an introduction to this, written in 1945, he says 'the chief difficulty for most people was to realise that they had really heard *new things*'.

The reason was that 'they always tried to contradict this in their minds and translate what they heard into their habitual language'. Ouspensky adds: 'We are so accustomed to the old tunes, the old motives, that long ago we ceased to hope and ceased to believe that there might be anything new.'

Today, the proliferation of so-called New Age movements generated by the cosmic transition from the Piscean to the Aquarian Age is becoming an additional cause of people's failure to recognise the newness of Work ideas. Having been disillusioned by one cult, people may think that somewhat similar phrases must mark another such. (Orage would not have been flattered by the adoption of his literary title for some of its modern associations.)

In the first lecture of the series in 1934, Ouspensky gave notice that he was introducing a different type of psychology to any his audience had known. At the same time, this psychology was 'perhaps the oldest science', having taken the guise in different eras of philosophy, yoga, religion, art, architecture and Mysteries or of various symbolic teachings including astrology, alchemy, magic, Masonry, occultism and theosophy.

Genuine modern systems study man from the perspective of

what he *might become* – which, incidentally indicates the aptness of incorporating '*Possible* Evolution' in the title of the book of the lectures. Ouspensky denied the possibility of any mechanical evolution; that is, regeneration happening through heredity or natural selection without the contribution of conscious effort on man's part.

His key points, that Nature leaves man in an incomplete condition and that further development depends on his own efforts, would have called for a sweeping reassessment of outlook by most of his listeners. Just as sobering was his next claim: man cannot complete himself without help. He pointed out that the reason most people do not seek help to attain new powers and qualities in order to 'become different beings' is simple: they imagine they already possess them.

In stating that man is mechanical, he meant he has no independent movements. In that first lecture Ouspensky also dared to level the potentially offensive judgment that *man cannot do*, that everything he thinks he does just happens as a result of external influences. He backed this up with a criticism of man's disunity, due to the instability resulting from his many 'I's.

What are those powers man imagines he has already and can utilise with no trouble? The most important is consciousness. At that early stage in his listeners' re-education, Ouspensky simply explained it as embracing varying degrees of a particular type of awareness, adding that some modern psychologists confused it with psychic functions. The Work's new idea, known of old, is that consciousness 'can be made continuous and controllable by special efforts and special study'.

In a 'general description', he said man has four possible states of consciousness: sleep, waking state, self-consciousness and objective consciousness, but usually lives in only the first two. Asking his audience to observe their memories, he explained that they recalled little vividly because 'you remember only *the moments when you were conscious*'. The most important question is whether it is possible to gain command over those 'fleeting moments of consciousness'.

The mind-stretching first lecture also enlightened newcomers on the seven functions (including two higher ones) of the human machine. Ouspensky stressed that self-study begins with the four accessible functions – thinking, feeling, instinctive and moving – and postponed any discussion of the sex function. He also disclosed a fact that they would hear repeated in many forms: Self-Observation is the beginning of psychology.

In the second lecture Ouspensky gave more details about states of awareness and did not disguise the fact that long work is required to acquire self-consciousness. To any who dreamt that they were self-motivated individuals, he divulged that no evolution of the kind he had in mind is possible without School. The current lectures were 'not even the beginning of a school' but they could give an idea of how Schools work and 'how they can be found'.

Ouspensky also introduced one of his favourite teaching topics – lying; that is, pretending that we know the truth. He said that 'lying fills all our lives', to the extent that psychology becomes 'the study of lying'.

Any listeners sufficiently self-satisfied to be rattled by that broadside had to immediately shield their egos from further salvos. The lecturer's next charge was that it is impossible to study man as a whole because he is divided into the 'almost real' and the 'almost all imaginary', otherwise known in Work language as Essence and Personality, respectively.

Then it was revealed that 'to know onself' actually means to know the structure of one's *machine*. One of the first mechanical manifestations to be observed is the expression of negative emotions. This weakness is one of the many results of the 'curious state' of identification, in which everything absorbs a person, who cannot separate something real in himself or herself from the idea, feeling or even object that has temporarily seized the attention.

The second sleep-producing state is 'internal considering', which is really a state of identification with people, in which, for instance, one worries what others are thinking of one.

Ouspensky explained that the definition of 'man' in ordinary language is too vague, so the Work divides men into seven categories. The first three – Man No. 1 being ruled by Moving Centre or Instinctive Centre, No. 2 by Emotional Centre and No. 3 by Intellectual Centre – are practically on the same level; Man No. 4, 'a product of School culture', has a permanent centre of gravity and balanced functions; No. 5 has unity and self-consciousness; No. 6 has acquired objective consciousness and No. 7 has attained a permanent 'I' and free will.

The third lecture – which differed slightly from the divisions in the book, but not significantly – broached the readily observed fact that the centres rarely work as they should. A major fault is that, in an untrained machine, the centres misuse a built-in safeguard that allows them to replace one another in an emergency, although with a loss in quality because each function ideally uses a specific grade of energy. Genuine results are compromised when, for instance, Moving Centre imitates Intellectual Centre, or vice versa. The wrong use of centres causes much of man's identification.

After what they had heard so far, Ouspensky's assurance that mechanical man is not entirely under the Law of Accident would have come as a relief. Man escapes this absolutely hazardous fate because he lives under two main sets of influences. The first, called A influences, are created by life itself and interest only the outer man. B influences are created originally by School and then become mixed with and watered down by those of the first kind.

Despite the admixture, B influences retain enough of a certain energy to empower some people to feel and think differently from the way of the world. When this happens the influences may fuse a group of interests, a number of 'I's, in the Personality to form a magnetic centre, which will attract more B influences.

There is a third influence, designated C, but this comes directly from a School and can be transmitted only by word of mouth.

School work, Ouspensky said, has to be conducted on three lines – for oneself, with other people, and for the School – because 'one line awakes a man who falls asleep over another line'.

The fourth lecture produced a detailed examination of centres, each of which occupies the whole body but has its centre of gravity in a particular location; such as the brain for Intellectual Centre. Each operates at a different speed, Intellectual Centre being the slowest, the variation from one to another being in the order of 30,000. This means that in effect they have different times.

Imagination and identification, Ouspensky said, make it impossible for ordinary, mechanical man to have positive emotions; that is, feelings that cannot become negative. For 'all our pleasant emotions such as joy, sympathy, affection, self-confidence, can, at any moment, turn into boredom, irritation, envy, fear and so on'. This seems to doom us to a miserable existence. Again, however, there is a bright side to one of our main failings.

Ouspensky showed that negative emotions cannot exist apart from imagination and identification. Then he explained that it is precisely because these emotions are artificial and have no useful purpose that it is safe to destroy them, which is not always the case with other unfortunate characteristics. Were this not so, he declared, man would have no chance of changing himself.

Effecting a change for the better involves one of the Work's paradoxes – for to do this man has to sacrifice his unnecessary and useless suffering. It takes long work to appreciate that it is extremely difficult to forgo 'imaginary' suffering.

In the meantime, Ouspensky was content to disclose that all difficulties in the Work occur because we can't remember ourselves. He assured the meeting, however, that we can remember ourselves at will, at least for a short time, 'if we try sufficiently hard and in the right way'. The knowledge that we don't remember ourselves is 'the weak spot in our mechanicalness'. For once we realise the need to remember we are already less mechanical. Work, he said, begins with 'understanding the necessity for actual change in ourselves'.

The fifth lecture opened with a revelation that two lines of development must proceed simultaneously in man: knowledge and Being. If one outgrows the other, lopsided development results. Knowing, Ouspensky pointed out, is not the same as understanding. In understanding, one can always see a connection with a bigger whole.

(The connection between a perceived phenomenon and its embracing noumena, part and whole, may suggest to readers yet another variety of perceived 'fragments' and invisible complete system. From there, it is possible to mentate on the inevitability of our fragmented view of reality.)

Ouspensky defined understanding as the arithmetical mean between knowing and Being.

He gave his listeners further food for thought:

'You can understand other people only as much as you understand yourself and only on the level of your own Being. You can see in others only as much as you have in yourself.'

Returning to centres, he further divided each into three parts, intellectual, emotional and mechanical – and then divided each part into similar segments. Those who would be staying on as students heard a term that would become very familiar to them unless they took pains to formulate their thoughts and feeling accurately. Ouspensky told them that the mechanical part of Intellectual Centre is the 'formatory apparatus', sometimes even called the 'formatory centre'. Its work, he said, should be confined to 'the registration of impressions, memories, and associations' but it usurps the role of answering questions addressed to the whole centre, making decisions and trying to solve problems. The majority of people live their entire lives by means of the formatory centre, he claimed.

His final point: 'all your work upon yourself is connected with Self-remembering . . . no work can be done in sleep'.

At the conclusion of the 'psychological' lectures, those still interested in following The Fourth Way could attend another five, sometimes called the 'cosmological lectures', based on readings from the manuscript of *Fragments of an Unknown Teaching*, mainly from chapters seven and nine. Ouspensky probably skipped the part where Gurdjieff tells him his idea of 'cosmic consciousness' is 'rubbish, the usual scientific sophistry', but certainly would have explained the Law of Seven and the Ray of Creation. This leads to the teaching of three octaves of radiation – Absolute to Sun, Sun to Earth and Earth to Moon – and the role of organic life on Earth in giving the shock that fills one of the three intervals where the process needs to be supplemented from outside.

Preparation of this talk on the structure of matter would have reminded Ouspensky of the lectures he heard in St Petersburg. For he recounts that Gurdjieff asked why he was not paying attention to one talk on this subject, to which he replied he had already heard it. Afterwards he found he could not remember one point that had been explained and wished he had listened when he had the chance.

Two years later, in 1917, while living with a small group in the Caucasus, he asked Gurdjieff about an apparent discrepancy in a diagram. He was told that particular point was explained in the Petersburg lecture he claimed to have known already. Gurdjieff asked whether, if he now heard that the same lecture was being repeated in Tuapse, he would walk the twenty-five miles there through dark, snow and wind.

Ouspensky said he would go 'without a word', seeing that he had previously walked that distance for no reward but simply because there was no room for him in the cart. Gurdjieff commended this reasoning, remarking that people rarely wanted to pay for the things that were most important to them (*In Search of the Miraculous*, pp. 177-8).

The large increase in the number of people receiving Ouspensky's instruction in London in the 1930s did not automatically mean a corresponding rise in understanding of the Work. At a meeting in September 1935, a year after the start of the lecture series, he reminded his pupils that he had asked them to bring more questions so he could determine whether they had learnt enough to justify his continuing the meetings.

'And I see that it is not worth while. So it will be the last meeting. Those who want to continue can write to me and explain why they should continue and why I should lose my time to continue.'

Many doubtlessly were shocked when he told them 'if we go on in this way we need at least three hundred years to achieve some results. It is useless to continue in this way.' Life was not long enough to change Being if they worked 'like we do everything else in life'.

He went on:

'Theoretical study of the system is impossible. It must be practical. And this means work on emotions and will. Without this it is impossible. Influences C, if not taken in the right way, become influences B. This means that the System becomes ordinary philosophy.'

He said 'a kind of perfected method' was needed.

'The first condition is understanding. All the rest is proportionate to understanding. There must also be efforts in connection with emotions and will. One must be able to go against oneself, to give up one's will. I mentioned it before but nobody noticed it or thought what it means to give up will, and how one can do it and when.'

'You mean going against what one likes?' someone asked.

This is too general. First you must ask yourself – what is will? We have no will. So how to give up what we don't have? It means, first, that you never agree that you have no will. You only agree in words. Secondly, we don't always have will but only at times. Will means a strong desire. If there is no strong desire there is nothing to give up, there is no will. Another moment we have a strong desire that is against Work, and, if we stop it, it means that we give up will. It is not every moment that we can give up will, but only at special moments.'

After dealing with a number of ensuing questions, Ouspensky said his listeners were mixing many things.

'You don't know how to think about it. On one side you

realise you are machines, but the next moment you want to act according to your own opinion. Then, at this moment, you must be able to stop, not to do what you want. But not at moments when you have no intention of doing anything. You must be able to stop if it goes against rules, or principles, or against what you are told. It often happens that people go on studying and miss these moments. They think they work when nothing happens. And when such moments come they miss them. We cannot work equally always. At one moment passive study, theories are sufficient. At another moment it is necessary to oppose your movement, to stop.'

Asked what causes these moments, he said:

'Desire. Resultant of desires is will. If one strong desire conquers, it gives direction to desires.'

It is apparent that the foregoing meeting notes (from *A Record of Meetings 1930-1947*, pp. 67-9) weaken claims that the powerfully intellectual lecturer lacked an emotional approach to the Work or that he preferred theory to practice. Whether or not he seemed to some to be emotional, he constantly pointed to the need to use all centres. As well as stressing the need for emotional involvement, the above passage also indicates the vital role of theory. Inevitably, 'practice' is a later stage in the learning process. At first, most people take in the Work ideas mainly through Intellectual Centre, although there is of course an emotional element in the intuition that they contain meaning. It is after newcomers study and apply the Work principles that a more potent emotion enters and can lead to understanding.

Ouspensky wrote in the 1927 version of *Fragments*:

'This system is waiting for workers. There is no statement and no thought in it which would not admit further development and elaboration. But there are great difficulties in the way of training people for this work, since an ordinary intellectual study of the system is quite insufficient; and there are few people who agree to other methods of study who are at the same time capable of working by these methods.'

This leaves no doubt that Ouspensky understood perfectly

well that an intellectual grasp of Work principles is insufficient. His difficulty did not lie in seeing what was needed but in finding people capable of receiving the ideas on any part of their Being other than the intellect. The passage also indicates that it was not by his own choice that he did not, as it is said, allow the London groups to develop for a decade, for he says there is no part of the System that cannot be taken further.

Anyhow, students confused by the new thoughts and feelings prompted in them by the System might have been reassured by a glimpse of Ouspensky's own emotions as described in his 1927 manuscript of an 'Introduction to *Fragments*':

'The predominant emotion in me was fear – fear to lose myself, fear to disappear in something unknown. . . I remember a phrase in a letter I wrote at that time: "I am writing this letter to you, but who will write the next letter, signing it with my name, and what he will say I do not know" This was the fear. But there were many other elements in it as well: the fear of taking a wrong way, the fear of making an irreversible mistake, the fear of losing some other possibilities. All this left me later on, when on the one hand I began to gain confidence in myself and on the other to have practical faith in the system.'

In 1936, one newcomer to the Work, Robert de Ropp, found that he and other students like him were too weak and disunited to submit themselves to the discipline needed for a System such as The Fourth Way 'therefore it has to be imposed on us by our teacher. We have to trust him and do the tasks he gives us' (*Warrior's Way*, p. 100).

On the other hand, he found this authoritarianism caused a conflict with another principle Ouspensky had stressed: 'Do nothing you do not understand. This is the way of understanding, not the way of faith.'

This seeming contradiction reflects Ouspensky's own quandary in the Caucasus, when he felt that Gurdjieff was asking his followers to do things they did not at all understand.

De Ropp is a convincing observer of the Ouspensky he knew at Lyne Place because he produces such a warts and all portrayal of his teacher, with a perception enhanced by his sharing of some of the weaknesses he depicts. On the frequently raised characteristic of authoritarianism, he notes that Ouspensky was

'Russian to the core – so much so that a saying circulated among the more objective of his followers: "One must distinguish between what is the teaching and what is just Russian." It seems to be the essence of Russianism that the Russian is either a complete slave or a complete tyrant.' (ibid., p. 99)

Despite this, Ouspensky rarely interfered in his followers' personal lives, de Ropp points out. 'At the time when I knew him he kept fairly aloof.' However, after lectures at Warwick Gardens he was driven back to Lyne Place where he relaxed over food and drink. 'Some of the men who lived in the house would sit up with him to keep him company. Never any women. This was *streng verboten* by Madame Ouspensky' (ibid., p. 101).

Recounting the many times he sat up drinking with his teacher, 'waiting in vain for him to let fall pearls of wisdom', de Ropp says he and others were usually regaled only by tales of Moscow and Petersburg. 'For this was one of Ouspensky's weaknesses. *He could not leave Russia*.' So the long night sessions became 'something of a bore'. But not always.

Once, he seemed to go into a trance and spoke of the 'week of miracles' in Finland. 'He must have been a very strange man, that Mr Gurdjieff,' commented de Ropp, hoping to restart 'this intriguing conversation'.

'Ouspensky gazed at me as if I had said something ridiculous. "Strange! He was extraordinary! You cannot possibly imagine how extraordinary Gurdjieff was."

Comments de Ropp: 'So many emotional elements entered into that simple statement: wonder, admiration, regret, bewilderment. . . . He had played the great game with a master and had been checkmated, but he still could not figure out quite how it had happened.'

In that kitchen talk, Ouspensky next relived an episode of sitting in a café in Constantinople very late at night:

'Suddenly Gurdjieff began to sing something in Persian, "The Song of the Dervish". He translated it into Russian. It was some special knowledge, very sacred. But we were both very tired. I wrote down what he said. Maybe five verses. . . .

'At that time I felt sure I could work with him again. That was again the real Gurdjieff. But next night I tried to get him to continue "The Song of the Dervish". Nothing! Nothing but dirty jokes' (ibid., pp. 102-4).

A pupil that de Ropp introduced to Ouspensky's group in 1936, Rodney Collin Smith (later well-known as the author Rodney Collin), felt the System was complete in itself yet inseparable from the Being of the teacher who expounded it, 'from O. himself'.

'When anyone else tried to explain it, the 'system' degenerated, lost quality in some way. And although no one could entirely neutralise the great strength of the ideas in themselves, it was clear that the "system" could not be taken apart from a man of a certain quite unusual level of consciousness and being. For only such a man could induce in others the fundamental changes of understanding and attitude which were necessary to grasp it (*The Theory of Celestial Influence*, pp. xviii-xix).

When he met Ouspensky privately and asked about his position in the group as a writer, Collin was advised 'not to get too involved' just yet; later there might be something for him to write.

'O. tirelessly explained, tirelessly showed us our illusions, tirelessly pointed the way – yet so subtly that if one was not ready to understand, his lessons could pass one by, and it was only years later that one might remember the incident, and realise what he had been demonstrating.' (ibid.)

Collin adds that Ouspensky never worked for the moment, only for recurrence.

All the same, Ouspensky knew that *time was a factor* in planning how to address the growing number of groups. In

September 1937 he spoke to the Lyne group about the Society and 'what you call expansion' of the teaching, mainly because he saw they did not know how these things should be organised. Previously, he said, he knew people in the group personally but with six hundred members expected to join in the next couple of years that would be impossible. Even with only ten groups of thirty each they would need a house with a number of rooms 'because, if they meet in different places, in private houses, it is not the same thing'. To save his repeating the same talk to a number of groups, they also needed a larger meeting room.

'This is connected with the idea of Society,' he said. 'Also, a name is necessary. On the technical side, the formation of the Society is finished. At a certain moment it is necessary to register it. . . . Running or buying a house needs money, and at present, with the means we have, we can only exist as we are. We are short of money. . .'

Ouspensky said he had decided to make an experiment in raising money, explaining:

'I have certain books I want to publish: one novel, a new edition of *Tertium Organum*, maybe some lectures. But that will take time. . . in three years' time we shall have the *New Model* in our hands – until then it is in the hands of the publishers, and it is not satisfactory; in many places it cannot be found and it is too little known. It would be useful to publish a cheap edition of it, and then it may sell very well. In Russia I published all my books myself and had quite a good income from them. . . . The novel is connected with the idea of Eternal Recurrence. Some of you may have read it. It needs time to prepare it for publication. First I must go through the Russian text (for it was written and published in Russian long ago) and then through the translation and work on the translation takes a great deal of time. Then these lectures may be rewritten, and may be published. Then I have for a long time wanted to bring *Tertium Organum* up to date, to connect it with the New Model – at present some of the terminology is different. . . . All this I can do only if I have more time. So you must not expect me to give so much time to these lectures. I will come when I can, from time to time, but not to every meeting. . . so you must be able to go on and do your own work and the work you can do for other people and for the school, and you must try to understand why this is necessary. If books are published and are successful, all our problems are solved' *(A Record of Meetings 1930-1947*, pp. 126-7).

One man protested that it was 'asking too much of Mr Ouspensky that the development of the Society should depend on profits derived from the sale of his books. It is more up to us than up to him to provide funds for the expansion, since the Society is for our benefit'.

Ouspensky did not disagree, but pointed out that 'if we do it in the right way, we will have quite a good income from publishing'.

Later in the same month, a woman said during a meeting at Lyne: 'To know people better one must do practical work together, not only talk. Can Lyne be made bigger?'

Ouspensky replied that Lyne could not grow physically. 'Now the order of the day is the Society and a house in London. When this is organised then perhaps we can think of how we can make Lyne grow.'

He told another questioner: 'I do not want to organise a search for a house yet, but everyone must know what we need – some kind of big studio or room, or hall, big enough for two hundred people, and then several rooms for groups.'

What, a woman asked, was the difference between the present and the proposed groups. Ouspensky replied:

'These are not groups: these are lectures. Groups should be, first of all, much smaller; maxium thirty people, better less. And sometimes (I do not say necessarily always) a group must be selected in a special way. It wants a variety of types. If all people are of the same type, then it will not work. Then special tasks are given, one to one group, another to another' (ibid., p. 130).

The so-called expansion did not mean that Ouspensky was widening, or diluting, his original perception of the principles set by Gurdjieff. These standards applied to the kind of people he accepted into the groups. For example, in October 1935 Gurdjieff had sent one of his pupils, Jane Heap, a well-known American writer, to London to work with English pupils of the Work. She asked to join one of the Ouspensky groups, but he rejected her request, almost certainly because she was a lesbian.

He would seem to have had some authority for this, having quoted Gurdjieff as saying that 'only a person who is completely normal as regards sex has any chance in the work' (*In Search of the Miraculous*, pp. 256-7). It seems that he stuck strictly to that judgment. Gurdjieff's own association with several lesbian women writers in Paris conceivably indicated that he was not to be held hidebound to statements he had made earlier in a particular context, a stipulation that Ouspensky himself frequently declared in reference to his own pronouncements.

It seems more than a coincidence that, a few days after this rejection of Jane Heap, Gurdjieff formed several lesbians living in Paris – Solita Solano, Kathryn Hulme and Louise Davidson, initially – into a Work group which called itself the Rope. Its title was a reminder that, like mountaineers climbing a hazardous slope, they were interdependently bound to a rope, which afforded security and assistance but also restricted their movements. The 'rope' is a reminder of one of The Fourth Way principles stressed by Ouspensky, that it is necessary for a teacher to bring a certain number of pupils up to his own level before he may ascend higher.

In London, the expansion gathered pace in 1938 when the group acquired a larger house, in Colet Gardens, West Kensington, with a studio that could hold more than 300 people, to cater for the influx of Fourth Way aspirants and prepare them for practical work under Madame at Lyne Place.

This was accompanied by the formation of the Historico-Psychological Society, which gave the group an outer form, with a title to allay any suspicions by people, particularly the powers-that-be, of an otherwise mysterious assembly; a title also that would attract few people not specifically directed to the group.

Mme Ouspensky, accustomed to Gurdjieff's more informal technique, might have been expected to treat the Society's pompous title and articles of association with a modicum of levity. In the event, she subjected them to outright ridicule. Ouspensky

'was sitting at one end of the long tea table, Madame at the other. As he read Madame began to laugh. She laughed till she wept, dabbing her eyes with a tiny lace handkerchief. She always laughed a great deal, but that afternoon I thought she would never stop. Poor Ouspensky was embarrassed. He took his society seriously and could not understand why she found it so funny' (*Warrior's Way*, p. 109).

The speaker, Robert de Ropp, comments that later he understood her merriment:

'We completely failed to realise that so far as knowledge was concerned, we already had more than enough. What we had to learn was how to put that knowledge into practice. . . . All the necessary conditions for work on Being were right there at Lyne Place. . .' (ibid.)

His opinion of Madame concurred with that of John Bennett: 'Madame Ouspensky was one of the most formidable Warriors I met during my journey through time. I established with her a strong *guru/chela* relationship.'

At first hearing, the objectives drawn up by Ouspensky do sound academically smug, but a closer study leaves little doubt that they are aimed at the transformation of man's psychology. He set the following aims for the Society's operation:

1. *The study of problems of the evolution of man and particularly of the idea of psycho-transformism.* An outsider's eyes might well glaze at the pseudo-scientific sound of this declaration of intent. But for people in the know it signified the core of the Work: first to study the in-built barriers to man's true, not Darwinian, evolution – that is to say, regeneration. Then to find ways of overcoming those obstacles and of transforming oneself.

2. *The study of psychological schools in different historical periods and in different countries, and the study of their influence on the moral and intellectual development of humanity*. Schools in this context would be taken in a vague, general way by the public. The word 'moral' also would have a personal meaning only for those not in the Work, which is concerned with conscience, not any arbitrary morality. Those with knowledge of the teaching might note the implication that psychological schools have existed historically and are not a modern invention.

3. *Practical investigation of methods of self-study and self-development according to principles and methods of psychological schools*. The repetition of 'psychological schools' underlines the society's actual purpose, and emphasises that for a person entering The Fourth Way self-study, knowing oneself, leads to practical work on themselves.

4. *Research work in the history of religions, of philosophy, of science, and of art with the object of establishing their common origin when it can be found and different psychological levels in each of them*. There is a reminder here of Ouspensky's contention even before meeting Gurdjieff that a true application of science must include an appreciation of human psychology. It is easier for the layman to see how this applies also to religion, philosophy and art. Both Work people and outsiders might find the suggestion of a common origin interesting.

The emphasis on finding a School gives the clue to Madame's hilarity, if one considers laughter to be the physical expression of a reconciliation of mentally or emotionally perceived opposites. It may have been triggered by the spectacle of Ouspensky, who counselled others about the danger of taking things too seriously, proposing something of such a portentous nature. However, the main incongruity was provided by this so-serious gathering dreaming of searching for a real School when already in their own selves was the beginnings of that very sort of School, which Madame was trying to lead them to recognise and which de Ropp obviously came to realise.

Further to guideline 4, Ouspensky told one meeting:

'I spoke about modern scientific ideas coming nearer to the ideas of the System. For some people it may be strange why we speak about the origin of worlds. But people cannot help thinking it in one or another way, and it is better to have right ideas about it than quite wrong ideas. It is interesting that, although modern psychology recedes further and further from the ideas of the System, physics comes nearer.'

After an article on 'the expanding universe' was read at the meeting, Ouspensky commented:

'What is interesting is that it is almost the same as the origin of the worlds in this System. The whole explodes and each subsequent unit explodes and produces smaller and smaller worlds. Also this idea of finite but limitless universe – it existed thousands of years ago in teachings similar to this System' (*A Record of Meetings 1930-1947*, pp. 86-7).

The reading could also be meant to show people that the principle 'as above so below' reveals among other things that cosmological and self studies go hand in hand.

At another meeting, in September 1935, Ouspensky told a person who asked whether much more effort was needed on the psychological side of the Work: 'It is all psychological.'

A man asked: "Is it against School if one tries to study other systems?'

'It depends what system,' Ouspensky answered. 'Mathematics is harmless, study of astrology is stupid.'

His questioner specified: 'Systems that increase our knowledge.'

'If you run after two hares, you lose both,' said Ouspensky.

While he spoke now to a wider audience, Ouspensky did not drop all his safeguards aimed at preserving the purity of the teaching. With the relaxation of some of the secrecy, he was asked more frequently whether both humanity and School would not benefit if the System were presented to the general public. He answered one such question in October, 1937:

'It will happen by itself. There is no need for us to worry about it. Ideas will spread, maybe in our lifetime and maybe after us. Most of these ideas will enter into scientific or philosophical language, but they will enter in the wrong form. There will be no right distinction between doing and happening, and many thoughts of ordinary thinking will be mixed with these ideas; so they will not be ideas we know now, only words will be similar. If you don't understand this, you will lose in this way' (*Remembering Pyotr Demianovich Ouspensky*, p. 36).

Another sign that Ouspensky resisted exposing the System to the general public – or even a theatre audience – emerged from his attitude to playwright J.B. Priestley's time plays. The dramatist, recognised as a commonsense spokesman for the common man, acknowledged after performances of his *Time and the Conways* and *I Have Been Here Before* in the 1930s that he had 'borrowed' the ideas of recurrence and parallel times from Ouspensky and psychologist J.W. Dunne.

Ouspensky may not have regarded this as much of a tribute when Priestley added that he himself did not believe in those ideas, possibly making it appear that they were used in the stage thrillers merely to captivate the audience with the mystery of time's dimensions and the chance of freeing oneself from the consequences of past mistakes in repeating life cycles.

At any rate, he refused the playwright's attempts to meet him. Ouspensky's pupil Maurice Nicoll, on the other hand, tried to enlist Priestley's creative talent to popularize the idea of inner travel to different parts of one's time-body.

In her biography Beryl Pogson reveals that during the years his group was based at Great Amwell House (1946-53) Dr Nicoll had practised 'being conscious in different points of his life'. This led him to write to Priestley:

'Now, could you write a play of a man, say of sixty, visiting 'himself' as he was (say) a lad of twenty at Cambridge and seeing what he could advise this lad to do? To move through "Time-body" was one of the exercises I was taught by Gurdjieff. Only you, with your fine dramatic sense, could do this play (*Maurice Nicoll: A Portrait*, p. 252).

That idea was not taken up. Still, members of the Nicoll group appreciated the time plays.

Ouspensky, though, perhaps suspected that if Work ideas – not that 'recurrence' was explicitly sanctioned – proved a profitable source of entertainment they would soon be distorted to suit inappropriate scripts and programs. Such a presentiment appears justified if applied to the comparatively recent adaptation of the enneagram to various popular purposes.

Ouspensky is reported to have told a group in October 1937:

'When I met Gurdjieff I began to work with him on the basis of certain principles which I could understand and accept. He said: "First of all you must not believe anything and, second, you must not do anything you don't understand." I accepted him because of that. Then after two or three years I saw him going against these principles. He demanded from people to accept what they did not believe and to do what they did not understand. Why this happened I don't pretend to offer any theory' (*Remembering Pyotr Demianovich Ouspensky*, p. 30).

In November 1937, Ouspensky spoke more appreciatively of his teacher, when he told a meeting:

'Gurdjieff gave me many new ideas I did not know before, and he gave a System I did not know before. About Schools I did know for I had been travelling and looking for Schools for ten years. He had an extraordinary System, and quite new. Some separate fragments of it could be found elsewhere, but not connected and put together like they are in this System. And certain things, particularly belonging to the psychological side, were quite a revelation. And also on many other lines. This was sufficient proof for me that this System was not a thing one can meet with every day. And I had already met with a sufficient number of Schools to be able to judge' (ibid., p. 31).

This is a significantly different way of evaluating Gurdjieff's 'fragments' of esoteric knowledge. Here Ouspensky says that others throughout history had managed to gain fragments but, at least in comparison with that, Gurdjieff had it all together.

Well, he could afford to give Gurdjieff the recognition due to him. In contrast to the difficulties his former teacher was experiencing in France and America, Ouspensky in the late

1930s was living through the most satisfying period of his life. He could ride through the pleasant grounds of Lyne Place daily on one of his horses (seated on his favourite Cossack saddle, which had been presented by a pupil), read or write in his study, organise his presentation of the System – all the while feeling relaxed in the awareness that Madame was capably marshalling the troops for practical work on the farm, assiduously pointing out the regrettable features of their Personalities.

Apart from the tardiness of the Higher Source in opening communication, the only dark cloud was Mme Ouspensky's increasingly frequent confinement to bed. Ouspensky 'discussed her illness with a psychiatrist pupil and both concluded that the cause was a form of neurasthenia' (*The Harmonious Circle*, p. 411).

In May 1939 Stanley Nott tried to gain Gurdjieff's help in combating her ailment, identified by some commentators as Parkinson's disease. Nott had been surprised when one of Ouspensky's senior pupils, pledging him to secrecy, confided that he believed Gurdjieff was the only man who could do anything for her but feared 'he is not the man he was'. Nott retorted 'he is even much more so. He also is perfecting himself and is doing it in his own way. Not only is he not mad as some of you seem to think, on the contrary his is absolute sanity – the sanity of objective reason' (*Journey Through This World*, p. 122).

In Paris, Nott asked Gurdjieff if he would come to England if it could be arranged and see Madame. 'If possible I will come. But she also must make effort.' However, 'a few days before his expected arrival in London war broke out. . . . Madame Ouspensky slowly got better and later was able to go to America' (ibid., p. 123).

James Moore has a blunter explanation for Gurdjieff's failure to return to England. He writes of Ouspensky:

'Twice before he had seen Gurdjieff sweep in and capture virtually his entire flock. This time he retired behind a Maginot Line of prior engagements . . . In its own minor key,

Ouspensky's manoeuvring to frustrate Gurdjieff's reception at Lyne echoed the diplomatic frenzy to restrain Adolf Hitler' (*Gurdjieff: The Anatomy of a Myth*, p. 270).

Earlier, in the spring of 1939, Ouspensky had spoken again to a few pupils of his 'fading hope of making contact with the source of Gurdjieff's ideas'. In response to this, John Bennett wrote to the Bash Chelebi, hereditary chief of the Mevlevi Dervish Order, then in exile at Aleppo, Syria, and was invited to visit him. 'When I told Ouspensky he was delighted. He borrowed the letter and showed it to the people at Lyne,' says Bennett (*Witness*, p. 185).

Again, World War II intervened, preventing Bennett's trip to Syria, but anecdotes like this leave little doubt that Ouspensky genuinely hoped to contact an esoteric School.

In October 1938, after a meeting between Britain's Neville Chamberlain and Germany's Adolf Hitler had postponed war, Ouspensky spoke about the future of the Work, his words carrying an undertone of imminent and dramatic change. He reminded his groups that the chief point is understanding – 'understanding of the Work, of the necessity of work, of the general plan of the Work'. Interest in that, he said, is obligatory. One must follow three lines of study: of oneself, of the universe, of Schools (*Remembering Pyotr Demianovich Ouspensky*, Epilogue).

Intriguingly, he said that 'work is a particular phenomenon in life, and it becomes less and less'. On that, he commented that 'one of the aims of School is to find a School'. This was because usually 'schools which can have a future began with little material, not with a definite connection with another school . . .'

Ouspensky warned that if one avoided one's share in this Work 'then one loses everything, or in any case one cannot acquire anything more'. He quoted a Russian proverb: 'If you like coasting downhill, you must like pulling the toboggan uphill.'

This gave notice of harder times ahead. He concluded: 'Try to think that I may go away and the Work, as it is now, may disappear. Look at it from this point of view, do not take it as a permanent institution' (ibid.).

Chapter 16

TRANSATLANTIC TRANSMISSION

BACK IN 1922, OUSPENSKY had considered moving to America if Gurdjieff established his Institute for the Harmonious Development of Man in England. As events transpired, or conspired, it was the Nazis' threat of crossing the Channel that finally sent him across the Atlantic. Ouspensky believed Germany would win its bid for hegemony of Europe, and that this would instigate a Communist revolution that would engulf Britain.

Evidently he had not forgotten the Russian Revolution, nor had events changed his view of the unhealthy mix of German, Russian and Communist politics. In his 1919 articles from Russia he argued that the catastrophe known as Bolshevism was 'made in Germany'. He had reported:

'Employing Bolshevism in 1917 to break up the Russian Army, Germany destroyed the danger menacing her Eastern front. You [the British] were in great peril, and you know it. But now you have decided the peril is gone, and you are mistaken. Germany is not annihilated or even weakened. She is energetically and cleverly preparing a revanche. Her chief enemy is England, and the chief trump card in her pack is Russian Bolshevism' (*Letters From Russia 1919*, Letter II, p. 16).

At any rate, even without invading Communists wiping out the intelligentsia and all cultural values, England's own military and industrial conscription made it difficult for Work groups to function there in an organised manner.

He was possibly struck by the similarity of his situation in 1940 with those in St Petersburg in 1917 and Essentuki in 1918-19 when, until almost too late, he had postponed moving to a safer place because he did not want to curtail his association with Gurdjieff. As early as 1936, Gerald Heard, writer on subjects scientific and religious, and Aldous Huxley, satirical novelist, essayist and author of *The Perennial Philosophy* and *The Doors of Perception*, had urged Ouspensky to follow their example and escape from England while the 'going' was good. They, too, thought America would stand clear of the coming 'dark age'.

Robert de Ropp reports that the two writers were invited to Lyne Place after he had persuaded them to attend the Colet Gardens lectures. Ouspensky enjoyed his first meeting in England with 'what we in Russia called intelligentsia' (*Warrior's Way*, p. 98). Apparently what he principally enjoyed was their confirmation of his low opinion of such intellectuals' ability to deal with practical matters. Similarly, de Ropp derided 'Heard's idea that by exerting "soul force" through meditation one might be able to influence the dictators'.

Madame also shared this view of intellectuals, as became evident one hot August day after she had directed very strenuous work harvesting with scythes and sickles on the farm at Lyne Place. Ouspensky 'had trotted up on the small horse he used for riding around the estate . . . "Now you can understand," he said, "why Russian word for harvest same as for suffering" ' (ibid., pp. 110-1). Madame used such hard labour to undress the False Personality. On this occasion she remarked that de Ropp, usually 'full of self-importance, like bishop' was now 'man after hard day's work, like peasant'. She asked de Ropp why his friends Heard and Huxley were absent; he suggested they might not like hard work. ' "They intelligentsia," said Madame Ouspensky, as if that explained everything' (ibid., p. 113).

An air-raid warning shortly before noon on Sunday, 3 September 1939, alerted people at Lyne Place to the outbreak of hostilities. Adults and children hurried down to a basement room that had been prepared as an air-raid shelter. Food stores had been built up so that evacuees from London could find refuge at Virginia Water. Madame did not intend to endure again the sparse diet that remained vivid in her memories of their ordeal when the Gurdjieff group holed up in the Caucasus mountains. To supplement the larder, members of the group operated a fruit drier to hoard a large supply of apples.

Nick Roles records that at the outbreak of war Lyne Place became home for several families of group members.

'We children were allotted a large playroom with a piano and were allowed to roam freely over the property with the exception of the two ends of the large house – Mr Ouspensky's end where his green drawing room looked out on to the gardens, and Mme Ouspensky's apartments at the opposite end above the large dining room where the adults ate in silence. . . . Mr Ouspensky loved cats and I remember a very handsome orange Persian called Chijck and also a very large Irish setter called Spark who terrified us. Then there was Mr Ouspensky's horse Suzette and two cart-horses, Bess and Blossom, the former a vicious animal with a nasty bite but the latter a gentle creature with huge hairy fetlocks. There was a herd of cows and a flock of sheep. . . There was a row of pigsties with occupants and three or four ferret hutches whose inmates we used to tease, trying not to get bitten in the process. There were free-range chickens and turkeys. I remember the turkey cocks as very frightening. Miss Ripman, whose job it was to feed them, had her skirt torn off. There was a small spinney not far from the house with five or six beehives looked after by Roger Nickalls. I well remember him staggering up the drive and collapsing, having been severely stung while collecting honey. It took him several days to recover. The lake and ravine in the grounds were our favourite haunts. The lake contained perch, roach and enormous carp . . . I remember Mr Ouspensky as a short, stocky, near-sighted man with pince-nez. . . . He was always kind to us children, but I remember being frightened of him. He spoke in broken English, rather abruptly but not unkindly. My memories of Mme Ouspensky are of her lying in a huge bed propped up with pillows . . .' (*The Bridge*, No.12, pp. 113-4).

In this tense period there was no telegram from Gurdjieff to come and 'rest', which had been the signal to quit St Petersburg. In 1939, Ouspensky had no way of knowing that his old teacher would sit out the German occupation of Paris, even continuing to lead a group of forty or more, and assist

Jewish members, no doubt engaging in some expedient wheeling and dealing with the conquerors. (A magistrate dismissed currency charges against him after the liberation.)

Ouspensky once again had time to debate whether he had left it too late to flee should that seem necessary. Against that, presumably, he would take into account that Lyne Place had been built as an ark – primarily as a means of preserving esoteric ideas against an assault by cultural barbarism, it is true, but now extending to the physical danger of a threatened blitzkrieg.

The 'phony war' period added to the uncertainty. Suspected German bombers seen in the distance from Lyne during one early mistaken air-raid alarm proved to be barrage balloons glinting silver in the sun over London. De Ropp records a later, deadly episode during bombing of the London docks that throws light on Ouspensky's thoughts:

'We stood on the roof of Lyne Place looking towards the city. The entire sky was lit up, a vast crimson backdrop. Streams of tracer bullets rose like flights of red birds. Searchlights combed the sky, which constantly sparkled with bursting shells. Every now and then huge explosions added fresh splashes of light on the infernal scene. . . .

'Ouspensky watched the fiery sky and shook his head. He was obsessed with the idea that he had lived before, had been endlessly recycled along the curve of eternal recurrence. He was always trying to remember events before they happened. But he shook his head over the Great Fire of London. 'This I cannot remember,' he muttered. 'This I cannot remember' (*Warrior's Way*, p. 138).

His perplexity is understandable. In the ordinary way of thinking, such a spectacle would seem certain to stick in the memory of a man putting his best effort into Self-remembering. Maybe its non-recall caused Ouspensky to consider whether the criminal act of war, possibly an accidental result of planetary influences, warranted a place in his Work memory, despite its effect on the course of his life.

Perhaps it even gave him pause to reflect whether he had

escaped the war earlier in previous existences. But this would have been mere speculation, because he later found other gaps in his 'memory' of the war. Stanley Nott recalls:

'When the news was announced that Germany had invaded Russia I happened to be with Ouspensky. He was shocked and astonished. 'It's incredible!' he said. 'How can it have happened? It does not seem possible!' (*Journey Through This World*, p. 165)

Nott reminded him that he had written in *A New Model of the Universe* that 'this kind of situation must occur' because great empires eventually turn on each other.

The shocks of the Battle of Britain were very nearly matched in the minds of many group members by the Ouspenskys' decision to flee to the United States. The effect varied from person to person. When Madame sailed on 4 January 1941, one member noted that the dismay evidently felt by many of her pupils was hardly evidence that years of 'work' had developed an inner self that could cope with any emergency.

She had told her pupils the previous October that it would be necessary for her to leave them. Those who remained would be responsible for continuing the Work at Lyne. At first she had thought they would be able to escape as a group but now that was impossible. There would be difficulties, she said, both for those who stayed and those who left (*Talks by Madame Ouspensky*, pp. 6-7).

These conditions, de Ropp thought, 'should have been perfect for what Ouspensky called intensive work' to break the bonds of mechanicalness. So when Ouspensky left to follow Madame to America on January 29, even the strong-minded de Ropp vented 'an outburst of righteous indignation'. He admits having been prone to such a psychological weakness, but his reaction was probably shared by others.

'The indignation remained unspoken, for so brainwashed were we and so accustomed to the authoritarianism of the Ouspenskys that we dared not criticise them openly. . . . I simply could not accept the idea that the Leader of the Work would abandon us at that point. It was true that, in the winter of 1940-41, the outlook did seem bleak. . . . Was it really right for the Ouspenskys to desert their followers, who had, after all, provided them with every creature comfort?' (*Warrior's Way*, pp. 138-9)

De Ropp, as it happened, was not one of the more affluent members, some of whom were able to respond differently to the departure, accepting Ouspensky's invitation to join him in America. Most of the remaining senior members treated their leader's absence – a temporary one, they believed – as a challenge, for he had entrusted them with continuing the teaching at Lyne. The ark would stay above the flood in the captain's absence.

John Bennett, still a stickler for the St Petersburg rules despite being the most intellectually versatile member of Ouspensky's circle, sought and received, sort of, the master's permission to 'write out the System as far as I can remember it'. However, he found Ouspensky's reply disheartening:

'In my opinion, writing is not useful. Mental recapitulation is better. In any case, the System cannot be written in ordinary form. If you do write, it can only be to convince yourself that it is impossible (*Witness* p. 186).

At this last meeting between the two men, all that Ouspensky could or would say about his plans was that he had considered only the work at Lyne. 'The rest, so far as I am concerned, is dissolved. I have given my instructions for continuing the work at Lyne as long as possible.'

Those instructions were directed at a nucleus of advanced pupils. Ouspensky also left a program of work for all members of the group. Based on a four-day rota, it divided the day into four or five hour intervals. At the start of each period, say at 9 a.m., 1 p.m., 6 p.m. and 10 p.m., the instruction was always: Remember Yourself (five minutes, never more). What varied was the activity that followed, also for a maximum of five minutes. The successive daily tasks, in addition to Self-remembering, were:

'First day: 1 (9 a.m.), Try to revise in your memory why you came to the Work. 2 (1 p.m.), Try to revise in your memory what you want to get through the Work and why. 3 (6 p.m.), Try to realise that ordinarily in life you identify with everything that interests you. 4 (10 p.m.), Try to understand that you can be interested in things without being identified with them.

Second day: 1, Try to understand that there are two ways of not identifying. First is to think about ideas of the system like laws of three and seven, diagrams, centres, etc. Second is to think about anything, remembering yourself all the time. 2, Think about three lines of work. 3, Think about man as a machine. 4, Think about sleeping men.

Third day: 1, Think about formatory apparatus. 2, Think about problems insoluble for our mind. 3, Think about consciousness and about relation of states of consciousness to functions. 4, Think about conscience. Why we cannot feel all our emotions at the same time.

Fourth day: 1, Think about your present state of consciousness and the rarity of glimpses of the third state of consciousness. 2, Think about negative emotions and right attitudes as a weapon against them. 3, Try to realise that all causes of your negative emotions are in you. 4, Think about imagination. Try to realise how many imaginary things are in your thinking, in your emotions and in your decisions.'

Ouspensky said in a footnote that Self-remembering could always be replaced by 'stopping thoughts'.

The attempt to stop thoughts was a regular exercise in Ouspensky's groups, but it may still have caused some confusion among the pupils left in England. Earlier, when one member questioned Maurice Nicoll about this practice he said he could not do it, and believed Ouspensky had recommended they try it only so they could prove this inability for themselves. (See also *Psychological Commentaries*, vol. 5, p. 1518.)

A more extreme view was formed years later by one of Ouspensky's successors as a Fourth Way leader, Dr Francis Roles. After he had shifted the emphasis of his group's work towards a form of meditation, Roles said in a lecture: 'Mr

Ouspensky did go wrong when he advised us to stop thoughts' (*Way of Liberation*, p.12).

But, by coupling 'stopping thoughts' with the vitally important exercise of 'Self-remembering' in his daily Work list, Ouspensky made it clear that he meant what he said. To gain an idea of just what he did mean, first it has to be remembered that Self-remembering is 'a method of inducing Self-consciousness'. He taught that as we are we can't work on consciousness but we *can* make efforts to control our thoughts. No one could believe Ouspensky was against thinking *per se*, for he also explained that people can begin to remember themselves by forming mental processes in a certain way. (It may tell us something about the usual level of Being that, having a shrewd idea of the quality of people's usual thoughts, he recommended stopping them.)

Again, Ouspensky pointed out that we had to do more than just think about things. When someone once asked whether people in the Work should meditate, he pretended he did not know the term, adding that if he thought the System needed any new words he would introduce them himself. (He persistently urged people to describe their experiences in their own words, but stamped on borrowings from other philosophical or psychological systems, which might have unhelpful connotations.)

Madame Ouspensky insisted that The Fourth Way was hard 'and could not be achieved by sitting around meditating which she said was a useless practice.

'"You meditate," she said, "stare at wall. Soon you see things – angels, devils, anything. All imagination. Must work" ' (*Ouspensky: the Unsung Genius*, p. 92).

A clue to what Ouspensky meant by stopping thoughts is given in this advice which he sometimes offered: 'We can eliminate useless thoughts and we can also put in the centre of our thinking the realisation of "I am" – "I am here", "I am thinking." '

It is the 'constant turning of thoughts' that prevent Self-remembering, and can be halted. He also pointed out that 'thinking of nothing' will not produce Self-remembering in a person who knows nothing about Self-remembering. Practice without theory does not work any better than theory without practice (see *The Fourth Way*, p. 116).

This latter point is worth noting, seeing that Ouspensky is sometimes imagined to have been sorely lacking in both practicality and emotions. In fact, he made his students aware that an emotional shock could produce Self-remembering without any theory – but in the usual conditions we forget to do it. He stressed that not just the intellectual and emotional functions are needed for a person to Self-remember, but all the centres. 'You may begin with two centres, but it is not sufficient, because other centres can interrupt your self-remembering and stop it. But if you put all centres to the work there is nothing that can stop it' (ibid.).

He recommended the detailed program above to his pupils because efforts to Self-remember had to be regular, 'if possible at the same times of the day'. He maintained that the stopping of thoughts – except for the one thought, 'I will stop thoughts' – would produce the same results as the effort to Self-remember. But it was not easy, and must not be practised for a long duration or one would begin imagining results. As well as thinking just one thought, one had of course to remember one's aim, to Self-remember.

After the circulation of that work list, it was farewell to Colet Gardens. Despite Ouspensky's earlier caution that the Work was not a fixed institution, he left widespread desolation and confusion in his wake.

While de Ropp had his reservations on the question of loyalty, no one would have accused the Ouspenskys of cowardice; they had proved their high tolerance to hardship in the previous world war. The deciding factor, as Bennett notes, was that Ouspensky believed a German victory would be the prelude to revolution and a Communist take-over of Europe, leaving an 'aloof' America as the likeliest accessible country where conditions could be found to nurture the Work (*Witness*, p. 186).

However, while the ark of Lyne rode out the storm that battered Europe, Ouspensky's reputation as a teacher barely remained afloat in his American refuge. At least, that is a widely accepted view. De Ropp, whose job took him to the United States, found a few of Ouspensky's lectures in New York so boring that he refused to attend any more (*Warrior's Way*, p. 170).

However, for others on whose ears the Work message fell as unexpectedly good news, the perception was entirely positive. One of these was Irmis Barret Popoff, who met Ouspensky at a reception held for him in New York in March 1941, when he answered questions after his step-grandson, Lonya Savitsky, had read out passages from the introductory lectures. She was struck first of all by the significant distinction Ouspensky made between psychological systems 'that took man as he is, or as he is supposed to be, and those that study man from the point of view of what he may become (*Gurdjieff: His Work on Myself... With Others... for the Work*, p.15).

To the irony that writers introduced by de Ropp first suggested that Ouspensky move to America can be added the fact that he also brought to the teaching Rodney Collin, whose wealthy wife, Janet, helped their teacher get started in the USA.

Mme Ouspensky stayed at first with some American pupils in Rumson, New Jersey, where she was visited by Stanley Nott, who reported her health seemed improved by the change. Then it seemed as though Lyne Place was being reborn on the other side of the Atlantic. A large, grey-granite house, formerly a state governor's mansion, and its 300-acre property, Franklin Farms, near Mendham, New Jersey, was put at their disposal for practical group work. Madame was again in charge. Although he had an office at Franklin Farms, Ouspensky concentrated on lecturing in New York which, as already indicated, generated both grateful response and bored reaction.

Nott as well as de Ropp found his talks dull, but they had established reasons, justified or not, to be critical. More to the point, the stern, authoritative teacher made no concessions to Orage's former pupils, who were accustomed to a more emotive rendering of Work ideas, with the result many typecast him as a professor rather than a fount of esoteric wisdom.

Ouspensky felt obliged to continue the expansion program begun in England with public lectures, but when the US entered the war in 1941 people had other issues to distract them from instruction about the battle between inner and outer man.

After the first flush of enthusiasm, Madame enjoyed no greater success on the farm. Soon, she withdrew to her sickbed and communicated with her pupils through messages, frequently scathing, passed on by two generally unloved intermediaries, dubbed by de Ropp 'Brother Archangel' and 'Sister Archangel'.

De Ropp also notes that the debilitating US east coast climate had 'a disastrous effect on both my teachers'. Both the Ouspenskys had 'the pale flabby faces of those who spend too much time indoors, who eat food not suited to the needs of their bodies, who get far too little exercise,' he says (*Warrior's Way*, p. 170). He adds that Ouspensky 'was quite obviously ill, drinking far too much, and still wandering in imagination through the streets of Moscow and Petersburg'; and 'his paranoid tendencies had become more pronounced. He was apt, at the slightest provocation, to throw people out of the Work. One of his oldest pupils, J.G. Bennett, was excommunicated, along with all the people who studied with him' (ibid.).

This latest rebuff followed a series of public lectures on the System that Bennett gave in London in the spring of 1945. When several Americans in his group were returning home, he gave them letters of introduction to Ouspensky.

'They must have given him very garbled accounts of what I was doing in London,' Bennett says in *Witness* (p. 214). 'Only much later did I learn that they had supposed that the lectures I was giving were copied from Ouspensky's lectures given before the war.'

Despite feeling bitter, Bennett resolved not to justify himself although 'I did not enjoy reading out to my group the letter [from Ouspensky's solicitor] in which I was described as a charlatan and a thief.'

He recalled, probably with fresh mentation on the meaning, that Ouspensky had once told him, on a night when he felt he had discovered a real part of himself: 'You are like Madame. Both of you have young souls. You have not the experience of living many times on this earth.'

Although he does not state as much, it seems likely that it was this type of premonition of recurrence that persuaded Bennett of the close biographical nature of *Strange Life of Ivan Osokin*, including a belief that Ouspensky had committed suicide in a previous life (*Witness*, p. 215).

One of Nott's anecdotes suggests that, never mind previous lives, Ouspensky was treading a dangerous path in the present one. Not long after Ouspensky arrived in America,

'I felt that he was a sick man, suffering from the weaknesses and lawful infirmities of old age, as well as from some specific disease [kidney], and he was drinking strong concoctions that I could not take. 'You must have a stomach of iron,' I said one day when he offered me one of them. 'It's too strong for me.'

He said, 'It's the only thing that relieves the boredom and depression that comes over me at times' (*Journey Through This World*, 161).

On the positive side, Irmis Popoff, as already indicated, saw Ouspensky in a different light. After hearing his first lecture in New York,

'I walked out of Mr Ouspensky's apartment feeling that I carried within myself a hallowed cathedral, and the services that would charge it with life, music, and meaning were about to begin' (*Gurdjieff . . .* , p. 18).

Obviously, the lecturer's words must have met an emotional response in Miss Popoff. This could indicate that those who found his talks 'coldly intellectual' were not receiving his message on the appropriate part of their psyche. When he turned his Russian 'deaf' ear to formatory questions, she thought him 'superb in his silence', but others were offended when he refused to spoon-feed them answers that they, he probably considered, could work out for themselves.

Miss Popoff says it became apparent that many in the audience imagined 'change of Being' involved supernormal faculties, like 'astral travelling' or acquiring a 'third eye'. Ouspensky simply pointed out that these attributes might belong to men of a higher category but as he was not one he could not speak of them. Ordinary men must work very hard to develop the powers they imagine they already have – consciousness, will and the power to do.

Told by one indignant person that 'there are groups where intelligent people are taught to develop these powers that you say we do not have', Ouspensky replied, 'Good. No reason why you should not join them. Maybe better suited to your taste' (ibid., p. 25). Miss Popoff says that while she thought this logical, many felt rebuffed and left 'giving no further thought to the work that he invited them to do in the inner kingdom that was their self'.

She remembered what he considered the most important point: the realisation 'that we never knew about self-remembering and now we do know'. She gives this testimonial to Ouspensky's teaching:

'System ideas were like manna from heaven for me: they fed my hunger for understanding, and things that had puzzled me, things that I had learned without digesting, that I had heard without listening, that I had seen without taking them in, all began to unfold within me as I comprehended their meaning. I pondered over System diagrams and System concepts and had unexpected flashes that showed me the relationship, the meaning of words, of whole sentences, of symbols, which I had until now used and talked about without knowing in the least what they really meant. Even old fairytales became eloquent in association with these new ideas that served as fuel for the new, wonderful trips that I was taking into the realm of my unexplored mind' (ibid., pp. 29-30).

Hearing this, some critics of her teacher may argue, inconsistently, that Mrs Popoff was being over-emotional. Ah well, if the lectures attracted a few pupils who responded with this type of feeling, what does it count in the final analysis if a greater number took umbrage and a walk?

Ouspensky comes highly recommended also from a successful businessman, publisher and artist, William Segal, who met him at the start of his New York visit. He was attracted mainly by Ouspensky's talks:

'There would be an average of thirty-five people in each of these weekly lectures which were wonderful because he didn't broach anything that was of a low quality or a low nature. He wouldn't permit any question unless it made sense. He was very near-sighted and held a book close to his eyes. Someone would ask a question, he would say, 'Who said that?' Someone asked another question, 'Next' . . . 'No good.' He dismissed them just like that. You had to be on your toes and you had to formulate a real question before you would get an answer.
Some subjects aroused a great deal of interest on the part of Mr Ouspensky. Time and relationship between different universes. I would ask a question about time, and then he would go off . . . "Time is the unique subjective" ' (*A Voice at the Borders of Silence*, p. 60).

(Did Ouspensky give the impression he had not read *Beelzebub's Tales*? This 'unique subjective' description suggests he at least reached page 124. Maybe, though, Gurdjieff had referred to the 'Ideally-Unique-Subjective-Phenomenon' earlier. Or perhaps Segal was confused about where he had first learned of the unique subjective.)

Segal says he often visited Ouspensky at Franklin Farms in the middle of the afternoon when no one else was present.

'We would talk. I remember Mrs [Jessmin] Howarth would come in, she was the head of 'the movements' and she would say, 'Mr Segal has to come with us and do the movements.' Ouspensky, instead of saying, 'Go ahead,' would (growling) say to me, 'Sit down. What are you bothering with movements for?' (*A Voice at the Borders of Silence*, p. 62)

The American businessman says he was impressed by the "dedication and the intelligence" of many of the English visitors to Franklin Farms. He also seems impressed with the social style at the Ouspenskys' headquarters.

'Ouspensky did not have an American way of life. He had Oxford dons at his disposal. He had a wine cellar. Every Sunday night we would have a formal dinner. We were farming people [Segal was in charge of work in the woods], and would dress up in black dinner jackets. I was being served by an English lord. One hot day, while working in the fields, a man took off his shirt and there was a crest embroidered on his underwear. Later on I found out that the man I was calling, "Hey, Pentland," was a Lord Pentland. Bissing had inherited half of Cyprus. I would work in the fields or the stalls, in the manure heap, and I'd come home and find that all of Bissing's shoes were made by Lobb. Lord Ramsbottom became the head of a big Buddhist monastery in India' (ibid., p. 63).

Another positive event at one of Ouspensky's lectures in New York, about 1944, occurred when Rodney Collin became inspired to accept the task of classifying the sciences according to the 'worlds' they studied, which later enabled him to transmit new meaning to thousands of readers.

One of Ouspensky's friends remembered him as a man who was always trying to help the ordinary person, the underdog.

'I well remember, while sitting in his New York studio during his absence through illness, the occasion when our friend the commissionaire of a big Longchamps restaurant arrived with an expensive bunch of flowers and said, 'I thought he must be ill as he hasn't come lately. I can't understand his books, but Mr Ouspensky is the only really kind man I ever met' (*Remembering Pyotr Demianovich Ouspensky*, p. 39).

At the same time, to all appearances, Ouspensky was not feeling kind towards himself. His growing despondency left little doubt that he felt his work had lost its true direction. As did others who knew him as well as anybody could; and who now applied the same precept to him as he did in his relationship with Gurdjieff: a need to separate the man from the System.

What of his plans for the Historico-Psychological Society that had so entertained Madame? Did the idea return that once again he might be searching for the miraculous too far from his own hearth – now represented by Lyne Place in England? Or perhaps he felt that having made a commitment he had a task to finish there.

In January 1947, looking pale and unwell, he rejected his doctor's advice and, despite protests from Madame – to whom the Society once again brought tears – boarded a ship for England.

Chapter 17

'OUSPENSKY FIFTH DIMENSION'

OUSPENSKY RETURNED TO SOUTHAMPTON on the Cunard liner Queen Elizabeth, just reconditioned after war service, in January 1947. As he studied the frozen countryside during the drive in a friend's limousine to Lyne Place, he began enacting a role that suggested this was a rehearsal for a return performance staged in another dimension.

Gurdjieff had prompt intelligence of his arrival and weakened condition and may have thought it time he revived his former pupil's flagging hopes. His chief disciple, Jeanne de Salzmann, sent a message inviting the old warrior to a reunion in Paris.

Ouspensky refused. As the two men did not meet again, we lack any indication whether Gurdjieff would have created more tension for his once chief pupil or bestowed a calming influence. Nor do we know whether the thought crossed Ouspensky's mind that Gurdjieff himself could benefit from reconciliation between them – through a lightening of the responsibility he bore. Of course, he could not know for certain whether his mysterious teacher/magician still inhabited a sphere where he needed to bring pupils to a higher level of development before he could ascend further.

Whatever his thoughts, Ouspensky evidently concluded that he could fulfil his final tasks only by his own efforts.

To some people, naturally, it looked as though that alleged Russian streak of obstinacy had surfaced again. Gurdjieff had several times made it impossible for them to co-operate in the Work; Ouspensky would rigidly maintain that separation to the grave, or so ran that line of thought. It might have been nearer the mark to admit the possibility that any taint of pig-headedness had been replaced by a dogged determination, strengthened by a new will. What had he, or the Work, to gain from a pilgrimage to Gurdjieff's flat in the Rue des Colonels Rénard? His inner task now had to do with memory, and in that enormous faculty his relationship with Gurdjieff was already deeply engraved.

It has been suggested that one of the difficulties of understanding Gurdjieff's actions was that few of his pupils took literally his caution that he was working on an agenda hidden from them. Madame Ouspensky seemed to sense something of this in regarding him as 'X', the unknown factor. Now her husband was in a corresponding situation in relation to *his* pupils. They thought that, with their teacher back, School would soon be re-opened at Lyne Place. But Ouspensky was looking to a different rebirth.

With only the final notes to sound on the completing octave of his present life, his working principle now was to be as aware as possible of the people and places close to him, with the aim of being conscious of his time-body and its many connections with the lives of others. His belief in eternal recurrence of the present life in historical duration permitted him to visualise a second dimension of time, that is, his fifth dimension.

Meanwhile, his fellows' perceptions in the fourth dimension led them to assume their expectations of a re-opened School were confirmed when Ouspensky instructed two of his disciples to arrange a meeting of three hundred or more people interested in the Work.

With these crossed wires, the outcome of the meeting in London, and five others that followed, inevitably was a shock to their psychological systems.

Yet there had been portents that unusual happenings were afoot. Ouspensky had often behaved in an inexplicable manner since his return. He had called his leading associates to Lyne for discussions, met them privately, and apparently said or did something that caused some of them to make various excuses against ever returning.

His former Personality hardly showed at all; the occasional whimsical remark was sorely missed. Some people could not understand his long silences. He seemed to find the house cats as worthy of attention as the handful of people who stayed to cater for his every need. Everyone saw that he was frail and very ill.

A number of those nearest him, however, detected something else, which they explained in various ways: he had gained control over his organism and was making his dying body obey his will, he had completed himself, he was realising life on a higher spiritual plane, he was reliving other periods in his mind, he was giving an example of how to die consciously; he was, said a few, a magician.

Not a stage magician. When the frail, wizened old teacher was helped onto the platform at Colet Gardens on February 24 what he had to say sounded far from magical to most in the large audience. They had come to hear words of enlightenment, to discover how they might nurture their Essence, or be shown how to contribute their talents to the resumption of the Group expansion that had started before the bombing of Britain.

In that atmosphere of expectancy, he dropped a different type of bombshell – he was 'abandoning' the System.

What disbelief, then what dismay when the faithful realised he was serious! More than a few saw in that cryptic statement an admission that his mission had failed, or, worse, that at an embarrassingly late stage his intellectual genius had detected a fatal flaw in the teaching to which he had devoted his life.

Others attributed it to the weakness, the delusion, of a gravely ill man. This led them to regard Ouspensky in his later years as a tragic figure, despite the incongruity of people on a lower level judging that such a man failed to live up to his potential or that he was deflected from his true path by Gurdjieff. Tragedy was not a state that Ouspensky indulged in. It is instructive to recall that he criticised Maurice Nicoll for speaking 'tragically', a habit that he diagnosed as being a sign of a bad neutralising force.

However, a sufficient number of his more devoted pupils – and also perhaps some newcomers who received the news on open minds – appreciated that he was not dismissing the System but telling them that it had become necessary for them to rebuild it, based on their own needs and understanding. For he also said that everyone must 'reconstruct everything for oneself'.

There had been strong signs that a radical shift was in the offing. As opposed to his usual careful screening of newcomers, he had asked group members to each gather several other people to hear the Colet House lectures. And he had told them not to use System language when inviting them to the meetings.

At the lectures, he turned his famous Russian deaf ear to questions couched in the Work terms he had formerly insisted upon. He spoke quietly, sometimes almost inaudibly, but they heard the old 'Moscow shout' when someone asked whether he wished *Fragments* to be published. He said with feeling: 'No.'

If he voiced the word 'abandon' perhaps it was what sprang to mind as a way of expressing in ordinary language an intuition he was experiencing on a higher plane. Remember that the only written record he left of overwhelming impressions he had felt in a raised state of consciousness of the connectedness of everything was a message that a simple ash-tray could send a man mad.

How could a mere man dismiss the System? He could abandon it like a passenger leaving a sinking ship, but could not do so in the sense of a person abandoning someone previously dependent on him or her. The latter would be to reverse the idea of scale.

On this question of scale, to observers on Earth the passage of the Moon across the face of the Sun does on rare occasions eclipse the solar light rays, due to the coincidence that although the Moon is four hundred times smaller than the Sun it is also four hundred times nearer the Earth than the Sun. This would be irrelevant except for the curious coincidence that the Greek word *ekleipsis* means 'omission' or 'abandonment'.

This makes it even more difficult to imagine Ouspensky ever believing he was eclipsing the System – or, to make it personal, Gurdjieff. He may have conceded he was many times smaller in stature than either, but would not have claimed to be just as many times closer to mankind. (It might also be noted, in connection with *ekleipsis*, that the translation of a man's thoughts from a higher plane to a lower inevitably produces many 'omissions'.)

In former ages, superstitious tribes interpreted a total eclipse as a bad omen. Ouspensky's 'abandonment' was treated in a similar manner by those who felt they had been left in the dark.

When Ouspensky was asked how they could live without the ideas and ideals they had come to rely on to guide them through life he said, 'The System is greater than any man.' This probably sounded cryptic, but it should at least have reminded everyone of the principle of scale. Perspective makes the Moon appear as large as the Sun, and the darkness produced by an eclipse is no illusion, but it can give a shock so that when light is restored it is better appreciated.

Ouspensky's assurance that 'the System is greater' may also have reminded people of the cliche that 'life goes on', which at least would be something to remember when his present life was eclipsed in its grand circuit of recurrence, the moment when life, death and birth are in transitory alignment.

Collin, who was with Ouspensky in his final days, discovered what he believed was the meaning of the 'abandonment' a fortnight before his mentor's death. He reports that 'after a strange and long preparation, he [Ouspensky] said to a few friends who were with him:

'You must start again. You must make a new beginning. You must reconstruct everything for yourselves – from the very beginning' (*The Theory of Celestial Influence*, p. xxi).

In his last meetings at Colet Gardens Ouspensky indicated how people could do this. More than once he asked them, 'What do you want?' Knowing that, he said, was the starting point of the path of Self-remembering and consciousness.

This question of what people really want was obviously important to Ouspensky. When he instructed two pupils to 'collect three hundred people', they asked what they should tell them. 'Why say anything? Ask them what they want,' he replied.

What one wants is connected with the equally fundamental question of what one needs. Seven years later, Ouspensky's sometime pupil John Bennett gave a good idea of what this means during a London lecture when he answered the question 'What can we rely on in ourselves?' He said:

'What happens when you breathe and the air goes out of your lungs and they are empty? You have to take air in. All other questions disappear beside that. If you have known what it is to be near suffocating, you know that all other questions disappear beside that. You can rely on this: that as long as you can breathe, you will breathe. . . . The only thing we can rely on is that kind of an experience of need.'

To a person who suggested that consciousness was all illusion and asked what, therefore, did any system of transformation of Being matter, Bennett replied:

'If you truly needed an answer to the question that you have just asked – that is, to discover whether there is a reality where things matter – and if you needed the answer like you need air, then I assure you, you would find it. And really you do need the answer just as much as you need air, only you don't know it' (*Man's Task and His Reward*, No. 3 of six lectures, London, March 1954).

This analogy with breathing may well have originated in Ouspensky's teaching, seeing that another of his pupils, Maurice Nicoll, cites the example of a student whose head was immersed in a bucket of water so that his gasps for air would give him an idea of what he really wanted.

'He was told that when he wanted the teacher's instruction as much as he wanted air, he would be given it' (*Psychological Commentaries*, vol. 5, p. 1517).

The practical yet whimsical psychologist commented: 'I imagine he was offended and took himself off.'

There is little doubt that Ouspensky intended an equal degree of urgency to attach to his question of what his people *wanted.* It was something they needed – only they did not know it. They needed to discover what they really wanted.

At a Colet Gardens meeting in May Ouspensky said the System had been tried in America and found not to work. A new way must be tried, and again he asked: 'What do you want?' When people tried to answer, he urged them to be more precise in their formulations.

From their perspective, it was his answers that did not seem precise. Surely he did not mean literally that the System did not work in the United States? It was, after all, universal. Was this a way of saying that the people at his lectures there had not worked? So that what was needed was not a new System but a new approach to it? A wrong approach did not imply a mistaken System.

The Fourth Way, as Ouspensky had pointed out, began from a point above an ordinary person's standpoint. Steps had to be climbed to reach the path. He implied that one way of ascending more surely was to formulate their questions accurately – he always regarded questions as an important part of the quest, with the effort of making them precise sometimes being sufficient to clear away uncertainties and reveal the answer.

In view of the list of instructions he had circulated to group members before leaving England, one woman probably thought she was on the right track when she disclosed that she wanted to stop thoughts. 'Why?' he demanded.

She is likely to have felt that this retort was unkind. Others may have seen it implied that a genuine effort to stop thoughts, a method of achieving the state of Self-remembering, would throw up more searching questions than such a general wish. In which case, her question would have been of value to the group.

When someone asked him to suggest a new method, he replied, 'There is no method. Really, there is no method.'

Here again, in his present state of consciousness he might well have had a far different conception of 'method' from that of people in a 'walking-sleep' state. He was concerned with levels of Being. For Being to reach its full potential there was no one method – there were innumerable methods. Beside the essential transformations of human experience needed to form Being, however, there was little to say on his then level of understanding about basic techniques.

Another person asked how they could get the knowledge they believed Ouspensky possessed, and was told, 'That is the whole thing. How can you get it?'

It is possible to view these replies in the light of Bennett's assurance that if people needed the answers like they needed air they would find them. There was still a lingering suspicion that Ouspensky would have liked to know the answers as much as his audience. For his call for everyone to reconstruct the System for themselves appeared to have resulted from his impression of failure in America. All the same, this was not necessarily an entirely negative experience, given that some great undertakings are destined to fail – consider the lines from Simone Weil's *Le Pesanteur et la Grace*: 'Isn't it the greatest of misfortunes, when one battles with God, not to be defeated?'

Maybe Ouspensky simply deduced that the method he had been using had run its course. Was it time for a new technique, for a new octave?

Ouspensky's whole teaching was structured to transmit Gurdjieff's ideas to people capable of receiving them. Gurdjieff meanwhile, it appears from what he has written, had accepted failure in efforts to prepare others to succeed him as School leaders and was urgently seeking the best way to transmit the wisdom he had collected to future generations, when conditions might be more amenable to esotericism. It is not surprising that a quick learner like Ouspensky would not be far behind him in reaching a similar conclusion over his own efforts.

He did not fault the basic ideas, the fragments of knowledge that he had helped reconstruct into a System – but he left no doubt he did not now consider it a fixed solution. It was the pattern of a System, he implied, that individuals must build for themselves.

In his own rebuilding, he was at the stage of life where he was primarily concerned with eternal recurrence. It became obvious to those caring for him at Lyne that he was intent on reviewing episodes in his life, as well as heightening his awareness of the present. They remarked how he drove his frail body on long days in a motor-car to visit places that held meaning for him.

The Sussex village of Sidlesham was one port of call, and recall. And Maurice Nicoll was glad that in 1947 he sent Ouspensky two of his paintings of Alley Cottage there, where he had felt closer to real life.

One of the most remarkable events in this recapitulation of his life, his time-body, was a visit to Lyne Place in May by one of his Moscow schoolboy friends, 'F', whom he had last seen in Constantinople after they fled the Russian Revolution. Ouspensky had cabled an invitation to F in Paris.

F was obviously bewildered by his warm welcome after so many years and also by the significance of Ouspensky's work, for which his old chum was obviously held in respect. Ouspensky showed his countryman postcards of old Moscow to take his mind back to the days of their youth. It might have appeared to be nostalgia running rampant, but there was a practical purpose behind it.

F, sounding like a character in *Strange Life of Ivan Osokin*, related incidents from their school life. He said that Ouspensky the schoolboy had been fond of talking about very unusual subjects, but they did not interest any of his classmates. He was glad, therefore, that a fellow weekday boarder in the form below was a good listener, and able to respond.

F recalled that they would talk for hours as they walked along the school corridors, dressed in holland smocks and grasping the back of each other's belt, a behavioural fashion among schoolboys at the time.

One of Ouspensky's ideas, he said, had been that a novel needed to be written about school life. While F was at Lyne, Ouspensky gave him *Osokin* to read, which may well have given him the impression that his old friend had retained some interest in 'unusual subjects'.

After a week, Ouspensky called another large meeting in London, which he said was for F. Though he did not speak

English, the Russian guest was fascinated by the special meeting, and the awe that his old school friend inspired.

The other companions at Lyne realised that this visit was part of Ouspensky's plan to reinforce his memory of his early life. It would be a bonus if the 'strange life' circumstances so impressed F that he, too, would have moments of deja vu in his next recurrence. That might spread new circles of ripples through the pond of life.

There was an undercurrent of eternal recurrence in the six meetings at Colet Gardens from February 24 to June 18, 1947.

At one meeting Ouspensky, often so silent and detached that he could be described as a non-lecturer, was asked whether it would not be better to think about group aim rather than personal questions. He replied: 'What questions are not personal?' He does not appear to have intended 'personal' in this context to have any egotistical connotation. No more than his focus on recurrence points to an overweening interest in his own spiritual welfare. If he could remember more of his past in another recurrence he would have forewarning of old mistakes, of wrong turnings on The Fourth Way, and could help others earlier than in their present existence.

To a person who wondered whether anyone has a 'right' to expect help, Ouspensky was positive:

'One has right to everything. One does not spend time wondering about has one right or not. One has right to everything (*Last Remembrances of a Magician*).

The more attuned of the audience reported that it was difficult to describe the atmosphere, the feeling of potency, at these meetings. Some suddenly found it possible there to silently formulate their individual aims, and see where they needed help.

At one stage during his last weeks at Lyne, Ouspensky turned everyday time on its head, which naturally changed the pattern of the day for the other residents too.

'O. seemed to find it difficult to sleep for long, and after two or three hours rest would wake again about 9 or 10 p.m., take breakfast coffee, rise, and begin another day. This would mean that Miss R. must serve "lunch" sometime after midnight, after which they might sit together for an hour or two, and then go back to bed again. Next day O. might wake at 10, there would be a second lunch at 2, supper at 6.30, he would retire once more, and so on. In this way, two complete days became compressed into 24 hours.

'As always when O. began a new experiment, they were at first deceived into thinking him at fault, and would naively demonstrate that it was night outside the still-closed shutters. At this he would laugh and say: "I don't believe it." Afterwards it seemed extraordinary to them that they could ever have imagined one whose instinctive time-sense was so preternaturally acute to be so mistaken. But this was a definite aspect of his experiments: their very originality ensured that they should always be taken as foolishness.

'. . . all ordinary ways of looking at the routine of life and passage of time were revealed as simply habits of thought. If a man were strong enough to create circumstances which broke such habits, quite new points of view became possible. Like everything else that summer, it was preparation. But for what?' (ibid.)

Ouspensky's amusement that his pupils thought they knew the real time indicates he was aware that they did not share his present certainty that *his* time was curving back to birth. A commentary by his pupil Maurice Nicoll throws light on this aspect:

'Time is not a straight line but infinite circles all turning on themselves and some inter-communicating with each other. The past is as living as the present or the future. From this grand conception we can gain hope. We can understand that what we do now affects other people, both in the past and in the present and in the future. Everything, the Work says, is connected together so that if a person works now on himself or herself and begins to change their level of Being they affect people not only in the past but in the future. . . . G. once said:

"If you want to change yourself, you must change your grandfather." What does this mean? One meaning is that by changing your attitude to your father and to your grandfather you will change them also, although apparently they are dead, and so when you are born once more in visible life, on the circle of your own life, when you meet your father and your grandfather again you will change them. . . . In other words, there is no Time as our senses conceive it and everything is living and everything is always present. . . . I sometimes think that this means you have to see the whole of your past as living and that by working now you can change the whole of the past and all that is connected with it. So you will agree with me that if you can catch this vision of something above the senses and the sensory mind there is hope of an extraordinary kind' (*Psychological Commentaries*, vol. 2, pp. 753-4).

Ouspensky had this extraordinary vision and hope.

Lyne residents were frequently aware of a 'preparation' by Ouspensky through the summer of 1947, but it had been even more pronounced earlier. In April he had grown much weaker and had to force himself to walk or eat. One day, when his illness was nearing a crisis, he spoke, with difficulty, about his planned return to America.

'He said to Miss Q: "Will you go to America?" She replied: "When you do, Mr. O." And he answered strangely: "I am not going anywhere at any visible date." By the evening Miss Q. was very white. "This is different," she said' (*Last Remembrances*).

On September 4, what seemed very different was not the state of Ouspensky's health – or whether the alternative to a 'visible date' was an invisible dimension of Time – but the extraordinary episode when he made as if physically to return to America. Passages for Ouspensky and others of the group were booked and their baggage already loaded on the Queen Mary at Southampton, when he announced at the gangplank that he did not intend to embark. 'Now we go home,' was, he thought, sufficient explanation for this dramatic change in direction.

Such unpredictability resulted in some people changing

their mind about the ambiguously 'disowned' System and dropping out of the Work. On the other hand, despite this culling of the ranks, it was inevitable that in the folklore that grew out of those happenings his talk of returning to America would be taken to allude to a return journey of a markedly different type.

At the height of such speculation, the enacting of organising a passage and then relinquishing it could even be seen as an intimation that he might not have to play another round in the eternal game of recurrence after all. Speculative as this may be, the people living with Ouspensky during his final days were unanimous in feeling they were in a powerful presence, and believed he was experiencing a high level of consciousness.

J.H. Reyner, whose book *Ouspensky: the Unsung Genius* proclaims the author as a firm believer in the Russian teacher's message, describes his last days in this way:

'His health began to deteriorate rapidly, perhaps because he felt he had done all that was required of him so that there was no longer any need to inhabit his ailing and uncomfortable body. It was evident that his death would not be long delayed, but when it finally happened on October 2nd, 1947, it had a strangely triumphant quality. The day before, he appeared unexpectedly, fully dressed, and summoned the household for a final briefing. He spoke to them in terms of great affection. He emphasised that each of them had to make a fresh start, reconstructing from the very beginning all that they had learned and then venturing boldly into the unknown territory wherein they would find help. The atmosphere was alive with conscious influences which were communicated wordlessly to the assembled company in such a way that each perceived individually the way ahead.

'Unseen presences were all around in what appeared to be the prelude to a conscious and joyous transition from the physical to the spiritual state. Ouspensky had at last cast off the shackles of his role. He left the room and retired to bed, where he died peacefully the following day' (ibid.).

All very uplifting, but that is how a disciple might be

expected to honour his master's manner of passing. Yet even Colin Wilson, who contends that Ouspensky lost his direction by following Gurdjieff's teaching and had consequently reached a dead-end and who takes a dim view of a possible alcohol connection with his fatal illness, speaks well of his passing:

'[Rodney] Collin seems to have taken it upon himself to try to make Ouspensky "die consciously", and to make sure that he did not "go gentle into that good night". Others state that Ouspensky needed no encouragement, and spent his last days making "super-efforts", even waking his pupils up in the middle of the night. It was, according to Collin, in his arms that Ouspensky finally died at dawn on 2 October 1947 . . . . Collin retreated to the dressing-room next to Ouspensky's bedroom and locked himself in for six days. . . . Finally, Collin rang the bell that Ouspensky rang when he needed attention. He was found sitting cross-legged on Ouspensky's bed, dirty and unshaven, and he asked his wife, Janet, to bring him lime juice. He later told her – and his sister-in-law, Joyce Collin Smith – that he had been in communication with Ouspensky during all this period, and that the disclosures were so important that he was determined not to be disturbed. The result of this communication led him to formulate a theory of 'four worlds', each on different vibrational rates, and to write a book called *The Theory of Celestial Influence* (*The Strange Life of P.D. Ouspensky*, p. 116).

What Wilson reports here as the inspired cause of *The Theory of Celestial Influence* may well be true. But the book is also the result of the already noted challenge Collin accepted at a 1940 New York meeting to classify the sciences according to the 'worlds' they studied.

John Bennett was at his group's headquarters, Coombe Springs, near Kingston, Surrey, when he learned that Ouspensky had died. A friend phoned him from New York that he had received a message that Bennett should see Janet Collin Smith. He found her at her London address, very surprised to hear of his message because, like all of

Ouspensky's pupils, she had been forbidden to speak to him. However, she told him of their teacher's last hours. Bennett's response:

'Throughout the day I felt a great love towards him, such as I had never known while he was alive. . . . Ouspensky's potentialities had been brought into time, and they had undergone an irreversible transformation. There was something that I could not understand and should not try to understand. A great cycle of my own life which had lasted nearly twenty-seven years had closed. I felt love and gratitude towards Ouspensky, but I felt no nearer to him than I had before' (*Witness*, pp. 226-7).

Maurice Nicoll, although the most practised in psychological insights and one of Ouspensky's closest friends, did not analyse his teacher's death. Instead he told his group at Great Amwell House about a dream he had had a fortnight after first meeting him. Nicoll's biographer, Beryl Pogson, reports that 'Ouspensky appeared in the dream as a bird which, when someone fluffed up his feathers and otherwise annoyed him, remained quite still'.

Nicoll connected the dream with a Chinese parable about Chishengtse, who raised fighting cocks for a king. The king repeatedly asked if a particular cock was ready to fight, but was told 'not yet' until the fortieth day, when Chishengtse said: 'He is about ready. When he hears other cocks crow, he does not even react. You look at him, and he appears like a wooden cock. His character is whole now. No other cock will dare to fight him but will run away at first sight.'

Mrs Pogson comments:

'We all delighted to think of Ouspensky as a 'cock of wood'. Thus with a kind of joy in our sadness we paid tribute to his memory. Dr Nicoll had once more made what was serious comprehensible through what was laughable (*Maurice Nicoll: A Portrait*, pp. 248-9).

In 1949, after Ouspensky's death, Nicoll related another dream he had had about his friend. Samuel Copley tells it thus, Nicoll speaking:

'Suspensky (sic) is having a good time upstairs. I was at one of his Groups last night. He was paying less attention to rules and having a gay time. He must have taken a leaf out of my book *Portrait of a Vertical Man*, p. 24).

Copley offers his opinion that conversations between the two group leaders during Ouspensky's lifetime were predominantly serious, which made Ouspensky's relaxation of the rules 'upstairs' worth noting.

In our consideration of a vital transition point in a great man's life, it is of interest to note that Nott once asked Ouspensky where perfected people – Socrates and Plato, for instance – went. He replied there was a possibility they went to another planet where conditions were more favourable (*Journey Through This World*, p. 100).

This, obviously, leads to a further question: favourable for what? In our present situation, difficult, distinctly unfavourable conditions are the grist of the mill in which our functions can be developed and consciousness raised. Ouspensky himself perpetuated this idea with a conversational remark that still serves as a definition of a 'good' day on The Fourth Way: one in which everything goes wrong, and so presents the person on the receiving end of mishaps with the chance to struggle against mechanical and selfish reactions and impulses.

That, however, is only what is favourable to those who need to struggle to raise their level of Being. We don't know whether perfected human beings must remain connected to Earth and its bounteous supply of 'good' days.

Ouspensky's ashes were buried in the Holy Trinity Churchyard at Lyne after a requiem service in the Russian Church in London's Pimlico.

Left suddenly without direction, the group leaders at Lyne Place eventually sent a delegation to see Mme Ouspensky in the United States, appealing for help to set a new course. In January 1948, Mme Ouspensky sent them a message from her sickbed at Franklin Farms to contact Mr Gurdjieff in Paris. Though not surprising advice from a lifelong pupil of Gurdjieff, it was at startling variance from her husband's instructions – and splintered the Historico-Psychological Society.

Consolidating this proposal, in June 1948 Gurdjieff sent the Society a telegram: 'You are sheep without a shepherd. Come to me.'

Several days after that invitation, Bennett visited Mme Ouspensky at Franklin Farms. She asked what he would do now her husband had gone. Bennett says:

'I learned afterwards she had put the same question to several others. I replied that I had hoped to find Mr Gurdjieff, but could not trace him. I supposed that he had either died, or, as someone had told me, had gone mad. She said: "He is not mad. He had never been mad. He is living in Paris now. Why do you not go to him?"

'. . . She told her companion . . . to read me a letter she had sent to Lyne, asking the group there the same question she had put to me, and inviting them to consider a return to Gurdjieff. This letter had provoked a storm. Some considered themselves bound by their promise to Ouspensky never again to have anything to do with Gurdjieff. Others wanted more information. Only two – those who had come to America – had already decided that they would make the attempt to work with Gurdjieff again. It transpired further that Madame Ouspensky, in inviting me, had aroused the indignation of the fanatical section, who held that every word spoken by Ouspensky was an immutable law, which no one could break without betraying a sacred trust'(*Witness*, pp. 240-1).

Bennett adds the comment that whenever a spiritual leader 'leaves the earthly scene' his followers split into factions, one preserving every word as though it were fixed for ever, another rejoicing to be freed from the teacher's constraint, and another keeping alive the spirit of the teaching even though the outer form may change. He believed Mme Ouspensky saw the living content rather than the form of Ouspensky's teaching.

'She looked beyond Ouspensky to Gurdjieff and beyond Gurdjieff to the Great Source from which comes every good gift and every perfect gift' (ibid., pp. 241-2).

Madame's ability to perceive the Work in that way seems itself to be a good gift, and an example for others to follow. After that consultation, Bennett said in a letter to his wife: 'Madame Ouspensky says she never had and never will allow herself to be looked upon as a teacher. . . . She set all the group here at Mendham the task of answering the question: "What would you do if a Higher Teacher came?" The answer must surely be that one puts oneself unreservedly in his hands' (ibid., p. 243).

As Bennett predicted, members of the Lyne group went their several ways, some to Gurdjieff, some to form new groups, and some to join Ouspensky's disciple Maurice Nicoll. Beryl Pogson writes that although Ouspensky's death was a shock, 'it was important for the [Nicoll] group as a year or so later a number of people who had been working with Ouspensky now came to us . . .'

She quotes the impression formed on one of these by his first visit to the group's headquarters at Great Amwell House:

'I met Mrs [Catherine] Nicoll at (I believe) the first meeting of Mr Sam Copley's sub-group for new people. The teaching was given to me all over again, under a new impact – the same teaching in its purity, but with a difference: a difference of emphasis, perhaps; also a great flexibility in applying the ideas – or so it seemed, but maybe, after the enforced abstinence, I was putting better efforts into directed attention. . . . my first impressions of Dr Nicoll in action inevitably reinforced a kind of dogged determination not to find in him a substitute for the revered "dead shepherd". Separate identities were in fact preserved by marked differences of "type" – the difference in manifestation between a Professor of Philosophy and the ideal Family Doctor. What I did find in my new Teacher – and came more and more thankfully to acknowledge – was a Being of similar rock-like integrity, catholic and encyclopaedic in mental range, radiating wisdom with gaiety in a setting starkly at variance with ordinary life-conditions, yet oddly simple and what might be called Plain English. The ritual "At Homes" in the local pub, for one who could not even imagine

Mr Ouspensky resorting to such places, remained for some time a kind of Holy Mystery. . . . Later I came to accept it as a lightly imposed discipline – which could be as compelling as any of Ouspensky's Rules – against the temptations of careless talking and uncontrolled behaviour (*Maurice Nicoll: A Portrait*, pp. 249-50).

It is apparent that although Ouspensky's group seemed to fragment at his passing, committed members were soon contributing to other branches of Gurdjieff's teaching. And a notable few reconstructed the teaching they had received from Ouspensky in ways that attracted many more people to the Work.

Maurice Nicoll had begun earlier to present the System in his own way, and his talks to his groups, later collected into the five volumes of *Psychological Commentaries on the Teaching of G.I. Gurdjieff and P.D. Ouspensky*, became accepted as a comprehensive and comprehendible exposition of Work ideas. His classic *Living Time* is a persuasive treatise based largely on Ouspensky's views of Time and of eternal recurrence.

Rodney Collin produced his *Theory of Celestial Influence* which, although he himself said it would have no scientific significance, provided a new way of seeing the analogies between different cosmoses – 'As above so below' put into a modern context.

John Bennett worked for 14 years writing and rewriting the four volumes of *The Dramatic Universe* into intellectually and emotionally demanding but virtually incontrovertible 'All and Everything' textbooks of the structures, facts, values and meaning of life, greatly extending the knowledge of life processes beyond the 'sacred' three and seven term systems that Gurdjieff and Ouspensky focused upon. He found in this work that his centre of gravity shifted from his head to his heart, largely he believed through his contact with Subud, which contact, many of the Work orthodox thought, was reconstructing the System in quite a different way to any that Ouspensky would have envisaged.

Opinions about this Eastern spiritual way vary, but the

following observation by Bennett after practising that method bears closely on Ouspensky's thinking:

'As the years go by, I become more and more convinced that an action is taking place in the world that does not originate in any human or earthly source. I believe that there is being performed on earth a mighty work of spiritual regeneration that will change the way of life of the entire human race. We shall not abandon our intellectual achievements; but we shall see the need to go beyond them and enter the realm of direct intuitive perception' (*Witness*, p. 374).

The words 'source', 'regeneration', 'intellectual' and 'intuition' in this context resound with significance in relation to Ouspensky's aim in life.

In a way, all the above mentioned writers did for Ouspensky's teaching what he had done for Gurdjieff's. Stanley Nott, often a critical friend of Ouspensky, considered that the Russian writer, through his intellectual integrity, had been able to stand apart from his personal feelings in order to compose a record of Gurdjieff's sayings 'beyond price' – 'and by this alone perhaps he has paid Nature for his "arising and existence"' (*Journey Through This World*, p. 194).

The point about paying for one's arising goes right to the nub of the issue, and we shall come back to it.

First, let us look at the book that has been identified as the currency of this transaction. It may be that the split with Gurdjieff gave the necessary impetus for it to be accomplished. And Ouspensky's reluctance to publish it gave him adequate time to hone the work into the form and quality he desired, producing a work that continues to inform and inspire many people. During the author's lifetime, however, *Fragments of an Unknown Teaching* had been seen only in manuscript form by relatively few people.

For years its publication was deemed to depend on whether Gurdjieff's *Beelzebub's Tales to His Grandson* was printed for public sale. It was not until New Year 1949 that Gurdjieff finally decided to release *Beelzebub.* (He saw final proofs of the First Series of his 'Objectively Impartial Criticism of the Life of

Man', titled *All and Everything*, just eight days before his death on 29 October 1949.)

In November 1948 Gurdjieff had visited Mme Ouspensky at Franklin Farms, when she is believed to have asked whether *Fragments* should be published. For his opinion of the book that formulated and preserved his ideas we have Bennett's testimony that once, after he had read an early chapter of the manuscript to him, Gurdjieff said: 'Before I hate Ouspensky: now I love him. This very exact, he tell what I say' (*Witness*, p. 260).

Evidently, Mme Ouspensky obtained his approval to print.

In Search of the Miraculous was published by Harcourt, Brace in New York during autumn 1949 and by Routledge in London in 1950. With the many references in Ouspensky's teaching to the concept of 'fragments' it is a pity the title he preferred did not accompany it to the printer's. 'However, Ouspensky was already [in 1925] acquainted with G.R.S. Mead, and when he learned that one of Mead's books had the title *Fragments of a Faith Forgotten*, he realised that his title would have to be changed' (*Remembering Pyotr Demianovich Ouspensky*, p. 28).

In Search of the Miraculous, the title of one of his public lectures in Russia, is an appropriate second choice, for the miraculous was what he always sought.

Strangely, except perhaps right at the end, he never lost his hope of finding 'facts' of the seemingly miraculous, invisible world on which he based his philosophy of life. This seemed to go beyond his newspaper writer's instinct to find something solid on which to base reports of his experiences.

Bennett's wife Winifred revealed that Ouspensky was almost in tears when she told him of her out-of-body experience and confessed he had desired a proof like that all his life (*Witness*, p. 184). Although he did not use the word 'faith' lightly, he obviously knew that, even without factual proof, there was no better prospect than to make the Work ideas part of his daily life.

Nott is probably right, as far as he goes, in suggesting that by his work to produce *In Search of the Miraculous* Ouspensky 'paid Nature' for his arising. In fact he may have paid his dues to more than what is generally thought of as Nature, for the regenerative nature of the Work includes more than the phenomena of nature, and sometimes opposes it (see *Beelzebub's Tales to His Grandson*, p. 196, to gain some idea of Great Nature). The force of Nature as we usually view it controls life and the universe with firm rules that extract due payment willy-nilly, and in this sense cannot be imagined as taking one person's voluntary contributions into separate account.

Ouspensky himself pointed out that it is when a small group of people are invisible to Nature that they are able to free themselves from some of her restrictive laws without inviting counter-measures. (On a cosmic time scale an individual's transformation of energies may be welcomed by the Intelligences behind Nature, but that is only theory for most of us.)

Leaving aside obligations to Nature, Ouspensky, for most of his life at any rate, was always conscious of a debt to Gurdjieff. Although the two men exchanged defamatory assessments of each other, Ouspensky remained grateful for the knowledge that he received from the teacher who found him in Moscow. And they shared the same fundamental aim, to awaken sleeping humanity.

Where Ouspensky can be seen to have repaid his debt is in introducing people to Gurdjieff's ideas. Without this, few would have known of the Work – which is not to imply that he was alone in this; other teachers, such as A.R. Orage and Mme Jeanne de Salzmann, also played their parts in holding up the pattern of the teaching so that it could be seen and appreciated by people with the appropriate magnetic centre. The writer of *In Search of the Miraculous*, however, produced the most illuminating and reliable guide to the basis of the Work.

This book does not, of course, tell the whole story. On the possibility of doing that, it is worth recalling that Beryl Pogson, during a fireside chat in the saloon at her group house,

'The Dicker', once remarked that the common newspaper front page inducement *Full story inside* always exaggerates. For a *fuller* story, then, the reader captured by Ouspensky must turn to Gurdjieff's own works.

He or she might then be in for a shock. While it was Ouspensky's intention, role even, to make his explanations of human psychology and possibilities clear, precise and unadorned, Gurdjieff endeavoured to make his obscure to the point of impenetrability. One of the English translators of *All and Everything*, John Bennett, has reported that the author often urged them to 'bury the dog deeper'. He firmly disabused them of their misapprehension that he meant 'bone' when he said 'dog' (*Gurdjieff: Making a New World*, p.274).

From one point of view this indicates how heavily he intended his message to be disguised, presumably because it is only by great effort, much digging for meaning, that one can hope to attain deep understanding. Bennett recounts that when chapters of *Beelzebub's Tales* were read to Gurdjieff's pupils, if he 'found that the key passages were taken too easily – and therefore almost inevitably too superficially – he would rewrite them . . .'

This view is supported by Sri Madhava Ashish's answer to a question about the 'deliberate obfuscation' of *Beelzebub's Tales*:

'When anything is presented in easily understood terms, there is the danger that people will understand with their minds only. . . . G made the book deliberately obscure . . . so that mankind would have to work hard at getting his meaning . . .' (*In Search of the Unitive Vision*, p.214).

Bennett adds the thought that the expression 'bury the dog deeper' also alluded to the Dog Star, Sirius (Canus Major), brightest star in the heavens and an ancient symbol of wisdom.

In this, again, the two writers can be considered as complementary: Ouspensky shows without leaving room for argument what can be done; Gurdjieff then demonstrates the practicalities, the sometimes harsh realities, of how to do it, once his code is deciphered. They were also complementary in a way that for Ouspensky at least was unintentional. While

Gurdjieff deliberately puzzled his questioners, 'Wraps Up the Thought' often bewildered them by the sheer thoroughness of his answers.

While on their more or less shared aim, it is also noteworthy that Gurdjieff explains that his second book, *Meetings with Remarkable Men*, was aimed at proving 'that there exist other ways of perceiving reality, and to indicate their direction' (*Life is Real Only Then, When 'I Am'*, p. 4). This, it may be recalled, is identical to the theme of Ouspensky's *Tertium Organum* and much of *A New Model of the Universe*.

It is also interesting that Gurdjieff speaks of 'the different fragments' he intended for publication, in view of Ouspensky's frequent use of that term.

Though their aim might be fundamentally the same, Gurdjieff remained the master, Ouspensky the disciple in exile. There is a theory that, by taking some of the responsibility off their teacher's shoulders by themselves gaining understanding through their intentional efforts, pupils can enable their teacher to ascend to a higher level, perhaps even free him or her from the circles of recurrence. It is a matter of conjecture what level of Being Gurdjieff inhabited during his recorded visit to Earth. That is to say, he may not have stood in need of freeing from recurrence. That said, it should also be noted that, while Gurdjieff was conscious of having a vital message for mankind, he did not suggest that his elevation of Beelzebub in *Beelzebub's Tales to His Grandson* to an extremely high graduation of reason was meant to be an autobiographical prediction or revelation of a previous existence. His final description of himself was simply the 'Teacher of Dancing' (*Beelzebub's Tales*, p. 50).

On that note, one of the unexpected spin-offs of Ouspensky's writing is fitting. His comments on the turning in *A New Model of the Universe* apparently gratified the Mevlevi dervishes. So much so that, when a successor of Ouspensky, Dr Francis Roles, expressed interest in the discipline, one of the chief sheikhs, Resuhi Baykara, went to the Work group's headquarters at Colet House in London in 1963 to teach the dancing technique.

This was of mutual benefit. Roles was following what he perceived as Ouspensky's instructions to seek a new method. Resuhi would have seen the move as a means of preserving his own teaching, following Mustafa Kemal Ataturk's banning of the whirling dervishes in 1925. The dervishes obviously agreed with Ouspensky's verdict that while they were the soul of Constantinople it was alive: 'Later it died.'

Resuhi trained twenty-six English pupils of the Work in the turning in a four-week crash course, pointing out that full training would take seven years. Similar groups were trained in New York in 1968, Wellington, New Zealand, in 1983 and in Mexico City in 1989 (*The Bridge*, No. 12, pp. 201-4).

Returning to Beelzebub's high promotion in the universal hierarchy, it did not seem that Ouspensky was entertaining any notion that he would advance to such a sphere at the completion of his life. He was evidently preparing for a return as he fixed people and places in his memory, as though a searching examination was in store.

His most ardent followers, however, did not view his position quite so unassumingly. J.H. Reyner sees his role as having been scripted by Conscious Humanity, utilising his skill in lucidity of expression to make him a forerunner of Aquarian Age heroes.

While touching on beings of a higher order, a séance attended by two notable *All and Everything* scholars, American Seymour Ginsburg and Russian-born Nicolas Tereshchenko, in Geneva in 1989 produced some thought-provoking claims about Gurdjieff's history that would suggest a further similarity to Ouspensky's. A self-styled 'minor initiate' known as Pastor, speaking through a psychic medium, told them it was in Gurdjieff's destiny 'to offer one message' and that

'this was in direct resonance with the disobedience he had committed a very long time ago, a very long time ago in history. . . . Although I speak of disobedience, we must not see it as being an error. It is simply something that happens. It is almost unavoidable in the development of the initiate. I would say it is even desirable, because it is where we can see that he really exists, that he is building himself, that he is beginning to understand the universe and he is beginning to appropriate the divinity. . . . But of course this commits the individual to a certain kind of karma; this is also certain' (*In Search of the Unitive Vision*, pp. 199-201).

This perception of inevitability, desirability even, of disobedience in the development of an individual strikes a chord with Ouspensky's refusal to accept his teacher's instructions. Strictly speaking, he may be said to have opted out of Gurdjieff's tutelage before he could be accused of disobedience, but a rebellious element was still present. The stage of 'beginning to understand the universe' is of course particularly apt in his case.

But the outstanding parallel in Pastor's message is between what he claimed was Gurdjieff's destiny and the 'callow' young Beelzebub's exile from the 'Sun Absolute' to our remote solar system for rebelling against what he saw as something illogical in the World government (*Beelzebub's Tales*, p. 52).

Ouspensky, too, saw something illogical in the leadership and, if an analogous 'exile' is seen in his life, this gives a new meaning to Gurdjieff's comments (at the London meetings in 1922) on the hardships of living in the English climate.

Very interesting . . . but this line of thought has an obvious weakness. It depends on the truth of Pastor's utterance, which was in answer to a question about what more is needed to be known for a student to understand in depth Gurdjieff's Law of Seven. Ginsburg realised that the medium could have 'telepathically picked up our own thoughts about Gurdjieff'. But he did not think so 'because Pastor's interpretation of G's life cycles was not entirely flattering, and we had no unflattering thoughts about Gurdjieff in our minds' (i*In Search of the Unitive Vision*, p. 204).

He agreed that 'disobedience is a trait that characterised Gurdjieff' and pointed out that one of his prime teachings 'was that one should never "do the expected thing" ' (ibid., p. 202).

Pastor recommended that Tereshchenko, if he wanted more details, should 'call Gurdjieff, be truly Gurdjieff's disciple', by a meditative technique he described. This is a curious point because Tereshchenko believed Ouspensky had an incomplete grasp of the Law of Seven (or 'heptaparaparshinokh') and he and British colleague Bert Sharp devised a fuller representation of the octave process (*The True Myth*, pp. 245-56).

Tereshchenko and Ginsburg asked themselves 'if it were possible that the being we know of as Gurdjieff could really have been expelled for "disobedience" from the unity of being in the very early history of the universe'.

Although Ouspensky is very unlikely to have wondered about that possibility, he certainly felt that he had lived many lives. From his own teaching he would be well aware that this posed two main possibilities: that of finally awakening and reaching a destination on The Fourth Way or failing to develop understanding and sliding down the scale of Being.

There were indications that 'Wraps Up The Thought' Ouspensky finally succeeded in unwrapping his innermost Being during the transition to another life.

Chapter 18

JOURNEY TO THE CENTRE

LIFE IS A JOURNEY AND a search. For some it is a zealous rush for riches of various kinds, from money to spiritual self-satisfaction; for others, a chase after fame and glory; for many, a striving for comfort, a condition that ranges from bare subsistence and relief from hunger and disease to sickening indulgence. For Peter Damian Ouspensky life was a quest for knowledge. In broad terms, this was an aim he shared with many men and women driven by intellectual or emotional curiosity about some aspect of life – science, the arts, politics, religion, technology. . . When it comes down to specifics, however, he was singularly eclectic: his perception of what constitutes knowledge embraced the impressions that could be received from the gamut of life, from a mathematical equation to a work, creature or scene of beauty.

This distinguished him from the ordinary run of seekers after truth in ordinary life. From the start, he was unusual in the select ranks of The Fourth Way, too, because he began at the top and worked down. As he himself explained, in the beginning he was found to be more useful to the general purpose of the Work, its third line, than to either the first line, work on oneself, or the second, work with and in support of his fellows on the same psychological journey.

Usually, people attracted to Work ideas devote considerable time and effort towards preparing themselves to be able to work with others and ultimately further the aims of the teaching. Gurdjieff saw that Ouspensky, however, was already intellectually trained to absorb the radical principles he disclosed and interpret them in an intelligible manner to novices in esoteric studies. His new pupil could also draw other suitable candidates to the System of self-change.

A personal minus to these System plusses was that his ready intellectual acceptance of Gurdjieff's ideas may have prevented him from registering as strong an emotional shock as did those who found them more surprising. Ouspensky himself said that he had evidenced 'extreme individualism' in his early years. While his fellows knew Ouspensky the teacher rewardingly well, few people had, or have now, a clear picture of the inner man. Judging by the secrecy surrounding his lectures on the System – even though, seeing that they dealt with esoteric knowledge, a certain degree of circumspection was demanded – it might be expected that work on his invisible self would definitely remain private.

It did. Despite that, some idea of this personal struggle with inner weaknesses can be gained from his words and actions. Psychologically, his journey was obviously always directed inwards. The following fragments of his life story suggest that spiritually he ventured right to the centre of his Being.

Perhaps it was not until late in life that he was able to work intensely on himself. It is apparent that while in the United States after World War II he decided to act on a sense of obligation he felt to his students in England. People often feel the binding effect of an obligation in a negative manner, so the fact that Ouspensky drove his fatally ill body to the other side of the world to fulfil this duty indicates the wish to do so arose from a central part of himself. According to people experienced in the Work, the carrying out of such a deeply felt obligation is possible only at an advanced stage of self-development. It requires real will, which can be exercised only after one's consciousness has been raised sufficiently to add a dimension beyond the temporal to one's Being. To *be* both *conscious* and *willing* is a far destination on The Fourth Way.

This stage of realising obligations is connected with an appreciation of the debt that one incurs for one's arising and existence. It is probable that in America Ouspensky felt that he could repay something of this debt and also play his part in the universal scheme of reciprocal maintenance by giving further direction to his group at Lyne Place in England.

Like the universal self-renewal process – in which everything eats of a lower level and in turn is food for a higher, while being nourished by both – the obligation that motivated him influenced several levels of his Being. He was obliged to help them by their need – or, at least, they would be able to receive help if they saw and accepted their need – and he also owed to higher beings that he pass on the knowledge that he had been assisted in transforming into understanding.

What he understood was indicated by what he could do. In the realm of Will, according to the Work teaching, *doing* is beyond personal abilities and implies that the doer is a conscious instrument of a higher power. Just as the same teaching regards fineness of spirit as the measure of one's power of consciousness, the transmutation of Being can be seen as the gestation of Soul. This techno-spiritual side of the Work is hinted at because those close to Ouspensky in the evening of his life were confident they saw signs that his soul was directing his actions and relationships. The spread of its embrace was suggested for one thing by his addressing the hundreds of people at his final London meetings as his family.

He was believed to be acting not only as one whose Essence had eliminated or relegated the respective aspects of Personality but who had attained to Individuality.

In paying a debt to Nature and the Work, as Stanley Nott suggested, Ouspensky would be following in his teacher's footsteps. In the introduction to the *Third Series* Gurdjieff said: 'I determined by this very series of books [*All and Everything*] consciously to acquit myself with Great Nature for my arising and existence.' He also said that 'thanks to my personal written explanations, a great benefit will arise for the majority of contemporary people as well as for future generations . . .' This latter effect can be seen to apply in no small measure to Ouspensky's writings too.

In an earlier but well remembered phase of his life Ouspensky had seen that Russian society was continuing only by momentum and foreseen the consequences of that lack of direction. It seems likely that while he was absent in America he became aware that his group centred on Lyne Place was similarly running solely on the force of its initiating impulse, and felt obliged to offer his guidance. He probably saw, too, that to a large extent the group was stuck in a rut because of restrictions he himself had imposed on development of the teaching. And he knew that when an involutionary process runs out of steam it needs a shock from outside.

It would have been no delusion of self-importance for him to have concluded that, as things stood, without him to steer the 'ark' it would drift off course. So he was obliged to return to England. That, however, could effect only a temporary correction as he had little time remaining to act as the great helmsman.

He found himself in a situation remarkably similar to that experienced by Gurdjieff in the latter part of his life. Somehow Ouspensky would have to open a way for the branch of the Work started in London and expanded at Lyne Place to continue, under new direction. Like Gurdjieff, he had no one to whom he could simply hand over control. There were a number of promising pupils, accomplished in his method – but that was the same method that he had judged to have missed the mark. Knowledge by itself could only ever perfect Function, after all. True, he had shown more than a few people the way to begin to develop Being through Consciousness. That was important, but what could one lecture about Will? First it was necessary to give up self-will. Many people, the teacher could not help observing, imagined they understood this, but extremely few really believed and accepted that they had no more than a trace of will. So how far could mere talk of understanding's connection with objective consciousness and a permanent 'I' lead?

Better to throw overboard all the old formulae. People would then have to formulate the ideas afresh for themselves. Ironically, this notion is reminiscent of Gurdjieff's reported remark to Frank Pinder after casting doubt on Ouspensky's qualification as a group leader at a London meeting in 1922: 'Now they [Ouspensky's pupils] will *have* to choose a teacher' (*Journey Through This World*, p. 99). Whoever they chose, it would be the act of choice that was of value.

As Gurdjieff had repeatedly found necessary, Ouspensky

now must act to prevent people continuing to depend on him. He would abandon the System to give his pupils the opportunity of being independent of his direct influence.

His separation from methods, techniques, can also be seen as the sacrifice, the relinquishing of what he had struggled to attain, that represents the 'down' side of paying what is owed. The 'up' side is the accomplishment of having cancelled the debt, and the freeing-up feeling that evokes. This two-way flow – involution, or generation, and evolution, or regeneration – can also be seen in his reaching the nadir of his life in America, for it was from that rock-bottom that he rebounded towards the inner freedom he had always sought. A special effort, typified in this instance as sacrifice or abandonment, is needed to shift from passive to active force.

To strengthen his resolve to carry out this tactic, misunderstood as it was likely to be, Ouspensky could reflect that the group aim had never been the acquisition of knowledge as an end in itself but as a stepping stone to Being. And, unlike the so-called System, Being is not a collection of *fragments*. Its defining quality is wholeness; that is how a person's inner unity can be determined.

It was this strengthened inner cohesion that Lyne residents felt distinguished their returned leader. They sensed that when they succeeded in communicating with him it was not with the instruments of his physical body. He had little further use for that part of himself; it was sufficient for his physical mechanism to move him about for a short time longer, enable him to take in impressions and articulate the occasional message. He was not interested in mundane things. Even at the Colet House meetings, he did not appear to register trivial questions, or waste energy replying if he thought the meaning of his answer would not be grasped.

It is bending a long bow to suggest it, but there may be a parallel between Ouspensky's situation then and the story in *Beelzebub's Tales* about the Martian Toof-Nef-Tef who in his final days wished to return to the place (on planet Earth) where he had spent his youth. The Martian is depicted as having reached the stage that Gurdjieff calls 'Ischmetch', which leaves him free of the need for the lower centres' energy transformations and dependent only on a substance derived from the Prime Source. At this level of perfection, his highest being body is said to be ready to be taken to the planet Purgatory (ibid., pp. 1147-9).

While Ouspensky's disciples may not have been considering whether he was ready for purification in Purgatory, some did think he had reached a very high graduation of Being. According to several reports, in the period of his death Ouspensky's presence was felt by different people in different localities at the same time, an attribute of beings who have grown what Rodney Collin calls the electronic body (*The Theory of Celestial Influence*, p. 202). So, perhaps the highest part of his reasoning was perfected to the degree necessary for Purgatory. . .

In accord with the principle that ultimately all Being is one, Ouspensky did not seek seclusion at this time but apparently shared the fine energy that was now invigorating him with others. Of course, this is to be expected, seeing that it is argued on economical grounds that one person does not have a right to use the force necessary for the Work unless it is shared with the community.

Such sharing is not necessarily simple to manage. Assuming that he was conscious of living in a higher dimension and of being connected with a Higher Source, it would be impossible for him to transmit what he was experiencing in the language of a lower level. It was noticeable that he insisted on repeating that 'really, there is no method'. At first his audience might see madness in this abnegation of method, but eventually they would surely grasp that they could not expect any system to automatically develop Essence and raise Being. Knowledge can improve functions; it takes another step to transform an inner part of oneself.

Previously Ouspensky could have been perceived as emphasising intellectual or emotional approaches over other aspects of self-development, to beginners at any rate.

Gurdjieff, on the other hand, consistently put equal stress on body, mind and feeling with the aim of harmonising them to transform the whole Being and open a connection with a higher force. In referring to 'feeling' he sometimes substituted 'soul'.

Both teachers agreed that a centre of gravity must be formed in Being before it can move to Will. 'What do you want?' Ouspensky asked his pupils. The intensity and realisation of one's want or need depends on the level of Being; a sudden realisation that in truth one's Being is void of anything of value can be the spur to promote understanding.

Genuinely perceiving this emptiness is not, as may be imagined, an early milestone in the Work. So it is in no way belittling to hypothesise that Ouspensky had such an insight during his American stay. Which would open the possibility that it was this shock of reality that led him to call a halt to his established methods and urge his pupils to begin again, though they would surely still need a technique, even if of their own making.

Of course, there are methods and *methods.* The term simply denotes a working guide of some kind, which is also the purpose of a map or a model. A progression of methods or models leading to Gurdjieff's ideal of harmony can be seen in various stages of the Work.

On a visit to American groups in 1930, Gurdjieff purported to ridicule his representative A.R. Orage's imagery, or as he put it, 'wiseacring', in devising 'The Local Map', 'The Boat', 'The Greater Map' and the 'Destination' (*Gurdjieff: The Anatomy of a Myth*, p. 238). Indeed, he made as though to wipe Orage right off the esoteric map by having all members of his group sign an oath to have no further relations with Orage without Gurdjieff's permission. But his approval of Orage's signing the declaration rather indicates that he did not really disapprove of maps per se as a guide to Work exercises, just that he thought the New Yorkers should redraw theirs (*Life is Real Only Then, When 'I Am'*, pp. 117-25).

Ouspensky's pupil Maurice Nicoll gave his group the

example of a novel aide-mémoire he used to facilitate travel in his own psychological territory. Nicoll's pupil Beryl Pogson in turn told her group about it: 'Dr Nicoll used to have London for his map. "Where am I? I'm in Soho..." You have to remember there is somewhere else to go' (*Mind and Energy*, p. 27/28 depending on edition).

For those unfamiliar with London, it can be assumed that Soho would represent a place, a state, an attitude, that Nicoll regarded as an unsuitable area to reside. Awareness of the map was a reminder that it was just as possible to move from one state of emotion to another as it was to travel from Swiss Cottage to Baker Street.

Ouspensky, of course, drew up a far grander scheme than a map of London: a veritable new model of the universe. Despite the many new territories, contours and alignments this model reveals, and although it certainly does not deserve Orage's jocular tag, 'New Muddle of the Universe' (*Journey Through This World*, p. 37), it is essentially one viewed from our customary Earth time-space plane. Not that it can be slighted; many people see it as a model suited to the new age.

Gurdjieff, with the help of the alien Beelzebub, goes a stage further to show how we on Earth appear from a higher point in the universe. So *All and Everything* can be studied as an impartially prepared map of the Being of humanity.

Although he professed not to have examined Gurdjieff's major work, Ouspensky evidently came to see that no single method was enough to achieve a transformation of the whole Being, that the processes of Function, Being and Will had to proceed in unison. His group at Lyne Place would have to discover that for themselves; a teacher can only point the direction.

While there was more at stake than Ouspensky's own development, by transforming his own Being he was freed of his own psychological clothing. For the greater part of his life he had been pretty well isolated from others, communicating mainly through functions. Most of his old pupils at Colet House failed to understand this new Ouspensky, but a few were inspired to follow his instructions and rebuild from the beginning, as he had done. He had taught them Gurdjieff's revelations about the working of triads, the Law of Three, in which Active Force is resisted by Passive Force and the conflict reconciled by Third Force. Previously he had given them the theory of the rare condition of freedom from ordinary restraints when Neutralising Force becomes the active element of a relationship. Now his closest pupils saw that he was giving them a living example of this.

One person in Ouspensky's circle commented that he

'not only opened the psychological door for us at Warwick Gardens through the System but also removed all obstacles for us and left us, at Colet Gardens at the end of his life, freer to enter the *esoteric* gate also. In fact, he led us through Wonderland in search of the Miraculous and at the end beckoned us to follow him through the Looking Glass (*Remembering Pyotr Demianovich Ouspensky*, p. 45).

This class of valuation does seem to recognise him as a harbinger of the new epoch, which is predicted to be marked by the breathing of life into the Soul as well as a refreshing of the Spirit. Well, that is an aim. To come down to actual happenings, what is rather fantastically described as an adventure through Wonderland translates in fact into a long, patient training to overcome our habitual state of identification. That advanced stage of Work, which reveals the reverse side of our mirror of reality, and to which Ouspensky's pupils were only beckoned, was indicated by their teacher's new-found freedom from mechanicalness.

The teaching illustrates Identification and Freedom as opposite ends of the stick of Choice. Or again, it may say that the risk of one is the price of gaining the other. For identification can be seen to begin in the moment a chance of freedom pops up – but when we habitually react to it in denial, in passivity, by taking the line of least resistance, behaving as we repeatedly do even when we have resolved to do the opposite. The positive side of choice is the exercise of freedom; it depends upon understanding, which is increased only by the transformation of Being – that is to say, power to choose is directly proportionate to the level of Being.

Struggle with identification is an exercise of (and for) freedom, an act of choice. That is why it is said that facing the threat posed by identification is the price man pays for the possibility of freedom. The currency of this payment is our attention and effort, as it is throughout the Work.

Ouspensky followed Gurdjieff's teaching that people need to increase their consciousness and that this can be achieved only by raising their level of Being.

In commenting on Ouspensky's death, John Bennett said that his 'potentialities had been brought into time, and they had undergone an irreversible transformation' (*Witness*, p. 227). This seems to imply that he had completed the downward, involutionary phase and was on the ascent, evolving from the actual to a higher level by building up potential. In Bennett's Systematics, this triad of transformation is shown to start with Second Force, the denying principle. There has to be a sacrifice of the actual for new possibilities to emerge. To illustrate this he points out that a seed is formed by a plant's sacrifice of its growth to produce a flower, which dies so that the seed, a storehouse of possibilities, can be born.

Such a transformation can be imagined as having taken place in Ouspensky: he responded to a crucial moment of potential freedom by choosing to sacrifice his teaching method, thus beginning the switch from passive to active, the start of an evolutionary process.

The next great triad of development is seen by Bennett as being formed by the relationship he designates Freedom, which gives life meaning. Gurdjieff, says Bennett, was the first to reveal it as such, and to show that it begins with a reconciling impulse, the Third Force. It is freedom, he explains, because it is the nature of the Third Force to relate to any situation, for it is not committed to either of the other two forces, making possible a triad in which neither active nor positive impulse dominates.

Ouspensky's decision to abandon his method might seem to have been designed to fault the whole System. However, in following this course he may be seen to be echoing Gurdjieff's realisation, at one point during his travels in Central Asia, of 'all my blunders and in general the imperfections of the methods previously applied by me' (*Life is Real Only Then, When 'I Am'*, p.18). He also says he then saw 'how I ought to have acted in this or that instance'.

Gurdjieff's disclosures invariably contain a number of meanings, but an obvious, possibly superficial, interpretation seems to relate to Ouspensky's seeing how he too might have acted differently. At the 1947 meetings he gave a clue to this by asking: 'What do you want?' He did not supply a theoretical answer. His listeners' own pondering on this question could have been a starting point for work on building up their capacity for Self-remembering and consciousness. The attainment of consciousness, an instrument of the Spirit, appears a long-range goal to most of us, but those closest to Ouspensky suspected he had moved beyond it to inhabit the Soul, which is in the province of Will.

Gurdjieff reports that on November 6, 1927, about 30 years after his memorable shock when he was on the edge of the Gobi Desert, he realised he needed something that would continually prompt him to Self-remember (ibid., p. 25). Ouspensky's perhaps similar experience, about January 1947, also came some 30 years after his life-changing experience of meeting the System.

Gurdjieff's second shock resulted in his thinking of what he calls a 'reminding factor" (ibid., pp. 24-25). 'Thinking and thinking, I came to the conclusion that if I should intentionally stop utilising the exceptional power in my possession which had been developed by me consciously in my common life with people, then there must be forced out of me such a reminding source.'

That power was generated by the psychic energy he termed 'hanbledzoin', which is produced by special exercises or conscious labour and intentional suffering and is used for spiritual development, as well as for the observable practices of telepathy and hypnotism. Gurdjieff seems to imply that saving the hanbledzoin from such uses would make it available for Self-remembering – and for writing the series of books that was currently his main aim.

In 1947 Ouspensky, on his scale, may also have decided on self-sacrifice to further his aim. He seems to have forsaken his power of formulating and explaining complex subjects to his students. In his last 'lectures' he threw the explaining back on his questioners.

His insistence that the group make a new beginning, coming as it did as he came to the end of his time, evokes a powerful saying of Gurdjieff: 'One of the strongest motives for wishing to work on yourself is the realisation that you may die at any moment.' Gurdjieff emphasised this by making a similar declaration Beelzebub's final message to the world (*Beelzebub's Tales*, p. 1183).

His state of health at that time would have left Ouspensky little choice but to bear in mind his physical death. But both Gurdjieff and Ouspensky made clear that it was also necessary to remain aware that death of another sort is a hazard every time there is a choice. If we do not make the right choice, part of us expires, psychologically. This is a reminder that man must hold in his consciousness the possibility of life or death for the spiritual Self that the Work names 'Real I'.

The necessary continual renewal of spiritual life depends on our capacity to choose. A special memory is needed to accomplish this. This indicates that Ouspensky's apparent preoccupation with memorising his life may have had an additional purpose to the generally assumed one of preparing for another round of earthly life.

What he was demonstrating in his dying days was largely what Nicoll suggests in *Living Time*: 'a rethinking of everything in terms of *all the life* and *now*'.

'Above space appears Time,' Nicoll says, 'and above the enduring World in Time the enduring World of all possibilities, which is the World of Eternity' (ibid., p. 238).

What Nicoll calls 'a new sense of environment' makes for the *integration* of the life. Although we do not have unity while under the illusion of 'passing time', Ouspensky, we may assume, was envisioning his whole Time-body, where all his lives, past, present and future, met in the Now, which is not the present moment and which has to be created; it is 'where one is present to oneself' (ibid., p. 224).

It was Nicoll who pointed out most clearly that the response of higher powers to request is always more than the petitioner expects. Ouspensky remarks in *In Search of the Miraculous* that this was noticeable also in Gurdjieff's answers; he gave more information than was necessary to cover the question. Unfortunately for our comfort, this over-supply phenomenon works in the other direction, too. When one fails to make a required effort, one is not simply marking-time. There is no accommodation in the Work discipline for standing still. It's always a case of either up or down. That is why the warning about remembering one's death is pertinent to every moment of choice, for then one is confronted by the alternatives of life or death, up or down, in relation to one's Real 'I'.

True, Ouspensky promulgated the idea of eternal recurrence, which in a fortunate life might promise to be the ultimate in marking-time, even of resting on one's laurels, but the duration of this recurrence is not *absolutely* eternal. Anyhow, on Ouspensky's own calculations, Eternity comprises both the fifth and sixth dimensions, so contains different levels of time; every level of Being has its own time. Certainly, recurrence may exist, but not indefinitely. Ouspensky described the repeating cycles of lives as being designed ideally as spirals; there are points on the circle where one can step up to another circle, provided a conscious choice is made. If, on the other hand, one is stuck in a rut, even a comfortable rut, one can revolve around that circuit for a time, but it would seem that sooner or later those cycles of lives will be exhausted.

Ouspensky explains:

'"Eternal life" is a term which has several meanings. . . . on the one hand eternal life belongs not only to all people but even to everything that exists, while on the other hand it is necessary to be born again in order to obtain it. This contradiction would be inexplicable, if the difference between the fifth and sixth dimensions had not been previously established. Both the one and the other are eternity. But one is unalterable repetition, always with the same end, and the other is escape from this repetition.

Thus we see two ideas of birth: birth on the same plane, continuation of life; and birth on another plane, regeneration, transformation, escape from the first plane' (*A New Model of the Universe*, p. 515).

Nicoll adds an important condition:

'In discussing the idea of recurrence, in connection with the conception of a six-dimensional world, composed first of the three visible dimensions of Space and the (to us) invisible fourth dimension of the world that we experience as Time, Mr Ouspensky said that the possibility of change begins only with the possibility of remembering yourself *now*. He said: "In this sense the idea of recurrence is not necessary." At that time, when I heard this, I thought that the idea of the repetition, the recurrence, of everything, would make one's Self-Remembering stronger – and I no longer think it but know it. . . . A Conscious Man need not recur – that is, return to the same place in Time. He may reincarnate – that is, go back and be born in another part of historical Time where he can prevent things from going as they did' (*Psychological Commentaries*, vol. 4, pp.1247-8).

Nicoll says further that Man No. 5 lives on the outer circle of the Conscious Circle of Humanity, the inner circles of which comprise men Nos. 6 and No. 7.

So, although Ouspensky appeared to be making strenuous efforts as a Balanced Man (No. 4) to retain his memory in his next recurrence, some of his disciples judged that he might not have to repeat the cycle. They would not have regarded it a great stretch of the imagination to picture him on at least the outer rim of the Circle of Conscious Humanity. Perhaps for one so interested in the possibility of reincarnation he would be allowed to revisit earlier parts of historical time and tie up some loose ends, or loosen knots, and thus defuse some future situations.

Those who regarded him in this light interpreted his 'abandonment' as a warning not to allow the System to degenerate into dogma. This view was supported by his instruction not to use System language when he asked each group member to invite three new people – a publicising of the movement that was itself radical – to the lectures (*The Bridge*, No. 12, p. 128). Nor did he answer questions in the System vernacular.

Obviously, it was natural for his associates to attribute deep inner meanings to his every word. After one lecture, he called a senior group member, Francis Roles, up to the platform and told him: 'Prepare them better next time' (ibid.). Ouspensky did not appear to have been thrilled with the way the meeting had gone, but some of his followers pondered whether he meant a preparation for the next round of life rather than the next lecture.

On another evening, one of his associates recalled that as they watched the crowd of people streaming down the long staircase at Colet House Ouspensky said quietly: '*Vse Ya sam.*' ('All this I did myself.') As recalled in the booklet *Remembering Pyotr Demianovich Ouspensky*, this is thought to have resulted from the realisation that because he had been unable to find representatives of ancient wisdom in the East he had reconstructed Eastern ideas for the West (p. 43). There is no suggestion there that it could also be interpreted as an acceptance of responsibility for the state in which he now found his pupils, who just happened to be *descending* the stairs.

The dramatically inclined thinker Rodney Collin writes that Ouspensky 'produced among his friends a play, of which they unwittingly but perfectly played their parts, and whose plot was his own death. Silent, he instructed them in their hearts, some recognising, some not. "I will always be with you," he too could say – but lightly and smoking a cigarette, so that none noticed' (*The Theory of Eternal Life*, p. 116).

What everyone concerned has noticed is that the provocative cause of many acts of Ouspensky's 'play', which often seemed to be a 'Struggle of the Magicians', was his physical and psychological, if not spiritual, separation from that celebrated Teacher of Dancing, George Gurdjieff. It is insufficient to offer as a reason for this that Ouspensky did not understand Gurdjieff's overall strategy, his big aim and plan. Who did? So it may be useful to review briefly the two men's approach to the drama of the Work

In June 1917 at Essentuki Gurdjieff collected some fourteen people and worked with unparalleled intensity to impress his ideas on them. Ouspensky says that he unfolded the whole plan of the Work. Gurdjieff later revealed that it was a test of methods to use in his Institute. As soon as he was satisfied on this, he dismissed the group, to general confusion and dismay (*In Search of the Miraculous*, p. 346) – much as Ouspensky did with his group thirty years on when perhaps he too had found what he needed to see.

Next Gurdjieff introduced, at Tuapse in March 1918, his special methods of rhythm and dance. The point of this Ouspensky understood less perfectly. Although he could see that people would have to work hard to master the exercises and would obviously learn something about themselves, he felt the Movements were not for him. All that he said later about this period shows that he did not realise that Gurdjieff was looking at a different time scale, working on a different agenda, and on an experiment unsuspected by those in it.

'Experiment' may strike some people as a demeaning reflection on the hard tests the pupils endured. In that case, Gurdjieff's own description as reported by Stanley Nott will sound rather less respectful: 'I needed rats for my experiments.' That was his sardonic reply when Nott, who says he was in a heated state, accused Gurdjieff of taking his students so far and then leaving them 'between two stools' (*Journey Through This World*, p. 38). Actually, the phrase 'between two stools' tends to throw responsibility for their situation back on the students, for to Gurdjieff on other occasions it denoted the position of people who tried to retain their old attitudes while acquiring new, esoteric ideas.

Of course, Gurdjieff's 'rats' remark must be subjected to the usual precaution: it may have been intended to have a special effect on the hearer. Even with this proviso, it adds weight to the widely accepted theory that Gurdjieff's main purpose was to investigate the psychology of all types of people to develop an antidote for their suggestibility.

Another remarkable phenomenon that Ouspensky did not understand at the time was how Gurdjieff's work could be furthered by his placing himself amid wars, revolutions, and trying situations in general. Only someone on Gurdjieff's level of Being could really realise how his creativity could be invigorated by intentional suffering, so that while his 'outer world gasped for breath; at the same time, nevertheless, the vivification produced by the ever opposing factors in my inner world increased to the highest degree'.

In this, the master's aim was 'to expound the very essence of all the material elucidated by me for the welfare of humanity'. Apparently, mankind was not ready to learn and was proving difficult to help. In 1927 he aimed to 'study and from all sides make clear to myself the details of some of the, for me, still obscure and very deep questions concerning the common psyche of man . . .' (*Life is Real Only Then, When I Am*, p. 35). He was convinced he would attain his aim through his 'Inner-World Revolution', the forces of which struggle he says produced Self-remembering of 'a never-before-experienced vigour' (ibid., p. 42).

Later, in order to think what was to be done next he 'retreated to my room and locked myself in, of course making preliminary arrangements that coffee be amply supplied . . .'

This seemingly incongruous note about 'coffee', when issues of humanity's welfare were under study, is particularly intriguing because similar references to this beverage appear in other records of Gurdjieff's unique work. For instance, when A.R. Orage finally emerged from the depths of despair at the Prieuré, having found that something had changed within himself and he was at last even enjoying hard labour, Gurdjieff said to him: 'Now, Orage, I think you dig enough. Let us go to the cafe and drink coffee' (*Teachings of Gurdjieff*, p. 28).

In another account of relief from hard labour at the Prieuré, Beryl Pogson reports: 'In the middle of the morning Gurdjieff would say: "We old men, Nicole, we have coffee," and would call for Big Nina, to bring coffee to the carpenter's shed. (Dr Nicoll at that time was nearly thirty-nine!' (*Maurice Nicoll: A Portrait*, p.86)

In both these cases he offered the stimulant, or stimulus, after they had transcended a crisis in their efforts to apply Work principles. From that moment, Orage said, 'things began to change'.

Perhaps 'coffee' had an even more significant meaning when Gurdjieff uttered it as one of his last words. An American doctor who rushed to his bedside as he lay dying in Paris in 1949 was met by the greeting: 'Bravo, America! Now we have some coffee' (according to several sources, including, with slightly different syntax, Gorham Munson in the spring 1988 issue of the *Gurdjieff International Review*).

Of course, black or white, it may just have illustrated his sense of humour, which rarely faltered.

That Gurdjieff wrote at all is yet another example of his unsettling ability to turn an accepted belief upside down, as well as to turn his hand to anything necessary. Book writing was Ouspensky's central activity before he came under Gurdjieff's influence. Afterwards he professed, no doubt under his teacher's influence, to see little merit in the written word for the transmission of esoteric ideas. He had come to believe the printed page lacked the energy that could give digestible meaning to spoken words, an energy he felt in Gurdjieff's vocal delivery.

This attitude rubbed off on Nicoll who, in his acclaimed *Living Time*, an example of power in print, replies to the question of what could awaken a higher level of consciousness in this dismissive retort: 'Nothing gained from books can possibly do this.' He concedes that attempts to present ideas in such a manner as he has essayed are probably legitimate 'though I am not quite convinced of this myself because, if taken literally, they can be nothing but poison, i.e. if they fall on the passive mind' (ibid., p. 233).

Ouspensky's negative attitude to books dealing with inner teaching was probably also engendered by his acquired fondness for secrecy. 'The idea of keeping secrets is connected in esotericism with the idea of conserving energy,' he explains. 'Silence, secrecy, create a closed circle, that is, an "accumulator" ' (*A New Model of the Universe*, p. 187).

Thus there seemed to be an unwritten agreement to prevent details of the Work leaking to the great unwashed through the printed word. Then, from 1924 to 1935, Gurdjieff, who Ouspensky reckoned to be the most effective lecturer he had heard but one of the most amateurish of writers, put the bulk of his energy into writing a series of books, encrypting his message for the world into a code that he believed future generations would decipher.

As a writer, Gurdjieff could be seen to be following Ouspensky's example, in choice of medium if not in style. By contrast, few would have agreed that Ouspensky was adopting Gurdjieff's type of behaviour when he shocked his followers by announcing that a new method was needed. There was no corresponding outcry when Gurdjieff made clear to Orage's American group on 13 November 1930, the day when they were ordered to repudiate their leader, that they must make a fresh start.

Gurdjieff, of course, was always an unknown factor while Ouspensky was usually predictable in the course he followed. People were ill prepared to suddenly face the unexpected with Ouspensky. His method was to present the Work ideas precisely as Gurdjieff had explained them to his early groups. To prevent their being misused he was equally careful to pass on the principles only to people who showed signs of being able to value them. This he did by meeting privately and laying down the law against discussing what transpired to outsiders; even group members were to talk of the ideas among themselves only when in an appropriate state and not risk lowering their force by gossiping or romancing about them.

Gurdjieff obviously did not believe such an arrangement would allow him to cast his net widely enough. Once he had changed his method to the printed word, he needed to broadcast to the general public the possibility of learning an efficient way of realising their potential. His precaution against the System's degenerating into a popular cult was to write in such a way that only the most determined seekers would be able to penetrate to the layers of meaning hidden deep in a literary minefield.

On this grand plan, Bennett says Gurdjieff wished to show as many people as possible how to transform the energies necessary for the evolution of mankind. On a nearer objective, he also needed initiates who could interpret *All and Everything* accurately enough to maintain interest in its ideas and so preserve them until such time as they would be more widely understood. Half a century after publication, there are strong signs that this hope is being realised, as more and more people try to unravel his books' conundrums.

In recorded anecdotes about the two men, the impression stands out that Ouspensky obeyed all the laws he saw clearly, particularly those of honesty and integrity, while Gurdjieff seemed to be under only the great universal laws and bent or broke rules designed for ordinary folk with impunity. A.R. Orage occasionally referred to Gurdjieff not as an Armenian Greek but a Pythagorean Greek, evoking impressions of ancient wisdom and an astute interpretation of number in his system of knowledge.

Orage's analogy is strikingly apt seeing that Pythagoras is credited with having discovered the numerical ratios that determine the main musical intervals, leading his School to interpret the world on the foundation of number, and that Gurdjieff emphasised three and sevenfoldness in his teaching, which was based on an understanding of scale.

Like his character Beelzebub, Gurdjieff could have come

from another planet for all the chance that even his closest associates had of fathoming his actions, let alone impulses. No one knew for certain whether he was his own man or a representative of an esoteric School. A few in his inner circle noticed that he received mail from the Turkestan area and calculated that several trips he made from France to Germany could have been extended secretly to Central Asia, and from this speculated that he was receiving instructions from a School.

He says himself in the *Third Series* that, in the period when he locked himself in his room (January 1 to April 23, 1928), with coffee laid on, to plan how to fulfil his mission, he also wrote 'letters of inquiry to some of my friends whom I respect'. None of his people knew of any friends from whom he would conceivably seek advice. He so conscientiously assumed full responsibility for his community's needs that his followers would find it hard to imagine that he would need advice from anyone, even in an esoteric school. So this is one of the unknown facets of his life.

Another is whether he intentionally forced his chief disciples to go their own ways. John Bennett says that at some point Gurdjieff made it impossible for all 'potential initiates' to continue to work with him, erecting obstacles that they had to overcome. Citing his own first teacher as the best known case, Bennett comments:

'Ouspensky was to the very end of his life devoted to Gurdjieff. He was convinced that Gurdjieff was no ordinary man. He knew that it was Gurdjieff alone that had given him hope that it would be possible to find a way out of the state of mechanicalness and confusion into which he saw the whole world plunged. He had no doubt that Gurdjieff had the secret of a method that would work and he had decided to devote his life to its propagation. Yet, within two years, Gurdjieff began to drive Ouspensky away from him (*Gurdjieff: Making a New World*, p. 234).

Opponents of this argument reject it as merely an excuse to cover up weaknesses of those, principally Ouspensky, Orage and Bennett himself, who were unable to put Gurdjieff's teaching into practice. Against this rebuttal, we have Gurdjieff's own description of his pains to remove his closest associates from his proximity, in order to maximise the suffering through which he produced the energy needed to accomplish his task.

Another contentious issue concerning Ouspensky is the question of 'faith'. Readers of *The Fourth Way* may have been struck by his assertions that 'faith does not enter into The Fourth Way' and 'this system teaches people to believe in absolutely nothing' (p. 6), on the premise that 'if you can understand, you do not need faith' (ibid., p. 137). But they will find that he introduces the idea of discipline to take the place of passive faith. It becomes apparent that what he attacked was not genuine faith but blind belief. For it is inescapable that Ouspensky was too intelligent to waste his time studying the world and his and others' inner experiences unless he believed they could be found to make sense, to have a purpose – that is to say, from a Work angle, faith that they could be understood.

Yet another debatable point is Ouspensky's preoccupation during a large part of the 1920s and 1930s with the possibility of contacting a Higher Source. In this connection it is noteworthy that Nicoll frequently remarks in his *Psychological Commentaries* that the Work is not a psychological system invented by ordinary man but a conscious influence that higher man transmits to our higher centres. Therefore it is what our own Higher Intellectual and Emotional Centres would teach us if only we would or could listen to them.

On this reasoning, would it not be his own higher centres that Ouspensky might have hoped to find – perhaps in the end did find – as his Higher Source? If the conscious influence was getting through, then he may have been telling his people at those final London meetings that they did not need an outside method but should look within themselves.

If they did, presumably they would see also that the whole is greater than the sum of all its fragments, or perhaps that it is only our restricted vision that creates the illusion of fragmentation. The illusions and delusions of our perceptions were constantly in Ouspensky's thoughts since his early experiments into his own psychology. It should not surprise us if the ultimate effect of this was a vision of a higher dimension of reality. He surely made every effort to remember this.

Peter Ouspensky's customary words of farewell, his devoted pupil Nicolai Rabeneck recollected, were *'Ne zabuyvayte.'* They translate as 'Don't forget' and were used colloquially in Russia in such phrases as 'Don't forget, call again,' and 'Don't forget, drop a line' (*The Bridge*, No. 12, p.143). Obviously, to Ouspensky the meaning was 'Remember.' He addressed it to himself as well as to all kindred spirits: '*Ne zabuyvayte*, Self-remember.'

CHAPTER 19

MYSTERY OF THE 'WEAK' LINK

'DON'T FORGET' – that is the anglicised form of Ouspensky's farewell. It evidently persisted to his final acts on Earth, which appeared to be connected with the kind of remembering that enables a man to understand himself and life more fully. His friends' accounts of his last months agree that he used his remaining strength consciously to fix episodes of his life in consciousness. Rodney Collin recounts in *The Theory of Eternal Life* (p. 101) that he frequently insisted on being driven all day to places that had been significant in his experiences, insulating himself from all distractions, including eating and drinking, and enduring feats of endurance that defied medical advice that he rest and exhausted his companions.

The effort in that aspect of revising and fixing memory was obvious to others. It indicated to them that he was preparing to take advantage of the raised consciousness and test of will that he believed death would open. What his colleagues naturally were not empowered to see was an accompanying psychological recapitulation. They might have speculated, however, that his renowned power of reasoning was now casting clear light on his relationship with Gurdjieff. For, despite anything he said at those final London meetings, his actions showed he himself had not abandoned the end results of the System that had directed his life. And, although he had barred any reference to his teacher from his group meetings, it is extremely unlikely that he would not now have reflected on the originator of that System.

Perhaps he even reconsidered his decision to cease following what he regarded to be Gurdjieff's changed Work direction. And could he have felt remorse in his last analysis of the emotions behind his suggestion that his former teacher might have gone mad?

In view of his extensive study of the *New Testament*, might not his position since 1924 appear to reflect his own view of

Judas Iscariot's attitude and role in the Gospel drama? This would demand of him a high degree of impartiality. In *A New Model of the Universe* Ouspensky dismisses not only the conventional 'traitor' interpretation but also the possibility hinted at by Gurdjieff that Judas sacrificed himself for the sake of man's redemption. Instead, he judges him to be 'a small man who found himself in the wrong place, an ordinary man full of distrust, of fears and suspicions ..." (ibid., p. 131).

Judas, he contends, had clung to his idea of Jesus as a potential king on Earth and was bewildered by His refusal to exploit this. Judas's tragedy sprang from his eventual wish 'to break and destroy that which he could not comprehend'.

In a final evaluation of the knowledge he had gathered, Ouspensky might have seen merit in Gurdjieff's interpretation that Judas was the most developed of the disciples, the only one who could play the real-life role of betraying the master and thus fulfilling scriptural prophecy, or scripted drama. Gurdjieff suggested that Judas's dealing with the chief priests and elders had been a necessary tactic to buy time for Christ to complete the initiation of his disciples, a process involving physical and spiritual modes and Time.

Through his study of the ancient mysteries of Egypt and Greece, Ouspensky would have been aware of a tradition that in a unit of twelve on such a mission one member has to be sacrificed. On this esoteric detail, Beryl Pogson explained to her students:

'In all stories of groups of twelve, there has to be a weak place so something can change. This represents something in oneself which will betray what is purest and force what is purest to suffer; suffering is what makes the transformation' (*The True Myth*, pp.615-6).

This view accords with the principle that in self-development, as in evolution in general, upward progress is made through places of weakness, by transformation of imperfections. When this is portrayed in mystery plays, the message can be scripted at leisure by those of the inner circle and acted in safety, whereas the Christian drama was performed in real life, involved real flesh and blood, and paradoxically produced a failure – but one that had the result of preserving the teaching through the ages.

Maurice Nicoll believed that to help achieve this, Judas had not only to act the part of a betrayer, the weak link, but to embody the role in real life, and suffer the consequences – a supreme example of what Gurdjieff meant by intentional suffering, accepting an essential task without hope of receiving a reward.

Whether or not Ouspensky came round to this point of view is a matter of speculation, but undeniably his actions late in life reversed his previous procedures. For instance, a feature of early Christianity of which he long approved was its advocacy of secrecy over its inner teaching, based on the precept 'let not thy left hand know what thy right hand doeth' (*St Matthew* 6:3). He considered that the practice of secrecy in the closed circle of esotericism accumulated energy. Yet, going against his custom of carefully screening those who attended his meetings, he surprised his followers by telling them to bring additional people to his final talks.

Apparently he hoped for a wide circulation of the shock announcement that he was abandoning the System he had taught. At this apparent renunciation his students in London felt something of the painful perplexity that, we are told, was experienced by eleven disciples in Jerusalem over Judas's defection.

It seems possible to some observers that Ouspensky was enacting (not previously consciously) a role corresponding in some degree to that of Judas. In the eyes of many of Gurdjieff's followers, he had already betrayed his master. Further aligning the events in modern England with those in ancient Palestine, he had finally rejected the teaching, or at least the System, if his words were taken at face value.

He disclosed fewer clues to his motivation than did Judas, who at least threw away the symbolic thirty pieces of silver and who, by hanging himself in remorse for betraying 'innocent blood', could be assumed to have put the accusations against

Christ in question and prompted some to ponder His real stature. Slander that Judas was driven by mercenary considerations would not concern personally an individual developed to the degree suggested here, but he might fear it would obscure the real lesson of the Crucifixion.

The difference in scale may well invite skepticism that Ouspensky's final scene mirrored in any way the Gospel mystery. However, those in the presence of the dying Work group leader did seem to detect a parallel. When Collin quotes (as reported earlier) that his teacher too could say, 'I will always be with you,' his use of 'too' points clearly to Christ's assurance '... and, lo, I am with you alway, even unto the end of the world' (*St Matthew*, 28: 20).

Collin, and of course Ouspensky, knew that *St Matthew*'s final verse has Christ making that promise after summoning his disciples to a Galilean mountain; that is, at a high level of consciousness, where they would be able to understand His words. Even at our ordinary low state of awareness, we know that the phrase 'the end of the world' has layers of meaning. The 'world' of the Authorised King James Version is interpreted in other translations of the *Bible* as 'age' or 'time'. We might regard it as the Aeon, the whole life of the Solar System.

Although Ouspensky, in his final talks, did not predict a similarly long life span for Gurdjieff's System, many of his followers responded to his words in the spirit of latter-day disciples of Gurdjieff's teaching. They understood that Christ's assurance of His continued presence encouraged His disciples to convey His commands to the world. Ouspensky's chief pupils, too, responded in individual ways to their teacher's request that they reformulate the ideas he had transmitted to them. Collin, as we have seen, classified the sciences according to the worlds they investigate to create his remarkable book *The Theory of Celestial Influence*.

We have also considered the suggestion that Ouspensky, while regarded by some as working in his own interest, was in fact carrying out a task in line with Gurdjieff's teaching. This, and the way he lived his whole life, are at odds with a literal interpretation of his abandoning the System. And if crediting his "always with you" pledge with having a Gospel origin is warranted, it can be taken as an affirmation that Fourth Way principles are timeless.

It is tempting to accept Nicoll's intuition that by the end of his life Ouspensky's character was complete. The idea of flaws being the gateway to perfection reinforces this opinion. For this aspect of imperfection, far from being a misconception of some secret cult, can be regarded as the cornerstone of the sciences of physics and chemistry – and of creation itself. Bert Sharp, a scientifically trained traveler on The Fourth Way, makes the point well in his privately published *Where Humanity Stands Today* (2000). Explaining the combining power of the elements, he says: 'The way in which such combinations take place is based on their imperfections, missing electrons in the outer orbits or shells.' We humans, too, 'can only relate as a result of our imperfections, since the perfect need nothing'.

Perhaps this is a law that Ouspensky took a lifetime to observe operating in himself, but which Gurdjieff, as a master, saw at the beginning – or at least in their confrontations in Finland and the Caucasus.

As for Ouspensky's imperfections, one was graphically illustrated by Gurdjieff's nickname for him, 'Wraps Up the Thought'. The sparsity of verbal exchanges during Ouspensky's last meetings was a reversal of this characteristic – to most in the audience, the lecturer became 'Wraps Up the Meaning'.

A more serious flaw from a School standpoint seems to have been his inability to obey his teacher's instructions fully. Against this, an assumption of this book has been that even in ways he did not suspect Ouspensky continued to act in accordance with Gurdjieff's unstated intentions for the preservation and spread of the Work ideas.

An undisputed general impression of his colleagues was that Ouspensky was a changed man at the end of his life. There is a parallel here with the Crucifixion story in that death and resurrection are essential elements in man's transformation. Ouspensky often emphasised the Work teaching that a beneficial change in Being cannot be achieved by improving man as he is: his rebirth as a New Man is necessary. In our ordinary condition, we can no more imagine this state than a caterpillar can entertain any idea of the butterfly it is to become – no more than his listeners could understand what it meant to 'abandon' the System.

We cannot know, of course, whether his transformation was complete or if, alternatively, he was conscious of the stages ahead, convinced that he would remain awake to that knowledge in another life. But it seems more than hopeful imagination to feel, in J.H. Reyner's words, 'Ouspensky had at last cast off the shackles of his role.' In that belief, we can farewell Piotr Demianovich Ouspensky by echoing, 'Ne zabuyvayte' – 'Don't forget' – with confidence that this pioneer of The Fourth Way will indeed remember his experience on Earth in the frequently tumultuous period from 1878 to 1947.

Grave of P.D.Ouspensky –
Holy Trinity Church, Botleys and Lyne

BIBLIOGRAPHY

Anon. *A Point in the Work* (two volumes), Eureka Editions, Utrecht, 2000 (first published by Work Books, London, 1985).

Anon. (probably by Rodney Collin) *Last Remembrances of a Magician*, Stourton Press, Cape Town.

Bechhofer (-Roberts), C.E. *In Denikin's Russia and the Caucasus, 1919-1920*, Collins, London, 1921.

Bennett, J.G. *The Dramatic Universe* (four volumes), Hodder & Stoughton, London, 1956. *Witness*, 1962. *A Spiritual Psychology*, 1964. *Gurdjieff: Making a New World*, Harper & Row, New York, 1973.

Bridge, The, No. 12 (P.D. Ouspensky commemorative issue), The Study Society, London, 1997.

Bucke, Richard M. *Cosmic Consciousness: A Study of the Evolution of the Human Mind*, Dutton, New York, 1969 (first printed by Innes & Sons, Philadelphia, 1901).

Butkovsky-Hewitt, Anna *With Gurdjieff in St Petersburg and Paris*, Weiser, New York, 1978.

Carpenter, Edward *From Adam's Peak to Elephanta: Sketches of Ceylon and India*, Asian Educational Services, 1999 (first published London, 1892).

Collin, Rodney *The Theory of Celestial Influence: Man, the Universe, and Cosmic Mystery*, Vincent Stuart, London, 1954. *The Theory of Eternal Life*, 1956 (first published by Stourton Press, Cape Town, 1950). (See also under Anon.)

Copley, Samuel *Portrait of a Vertical Man: An Appreciation of Doctor Maurice Nicoll and his work*, Swayne Publications, London, 1989.

de Hartmann, Thomas and Olga *Our Life with Mr Gurdjieff* (edited by T.C. and T.A.G. Daly), Arkana, Penguin Books, 1992 (first published by Cooper Square Publishers, 1964).

de Ropp, Robert S. *Warrior's Way*, George Allen & Unwin, London, 1980. *Talks by Madame Ouspensky*, Logos Press, Manchester, 1984.

Ginsburg, Seymour B. (compiler) *In Search of the Unitive Vision: Letters of Sri Madhava Ashish to an American Businessman, 1978-1997*, New Paradigm Books, Boca Raton, Fl., 2001.

Gurdjieff, G.I. *The Herald of Coming Good*, privately printed, Angers, France, 1933. *All and Everything: Beelzebub's Tales to His Grandson*, the First Series, Routledge & Kegan Paul, London, 1950. *Meetings with Remarkable Men*, the Second Series, 1963. *Life is Real Only Then, When 'I Am'*, the Third Series, Arkana, Penguin Books, London, 1999 (first published Triangle Editions, New York, 1975). *Struggle of the Magicians*, Stourton Press, Cape Town, 1957. *Views From the Real World: Early Talks of G.I. Gurdjieff*, Routledge, London, 1974 (first published by Dutton, USA, 1973).

Hunter, Bob *The True Myth: Beryl Pogson's teaching on Gurdjieff's All and Everything*, Eureka Editions, Utrecht, 2002.

James, William *The Varieties of Religious Experience*, Penguin Books, 1982 (first published by Longmans, Green and Co., USA, 1902).

Lermontoff, Mikhail *A Hero of Our Time*, Philip Allan, London 1928 (first Russian edition 1840). *Selected Works* (translated by Irina Zheleznova), 1976.

Moore, James *Gurdjieff: The Anatomy of a Myth*, Element, London, 1991.

Nicoll, Maurice *Psychological Commentaries on the Teaching of G.I. Gurdjieff and P.D. Ouspensky* (five volumes), Vincent Stuart, London, 1952. *Living Time and the Integration of the Life*, Eureka Editions, Utrecht, 1998 (first published by Vincent Stuart, London, 1952). *Informal Work Talks and Teachings 1940 to 1950* (compiled by Lewis Creed), Quacks Books, York, 1995 (now distributed by Eureka Editions, Utrecht).

Nott, C.S. *Teachings of Gurdjieff: The Journal of a Pupil*, Routledge & Kegan Paul, London, 1961. *Journey Through This World: The Second Journal of a Pupil*, 1969

Ouspensky, P.D. *Tertium Organum: The Third Canon of Thought* (translated from Russian by Nicholas Bessaraboff and Claude Bragdon), Manas Press, Rochester, NY, 1920; Knopf, New York, 1922; Kegan Paul, Trench, Trubner, London, 1923. *A New Model of the Universe: Principles of the Psychological Method in its Application to Problems of Science, Religion, and Art* (translated from Russian by R.R. Merton, supervised by author), Knopf, New York, and Routledge, London, 1931, revised 1934. *Strange Life of Ivan Osokin*, Faber & Faber, London, 1948 (printed by Stourton, London, 1947). *In Search of the Miraculous: Fragments of an Unknown Teaching*, Routledge, London, and Harcourt Brace, New York, 1949. *Letters From Russia 1919*, Arkana (published by Routledge & Kegan Paul, 1978; first published in New Age, 1919). *The Psychology of Man's Possible Evolution*, Vintage Books, New York, 1974 (first published by Hedgehog Press, New York, 1950). *A Further Record: Extracts from Meetings 1928-1945*, Arkana, 1986 (first published by Stourton Press, Cape Town, 1952). *The Fourth Way: A Record of Talks and Answers to Questions based on the teaching of G.I. Gurdjieff*, Routledge & Kegan Paul, London, 1957. *Talks With a Devil*, Samuel Weiser, New York, 2000 (first published by Turnstone Press, 1972).

Patterson, William Patrick *Struggle of the Magicians: Why Uspenski left Gurdjieff*, Arete Communications, Fairfax, Calif., 1996, second edition subtitled *Exploring the Teacher-Student Relationship*.

Pogson, Beryl *Maurice Nicoll: A Portrait*, Vincent Stuart, London, 1961. *The Work Life: Based on Teachings of G.I. Gurdjieff, P.D. Ouspensky and Maurice Nicoll*, Samuel Weiser, York Beach, Maine, 1994. *Centenary Fragments* (compiled by Lewis Creed), Quacks Books, York, 1995 (now distributed by Eureka Editions, Utrecht). *Mind and Energy*, Eureka Editions, 2000.

Popoff, Irmis B. *Gurdjieff: His Work on Myself... With Others . . . For the Work*, Eureka Editions, Utrecht, 2001 (first published by Vantage Press, New York, 1969).

Ravindra, Ravi *Heart without Measure: Work with Madame de Salzmann*, Shaila Press, Nova Scotia, 1999.

Reyner, J.H. *Ouspensky: the Unsung Genius*, George Allen & Unwin, London, 1981.

Roles, Francis C. *Way of Liberation: Two Lectures*, The Society for the Study of Human Being, Inc., New York, 1972.

Segal, William *A Voice at the Borders of Silence* (written with Marielle Barcon-Segal), Outlook Press, 2003, New York.

Sharp, H.J. (Bert) *Where Humanity Stands Today: Six Introductory Talks*, privately printed, UK, 2002.

Taylor, Merrily E. (editor) *Remembering Pyotr Demianovich Ouspensky*, Yale University Library, 1978.

Turgenev, Ivan Sergeevich *A Sportsman's Sketches*, 1847-52. *The Diary of a Superfluous Man*, 1850.

Walker, Kenneth *Venture with Ideas*, Jonathan Cape, London, 1951 (revised Luzac Oriental, London, 1995).

Webb, James *The Harmonious Circle: The Lives and Work of G.I. Gurdjieff, P.D. Ouspensky, and Their Followers*, Thames & Hudson, London, and G.P. Putnam's Sons, New York, 1980.

Welch, Louise *Orage With Gurdjieff in America*, Routledge & Kegan Paul, Boston & London, 1982.

Wilson, Colin *The Strange Life of P.D. Ouspensky*, Aquarian/Thorsons, London, 1993.

Studio photographs
of P.D.Ouspensky
(around 1926)

P.D.Ouspensky at Gadsden *(photo: Pierre Elliot)*

Gadsden *(photo: Pierre Elliot)*

At Alley Cottage

The Crab & Lobster Inn
and
Alley Cottage in 1999

Lyne Place in 1992 (Ouspensky's Group House 1935-1947)

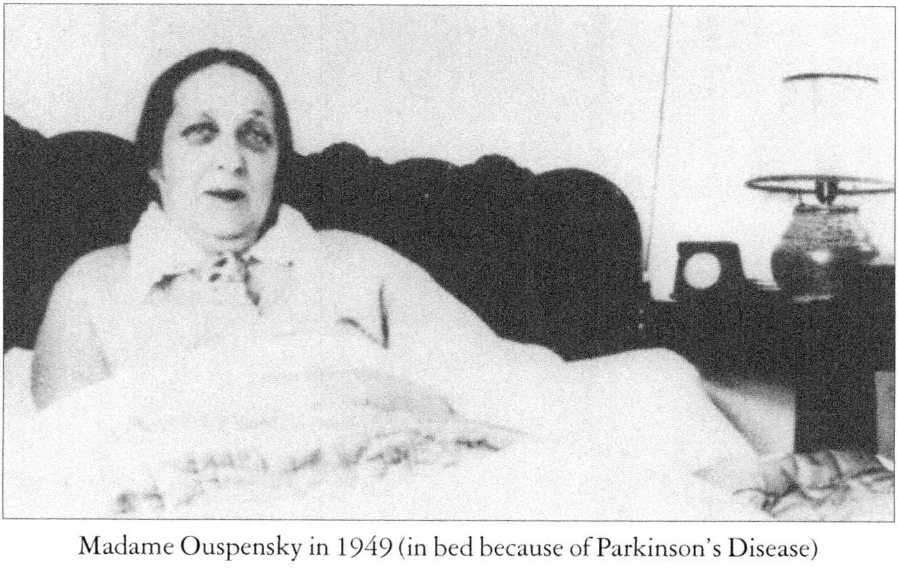

Madame Ouspensky in 1949 (in bed because of Parkinson's Disease)

(photo: Pierre Elliot)

Ouspensky in Ceylon 1916

Ouspensky at one of his meetings
at Lyne Place, Surrey. Circa 1938

Ouspensky and his horse 'Jingles' (1938)

Subject Index

Name Index

Available from Eureka Editions:

P.D. Ouspensky *A Record of Meetings*
P.D. Ouspensky *A Further Record*
Bob Hunter ***P.D. Ouspensky: Pioneer of the Fourth Way***
Bob Hunter ***The True Myth*** Beryl Pogson's teaching on Gurdjieff's *All and Everything*
Bob Hunter ***A Pupil's Postscript***
Bob Hunter/Beryl Pogson ***Brighton Work Talks***
Maurice Nicoll ***Psychological Commentaries on the Teaching of Gurdjieff & Ouspensky*** 6 Vols.
Maurice Nicoll ***The New Man***
Maurice Nicoll ***The Mark***
Maurice Nicoll ***Living Time***
Maurice Nicoll ***Selections from Meetings in 1953***
Maurice Nicoll ***Simple Explanation of Work Ideas***
Maurice Nicoll ***Notes taken at meetings in 1934***
A Few Recollections of Dr Nicoll and Amwell 1949-1953
Beryl Pogson ***Royalty of Nature***
Beryl Pogson ***In the East My Pleasure Lies***
Beryl Pogson ***Meeting taken by Beryl Pogson***
Beryl Pogson ***Maurice Nicoll: A Portrait***
Beryl Pogson ***Commentary on the Fourth Gospel***
Beryl Pogson/Bob Hunter ***Mind and Energy***
Bob Hunter ***Catherine Nicoll - A Wakeful Wife***
Beryl Pogson & Others ***Unforgotten Fragments***
Beryl Pogson & Others ***Centenary Fragments***
Beryl Pogson ***Work Talks at The Dicker***
Beryl Pogson ***More Work Talks***
Bob Hunter ***Ronald Oldham: A Life in three Acts***
Ronald & Muriel Oldham ***Work Teachings - Work Poems***
Samuel Copley ***Portrait of a Vertical Man: Maurice Nicoll***
Anon. ***Words on the Work***
Anon. ***A Recapitulation of the Lord's prayer***
Anon. ***A Point in the Work*** (Two Volumes)
Solange Claustres ***Becoming Conscious with G.I.Gurdjieff***
Paul Beekman Taylor ***Gurdjieff's Invention of America***
Paul Beekman Taylor ***G.I.Gurdjieff: A New Life***
Paul Beekman Taylor ***Gurdjieff in the Public Eye***
Paul Beekman Taylor ***Real Worlds of G.I.Gurdjieff***

Eureka Editions

info@eurekaeditions.com www.eurekaeditions.com

First published in 2000

This edition July 2021

©Eureka Editions 2021
ISBN: 978-94-92590-24-4

Eureka Editions
Herenstraat 4 A
3512 KC Utrecht
The Netherlands

info@eurekaeditions.com
www.eurekaeditions.com

Cover: Painting by Harold Wirk
© Eureka Editions

Printed in Great Britain
by Amazon

45592221R00189